IRON ROAD

The history of 100 years achievements of the

TO EMPIRE

of the progress and
Rock Island Lines

WILLIAM EDWARD HAYES

To Mimo

Contents

PART TWO

The Links and the Forge: 1869–1883

PART THREE

Beyond the Missouri: 1883–1901

PART FOUR

Pattern for Disaster: 1901–1933

PART FIVE

Re-birth and Regeneration: 1933–1952

Illustrations

following page 18

Foreword

The record of the hundred years of the birth and growth of the Rock Island Lines, as set forth here, differs from those innumerable volumes generally known as "company books." Frequently a corporation may employ a professional writer, pay him a flat fee, open the company's records to him, and stand the expense of the research he incurs. Such a contract between corporation and writer may provide that the finished manuscript shall be censored by the corporate officers, and the writer agrees to fashion his story as the company's officers desire. The writer also may be expected to relinquish all rights to any earnings that the book when published might enjoy, and to any subsidiary rights, such as serialization, motion pictures, or other use.

Obversely, this work was undertaken by the author solely as his own enterprise. He, although a salaried officer of the Rock Island Lines, was not assigned by the company to do this chore. The research and writing were done outside the performance of his duties, and his contract with the publishers is his own. The opinions expressed by the author and the conclusions drawn from his research are entirely his own, and are not in any way influenced by the opinions or conclusions of his employers.

You will find here no intricate reference work that sets forth the strict dry chronological development of a corporation together with endless tables of statistics and countless footnotes.

Nor is this in any sense a glowing record of one hundred years of glamorous achievements with the rough spots glossed over or left unrecorded. Rather it is a factual account of a century of growth and setbacks through periods of high prosperity and desperate decline.

In the evaluation of men and motives, the author has attempted to project, without bias or prejudice, his characters solely on the basis of the record they left—the record of the things they did, or failed to do.

Court records, magazine and newspaper stories, editorials, and the voluminous testimony taken at Interstate Commerce Commission investigations and at hearings before Congressional committees, were searched in an effort to get at the truth behind the conflicts that twice wrecked the Rock Island.

The author wishes here to express his grateful acknowledgement of the help he received from the following:

Arthur W. Large, retired Rock Island general agriculture agent, who not only lived through a long period in which he saw the history of this railroad made, but who upon leaving the service devoted many months to assembling the intricate research material on the corporate development and progress of the Rock Island and all the subsidiary lines that finally came into the system;

Carl Nyquist, retired vice-president and secretary-treasurer, who in his years of service in the financial department, sat through many of the dramatic meetings of directors and stockholders and saw, first-hand, dreams of empire rise and fall—whose remarkable memory for details helped to fill in important sequences in this story;

Joseph B. Fleming, surviving member of the three trustees appointed by the Federal Court in 1933, in the railroad's second and hectic receivership, who coöperated by permitting the author to examine his confidential files;

E. M. Durham, Jr., who in the railroad's darkest days in 1935, came from the senior vice-presidency of the Missouri Pacific to face the gigantic task of saving the Rock Island from dismemberment, and who gave freely of his personal reminiscences of the seven years he devoted to the inauguration and development of the great rehabilitation;

William F. Peter, retired Rock Island vice-president and general counsel, whose first-hand knowledge of the legal struggles to bring the property to its eventual reorganization proved invaluable;

L. B. Pritchett, assistant to President Farrington, who as secretary to Durham at the beginning of the long road back from desolation, provided intimate data from his personal records.

The author wishes in addition to express his thanks for the patient coöperation he received from Bruce Dwinell, vice-president and general counsel; E. Rigg, vice-president, freight traffic; W. H. Hillis, senior vice-president; Downing B. Jenks, executive vice-president; W. E. Bolton, vice-president; and to many other officers and employees who offered what they could to make this story complete.

Most of all, the author desires to record this special note of thanks to Rock Island's president, J. D. Farrington. His confidence and consideration were inspiring, and his modest reticence about his personal contribution was most endearing.

August 1, 1953   William Edward Hayes

PART ONE

The Dream and the Drama

Drama

1845-1869

1 The planners and the plan

A stooped man with lined face and straggly gray beard came out of Burrows' Store. He stared up Front Street then darted a quick glance at the river. His perturbed state of mind was indicated by the way he poked gnarled fingers into his beard, the quick steps he took toward the bench, where a thin little man sat quietly chewing on a large cud of tobacco.

The little man looked up at the tall figure, squinted and grunted a greeting. He moved over so that the other could sit beside him.

"Whut you so worried about, Lige?" the small man asked. He fixed his sight on a black ant in backward motion towing a bread-crust through the fringe of weeds beside the road. He spat—accurately.

"All that railroad talk," Lige, the tall man answered. "There in Burrows' Store—all them people, Pete, talkin' about nothin' else."

"What's talkin' gonna do?" Pete, the small one, queried.

"You know these fellers, Pete," Lige said. "They get t' talkin' about somethin' an' then they get to doin'. Just let Jim Grant get a-holt of an idee—"

"Jim Grant's likely to be right," Pete said. "If he's talkin' railroad he's on the track of somethin'. You gotta agree, Lige— he's done a lot for this town ever since he came here—'bout '38 wasn't it?"

"Yeh," Lige agreed. "Le's see, this is 1845—seven or more years ago—"

3

"Railroads is a comin' thing, Lige," Pete said. "I don't see nothin' to get so upset about."

"Well," Lige said, "I'm a river man, an' there's plenty to get upset about. I hear tell back East they're buildin' them things along rivers an' canals an' they're puttin' the boat men outta business."

"That's back East," Pete said. "That ain't here in Ioway."

"It's over there in Illinois," Lige said. He pointed a finger in the direction of the opposite bank of the Mississippi. "An' from the talk I hear in the store, Jim Grant an' some others from Davenport here plan on a big meetin' at the Colonel's house this evenin'."

Pete looked up at the tall man, his eyes widening, the rhythmic motion of his jaws arrested. "Over at Colonel Davenport's house, eh?" He smacked his lips. He glanced across the brownish river at the island just off the Illinois shore. He could see the white façade of the sprawling Davenport house against the green backdrop of the trees. "Sa-a-y," Pete drawled. "If the Colonel's in this with Jim Grant—must be somethin's really gonna happen!"

Lige gripped Pete's elbow. "There's Jim Grant now."

Grant was coming down Front Street.

"An' look who's with him," Pete whispered. "That feller Fulton that's been promotin' real estate deals around here, an' Eb Cook. If all three of them, along with the Colonel has got a railroad on their mind—man!"

Jim Grant, the North Carolinian, who studied law while he taught school, and who'd come to Davenport to put out his shingle when the town boasted no more than twenty-five or thirty houses, had a railroad on his mind. So had his companions in the boat that headed into midstream for the house on what they called Rock Island.

The lowering sun cast saffron light on the wide river. The air was still on that hot June afternoon. The grouping of houses and stores on the Illinois bank of the river, below the island, resembled a toy village. It was called Rock Island City. Be-

tween it and Davenport plied a busy ferry owned by Antoine
Le Claire, a huge gentleman who was part French-Canadian
and part Potawatomi. It was this man who with Colonel Davenport laid out in 1836 the Iowa town that bore the Colonel's
name.

Jim Grant and his companions tied up their boat at the
Colonel's pier and made their way up the walk to the wide
veranda. They didn't speak until the stocky man with a lion's
mane of hair that bushed up over his forehead and fell to his
shoulders called a greeting to them. George Davenport's ruddy
face glowed in the fading sunlight. His eyes did not conceal his
excitement.

"Sorry if we're late," Jim Grant said. He saw the group at
the other end of the porch—five men who had been talking
together and who now approached.

"Not at all," the Colonel said. "You know Lem Andrews
and Whittaker from Rock Island City."

The Davenport men exchanged greetings.

"And Charlie Atkinson from Moline," the Colonel continued. "And this is Nelson Elwood from Joliet, and Dick
Morgan, the railroad engineer—"

"We've heard of you," Grant said. "You're the gentleman
who's said to know so much about the matter we came here
to talk about."

The Colonel led the men into the long parlor. Ebenezer
Cook who, like Grant, was a Davenport lawyer of high repute,
and a leader in the town, found a seat beside the man from
Joliet.

"You came by stage?" Cook queried.

Elwood said that he had, and in answer to a further question
said, "I don't have to tell you about Illinois roads. A rough
trip. A mighty rough one. And these settlers heading west.
Some going to Iowa. Some to Missouri, some to the mountains,
and some just don't seem to know where they're going."

"West," Jim Grant said. "Always west. The pull of the
land. Each year the Iowa country sees more and more farms
staked out, and the population keeps growing."

"And that," said A. C. Fulton, "means crops, more stuff to market, more stuff to be shipped—"

"Which brings us to our subject," Colonel Davenport said. "Grant, will you take over and start things to going?"

Jim Grant drew himself to his full height. His face was sharp-featured. His eyes narrowed. He took a newspaper from his coat pocket, the *Chicago Daily Journal* of June 4, 1845. He spread out the front page and held it up. It was solid with advertising notices in plain and fancy borders.

"Railroads," Grant said—he pointed to the page. "One after another, telling us what they're doing." The group closed around the center table to get a closer look as Grant laid down the paper.

"The Indianapolis and Cincinnati Short Line," Grant resumed. "You see what it says. Trains ready to run. The Cleveland and Pittsburgh, nearly completed. Lines running from the Eastern Seaboard to the Alleghanies. They'll cross those mountains and they'll be looking to a connection with this great waterway." Grant made a sweeping gesture toward the river.

"We can have the connection for them," Grant continued after a brief pause. "The canal from Chicago to the Illinois River is now building."

"Yes," said the man from Joliet. "A railroad from Rock Island City to—"

"To La Salle or Peru," another in the group said excitedly.

"Such a rail link," said Fulton, "would give an overland outlet for our grain and produce to the Eastern markets. We could ship by rail from the Mississippi to the connection with the new canal and then into Chicago by boat."

"Also," said Richard Morgan, the engineer, "you'd be able to ship down the Illinois River to St. Louis and south when navigation on the Mississippi up this far would be closed in for winter. The possibilities—"

They all saw the possibilities. They all began talking at once. And they all realized how, in this year of 1845, the subject of a railroad in Illinois could be most unpopular.

They reviewed the sorry experience of 1837 when, by its internal improvement act, so-called, Illinois appropriated more than $10,000,000 which it didn't have in the treasury, to build a network of railroads between a number of the state's most important points. The farmers and businessmen subscribed to five million in bonds, and script for almost $1,000,000 was issued to contractors. The net result was a piece of railroad a little more than 50 miles long between Springfield and Meredosia that operated briefly at a considerable loss, and eventually was sold to private interests for virtually nothing.

What happened in 1837 would not deter these men now. They would develop their idea. Wasn't the whole country changing? The change was in the very air. And, besides, with George Davenport willing to play a major role in the promotion of this railroad they had a great power behind them.

George Davenport was an engineer and a builder in his own right. He was a man of means. He had come to this island with the American forces after the close of the War of 1812, and here in 1816 had built Fort Armstrong. He had laid claim to his land after the army had abandoned the post in 1836. Davenport had a close association with Le Claire, and Le Claire was a man of great wealth. It was pretty certain that Le Claire would come into the venture. They wouldn't worry too much about money now. The idea was to organize and get a charter. Somehow the money would come.

Long into the night, these men talked over every facet of the project. Then, at last, when they rose to take leave of their host, they knew that this night they had made history. A railroad from Rock Island to La Salle. That's what they would drive for. They couldn't fail. What was tonight a dream would tomorrow be a reality.

2 Rarin' for a railroad

The Illinois members of this group of railroad planners lost no time in getting to Springfield to set the machinery in motion for a charter. They were on their way before daylight the morning after their meeting with the Colonel on the island.

Meanwhile, the news broke at Sam Fisher's Store in Rock Island City. Before noon the word "railroad" was on the lips of everyone within miles around.

"The iron horse. I seen pictures of it—"

"Travel in them steam cars—they go fast—"

"Mebbe they'll build alongside my land, an' I can make money—"

"I got some ground north uh town that's good for buildin' lots—"

Hopes, dreams, magic in the warm June air.

A lean man at Fisher's Store gazing glumly across the river, muttering in his beard, "Me—I drive the stage to Beardstown. Let 'em get a railroad an' what happens to my livin'?"

"Feller that can handle them nags you drive oughtta be able to drive the iron horse," came the laughing reply.

They waited the days out for Lemuel Andrews to come home from Springfield. They hung on his words for a new spark of encouragement. They speculated on the date when the first ground would be broken.

Then, on the afternoon of July 4, Colonel George Davenport was murdered in his home. The sprawling mansion which had been the setting less than four weeks ago for the birth of this great new railroad project, suddenly had become a house of tragedy.

The death of Davenport at the hands of bandits cast a shadow of gloom over the men who had counted so much on his aid. Certainly the shock had telling effects on his associates. Some thought his passing would mean the end to their high hopes.

Jim Grant, of Iowa, however, was not a man easily shaken. Since 1841 he had been a member of the Iowa legislature from Scott County. He had faced tragic circumstances before, both in his arduous efforts to improve the town of Davenport, and to promote the progress of his State. He and his associates assured the people that no efforts would be spared to get the railroad for them.

No one, perhaps, will ever know the trials these men faced during the next year and a half—the conferences, the political considerations, the tiring trips back and forth to Springfield all took time and patience.

But, on February 27, 1847, the General Assembly of the State of Illinois approved the charter that established the Rock Island and La Salle Rail Road Company. The charter provided for the company's right to "survey, locate and construct and during its continuance to maintain and continue a railroad with single or double track and with such appendages as may be deemed necessary for the convenient use of the same, from the Town of Rock Island, on the Mississippi River, in the County of Rock Island to the Illinois River at the termination of the Illinois and Michigan Canal . . ."

The capital stock was fixed at $300,000, and under the terms of the charter this amount had to be subscribed before the company could be formally organized and the officers elected.

The charter named as commissioners to receive the stock subscriptions Joseph Knox, F. R. Brunot, N. B. Buford, William Vandever, and Nathaniel Belcher, of Rock Island County; Joshua Harper and James G. Bolmer, of Henry County; Cyrus Bryant, Justus Stevens, and R. T. Templeton of Bureau County; and J. V. Horr and William H. W. Cushman, of La Salle County.

The year 1847 was a year of crisis. Bank currency was depressed in the Illinois and Iowa country; credit had been expanded to the limit, and President James K. Polk's war with Mexico, for the acquisition of California and the territory east to the Texas border, had its deleterious effect on the general economy.

Money was hard to raise. Illinois was still feeling the effects of the panic of ten years ago, and the burden on the taxpayers that had followed the State's ill-fated venture into the railroad field was still a punishing one.

Despite the fact that only $5 was required for a down payment on each share of Rock Island and La Salle stock, with the balance to be paid as called, the commissioners seemed to get nowhere.

They held frequent meetings at Rock Island City to discuss their progress, or lack of it, and each time they went away more determined than ever to make a success of their venture. They called on every businessman and farmer between the river and La Salle, but their pleas, in most instances, were made to deaf ears.

It was not until early in 1848, after the fiercely contested march of the American forces from Vera Cruz to Mexico City resulted in the treaty of Guadalupe Hidalgo, that the economic picture brightened somewhat. President Polk had achieved his goal. California and the territory that is now Arizona, Nevada, New Mexico, and Utah, came under the American flag.

For the next two years and ten months the progress of the Rock Island and La Salle commissioners was slow but steady. Rock Island made the best showing; Henry County made the poorest.

Finally, on November 12, 1850, the commissioners met at Rock Island, and their eyes were grave as they glanced at one another. Discouragement was written on their faces. Early subscribers to Rock Island and La Salle stock wanted to know

what was happening to their money. Here it was getting close
to four years since the charter was granted and nothing tan-
gible had been done. The company had not been formally
organized. Richard Morgan, acting as engineer, had made a
survey of the line and it was down on the map of Illinois.
On paper, that was all. Was it possible that they again had
been played for suckers, again had lost their money in this
dubious railroad venture? Maybe they should have left it
alone in the first place.

Commissioner Buford reported for Rock Island County.
He called out the total subscription from that area—$75,800.
Next came Justus Stevens' report from Bureau County. His
books showed a total of $50,400. The men from La Salle
County reported $25,000, and Joshua Harper, from Henry
County, gave in his report—$20,000 subscribed.

The commissioners gazed about them in discouragement.
Three years and almost ten months, and they had just a
little more than half of what they needed to get this railroad
going. A grand total of $171,200 on the books; the charter
called for $300,000.

What was the matter with James Grant and Ebenezer Cook
and A. C. Fulton, and others from Scott County, Iowa, during all this time? True, Grant had met with them, discussed
their problems, knew their troubles. Surely had George Davenport lived there would not be this dilemma.

The door of the meeting room opened. The men around
the table looked up. They recognized the faces in the group
that entered. Of course Jim Grant was there, and Cook, and
others they knew.

"What now—" Hope kindled in tired eyes. These men from
Davenport. They must have some good tidings.

They did. They had subscriptions for $128,300 and they
put them on the table. The commissioners stared speechless,
then all began talking. There were handshaking and back-
slapping, and trembling fingers adding the totals together.

"Still five hundred short," one man shouted. "Five hundred. If we can get that five hundred we can elect a board of directors and—"

They got the five hundred. They made it up among themselves.

Right now was the time to elect the ten directors called for by the charter.

"Jim Grant, by all means," came the first nomination.

"By all means. We're all agreed on the Judge."

Grant smiled and bowed. The judicial title still pleased him, although he had been named to the bench of the Iowa District Court three years before.

"And Eb Cook," another said. "If it hadn't been for the Judge and Eb, with their Iowa friends over there in Scott County, we wouldn't be able to sit here and make nominations."

Thus it went. One by one the board was named. Judge James Grant and Ebenezer Cook, of Davenport, the latter now a member of the thriving banking firm of Cook and Sargent; N. B. Buford, who had taken the brunt of money-raising in Rock Island County; J. N. Allen; M. B. Osborne; Charles Atkinson, of Moline; and Lemuel Andrews, of Rock Island City, who had sat in on the historic meeting at the Davenport home five years ago; John Stevens; and Justus Stevens who did his best in Bureau County where the going had been extremely hard. The tenth man was L. D. Brewster, of La Salle County.

"Now that we're this close to formal organization of the company," Jim Grant said, "we've got the matter of construction to consider. Of course, we can't even think of contracting for anything until we comply with the clause in the charter that gives us thirty days from this date to meet again and elect officers. Personally, I think I'll have something to tell you within fifteen days."

"About a contractor?" someone asked.

"Henry Farnam," Grant said. "He is now in Chicago. I'd like to take a small committee with me to talk to him. I want to leave today."

In answer to another question Grant explained that he'd read about Farnam, a New Haven man, experienced in railroads, and presently contracting to finish building the Michigan Southern into Chicago from the East. Grant also explained that Mayor Ogden, of Chicago, was trying to interest Farnam in the building of the Galena and Chicago Union westward from its present terminus at Barrington, Illinois, to the Mississippi.

"It may be that we can convince Mr. Farnam that we have the most plausible route," Grant said.

"You pick your committee," someone suggested, "and if you think you'll be able to give us a report by November 27, let us set that date for our formal organization."

"I think I'll be able to give you a report," Grant answered.

"The railroad's a-comin'!"

The phrase was magic. People heard it in the store, they heard it on the streets of Rock Island City.

"Somethin's stirrin'," said the Beardstown stage driver in utter misery. "Only a few days ago them strangers was along the road between here an' Bureau. They had stakes down. They were sightin' along the prairie an' puttin' things on paper."

"The railroad's a-comin'!"

The excitement was electric. It filled the room where the directors of the Rock Island and La Salle Rail Road gathered around the table. It was November 27, 1850.

Judge Grant looked over his neighbors. He'd heard what they were saying on the streets. The others, too, had heard. They all looked at Grant.

"The first order of business, gentlemen," someone said, "is the election of officers. Nominations are open for the office of President."

"I say Judge Grant," a voice was quick to offer.

"Anyone else?"

There was no one else. The Judge was elected unanimously.

William Bailey was made treasurer and N. B. Buford was made secretary.

Grant took the chair. Now the directors were ready for his report on his conference with Henry Farnam, and the results.

"Henry Farnam will build our railroad, gentlemen," Grant reported. Then, after a dramatic pause, "—under certain conditions which I will now place before you."

The former North Carolinian told about his meeting with Farnam and the noted construction engineer's reaction to the plan. Farnam could see no point in such a railroad as had been chartered. A small link between two waterways. With roads from the East already forging their way to Chicago, the logical thing would be to build a railroad from Chicago through Joliet, Ottawa, and La Salle, thence on to Rock Island.

"Farnam has surveyed the proposed route, gentlemen," Grant continued. "He feels that he can interest his partner, Joseph Sheffield, provided we can get our charter amended. With Sheffield will come Eastern capital—all we will need. Once this line is completed we will have a solid line of rail from the Mississippi to New York. What such a project can accomplish in the opening of the West is beyond all imagination. I recommend that we comply with Mr. Farnam's suggestions and take the proper steps to have our charter amended."

There was some consternation. They all remembered how long it had taken to get their original charter, and how difficult it had been to get the stock subscribed to. Now here was a new problem.

Grant assured them that it wasn't too great a problem. Under his guidance the directors drew up a memorial to Congress to grant a right-of-way over all public lands across which the railroad might be constructed. A petition was drawn up asking the Illinois legislature to amend the original charter by authorizing a change in the corporate title and the extension of the railroad from the head of navigation of the Illinois and Michigan Canal (Peru - La Salle) to the city of Chicago.

Machinery also was set in motion to ask the legislature of Iowa to authorize the railroad to establish a depot in Davenport and to carry freight and passengers across the Mississippi River.

The railroad was on its way.

3 Enter: the builders

Previous to that historic meeting of November 27, 1850, the founders and commissioners of the Rock Island and La Salle had trouble only in raising money.

Now as the year 1851 dawned there were new troubles. That business of petitioning the Iowa legislature for the right to set up a depot in Davenport and transport freight and passengers across the river. Would the steamboat people stand for anything like that? Not without a fight.

And that business about extending from La Salle to Chicago. Right along the new Illinois and Michigan Canal. Would the canal people stand for a railroad taking their business? Most certainly they would not.

And the Illinois legislators had the interests of the canal at heart when, on February 7, 1851, they authorized the amended charter. A section was inserted which provided that the railroad would pay to the Board of Trustees of the Illinois and Michigan Canal a toll on all commodities, except livestock, that the canal could carry. The tolls were to be equal to the canal rates, and were to apply to shipments destined to or from any point between Chicago and a point twenty miles west of La Salle. The tolls were to be paid by the railroad only during the periods when navigation on the canal was open.

It is doubtful that the tolls section of the amended charter, as written, would have been acceptable to Judge Grant and his associates, had not Grant received a letter from Henry Farnam, written January 22, 1851.

In his letter the builder said:

> "Be sure to get the charter to make the road on the shortest route from La Salle to Chicago, even if they insist on your paying tolls on freights taken from points along the canal."

The directors met on April 8, 1851, and formally accepted the amended charter, including the canal tolls provision. The meeting officially terminated the corporate existence of the Rock Island and La Salle Rail Road Company. Chicago and Rock Island Rail Road Company became the new corporate title. Judge Grant was elected president, and the officers and directors of the first organization, with the exception of a few who dropped out, formed the new corporation.

Under the provisions of the amended charter additional directors were necessary, and the men elected to fill these posts were John B. Jervis, of Rome, New York, noted consulting engineer and a close friend and associate of Henry Farnam; Elihu C. Litchfield of Detroit; Charles Butler; and John Stryker. These men represented Joseph E. Sheffield's interests.

Sheffield was anxious to get into the building of the Chicago and Rock Island with his financial support but, according to the records, he didn't want to do it so long as the railroad was burdened with the canal tolls. This would indicate that he and Farnam didn't see eye to eye on this particular phase.

The tolls provision of the charter, however, was full of legal loopholes, and Judge Grant was pretty sure he saw a way out.

One part of the tolls section read, "If the Canal Board of

Trustees refuse to comply with this act by the first Monday in June following passage of this Act, then said railroad company shall have right to build and all restrictions with reference to tolls removed."

Judge Grant, shortly after the enactment of the revised charter, enclosed a copy of it to the president of the canal trustees. Grant received a reply that stated matters of such grave import to those whose interests he represented required serious deliberations. The canal president said he would refer the tolls provision of the charter to his associates at their next meeting.

The result of this action was explained by Judge Grant in his report to the stockholders for the year 1851 when he said, "The first Monday in June has passed and the Trustees of the Illinois and Michigan Canal, having failed to assent to the terms of the charter, our obligation to pay tolls to the Illinois and Michigan Canal ceases by the terms of the act of incorporation."

It was as simple as that.

Immediately, the new railroad came in for a battle in the courts. The canal trustees had been advised by counsel that the railroad could not exercise the power of eminent domain on the public lands that had been granted to the canal on either side of its channel for construction aids. The railroad went ahead to condemn the right-of-way over canal lands and other lands.

The canal trustees took the case to the Cook County (Illinois), court for an injunction against the Chicago and Rock Island. The court held that the power of eminent domain was lawfully exercised, and the ruling was upheld by the Illinois supreme court.

The way now having been cleared for building, Henry Farnam, on September 6, 1851, submitted the Farnam and Sheffield contract to build the road from Chicago to Rock Island, 181 miles, at a cost of $3,987,638. This price did not include right-of-way, station grounds, station buildings except in certain instances, fencing, and incidentals.

The railroad's directors on September 17, 1851, met at Rock Island and unanimously approved the Farnam and Sheffield contract.

That the contractors went into action at once is evidenced by Judge Grant's remarks at the first annual meeting on December 22, 1851. He said:

"Since that time (September 17, when the contract was approved), Messrs. Sheffield and Farnam have commenced and prosecuted the work in a manner highly creditable to them and which we were authorized to expect from their character for promptness and energy, and permit me to say that it was fortunate for us that men of such pecuniary means and personal worth were induced to embark in the enterprise, and we must endeavor to so fulfill the contract on our part that the work may be completed at the earliest practicable period."

At this meeting, which was held in the Tremont Hotel, in Chicago, Judge Grant announced that he would have to decline re-election to the presidency of the organization. He had again entered the Iowa legislature, and had been elected speaker of the house, and he felt that his law practice and legislative duties would not permit him to guide the destinies of this new railroad to the west.

As a result, the presidency went to John B. Jervis, the engineer and builder with whom Farnam was now associated in the building of the Michigan Southern toward Chicago. Judge Grant remained as vice-president. Nelson D. Elwood, of Joliet, who had met with Grant and those others at the Davenport home on Rock Island five and one-half years previously, was elected secretary. A. C. Flagg, of New York, became treasurer. Isaac Cook, of Chicago, became assistant secretary.

Judge Grant could turn over the gavel to Jervis with the satisfaction of having guided the railroad from the birth of an idea to the point where construction was under way, with great faith and perseverance. Now it was a job for hard-rock railroad men—builders and engineers.

1 John D. Farrington, Rock Island's president, who in mid-May 1936 came
from the Burlington to tackle the job of chief operating officer and map
out the program for the road's complete rehabilitation—a program of
"planned progress" that lifted the system from financial and physical
bankruptcy to rank with America's finest railroad properties.

2 Edward M. Durham, Jr., chief executive officer under the Rock Island
   Trustees, left the senior vice presidency of the Missouri Pacific in December 1935 to use his fine executive talents in the first big move to circum-
   vent dismemberment and route Rock Island back on the road to recovery.
   He retired in 1942.

3 Antoine Le Clair, enormous French-Indian pioneer, wealthy land-owner, and founder of Davenport, Iowa, played a leading role in early Rock Island history. He turned the first earth to mark the beginning of railroad building in Iowa.

4 James W. Grant, of Davenport, elected first president of the Rock Island and La Salle Rail Road, retained that post when by amended charter the name was changed to Chicago and Rock Island Rail Road Company. Chief among the road's founders, he led money-raising campaign from 1847, resigned presidency in December 1851.

F.M.Mayer

S.R.Arias

R.C.Ingersoll

M.A.Brown

E.E.Brown

J.D.Farrington

L.B.Neumiller

J.B.Faegre

W.F.Peter

H.L.Horton

J.N.Norris

A.O.Gibson

H.Crown

5-6   Henry Farnam (*opposite left*) Joseph E. Sheffield (*opposite right*); they, in partnership, were the contractors who built the Chicago and Rock Island. Farnam later served as Rock Island's president from December 1854 to June 1863.

7   (*Below*) Rock Island's "working" Board of Directors. Absent when this picture was made were Harry Darby, Chairman of the Board, Darby Corporation, Kansas City, Kansas; Charles Wiman, President, Deere and Company, Moline, Illinois; Robert McKinney, publisher, Santa Fe (New Mexico) New Mexican. Of the others, identified in the inset, James Norris is now deceased, was succeeded by his son, Bruce Norris. Arthur O. Gibson, secretary and treasurer, is not a member of the board.

8   Rock Island's first bridge across the Mississippi, begun in 1853 and completed in May 1856.

9   Subjected to fire and other acts of apparent sabotage, in long battle with steamship interests, the bridge fell victim in March 1868, to a devastating tornado.

10   Advertising its Palace Dining Cars in the late 1870's, Rock Island stressed complete table d'hote dinners for seventy-five cents with "a bottle of imported French wine 15 cents extra."

11 Camelback locomotive on the Choctaw, circa 1902, a rarity in the west.

12 Engine 46, ready to leave Indianola, Iowa for Des Moines. This "iron horse" of 1881 was typical of early-day motive power.

13 Rock Island's depot Des Moines, circa 1872, with Engine No. 3 heading out for Winterset.

14 Rock Island's 5000-class 4-8-4's, great among the high-speed tonnage haulers in World War II, now replaced by diesels.

15 Queen of the Rocket Fleet is Rock Island's Extra-Fare Golden State, between Chicago and Los Angeles. It was inaugurated in 1902.

16 (*Above*) La Salle Street Station at night and a streamliner ready to go—
the Corn Belt Rocket to Omaha precedes the departure of the Imperial
to California.

17 (*Below*) The diesel switcher, now doing all Rock Island's yard work,
has played an important part in the road's complete dieselization.

18 Popular Twin-Star Rocket, shown here at a station pause, connects Min-
neapolis-St. Paul with Houston, Texas, in a fast daily run.

19 Fast freight out of Memphis, crossing the Mississippi, follows a route
to Oklahoma, Texas and beyond where early history was hectic.

20 Samson of the Cimarron, symbol of the reborn Rock Island, was first
great major improvement on California route.

21   Train-side bus arrival from Peoria brings passengers to connect at Bureau with Golden State and other main line trains.

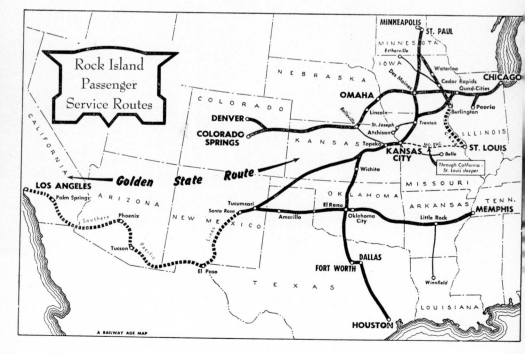

22   Route of the Rockets—this map shows Rock Island's passenger service coverage.

23 Armourdale (Kansas City, Kansas) automatically-controlled hump yard, can handle classification of 4,000 cars daily.

24 (*Above*) Last word in modern diesel repair facilities housed in remodeled shop at Silvis, Illinois.

25 (*Below*) This veteran agent-telegrapher, G. C. Cornett, of Shawnee, Okla., is typical of Rock Island's old-timers who help keep trains always on the move.

4 The Rocket—the first train West

Through the fall and winter of 1851-52 Farnam and his forces completed and rechecked their surveys, made all arrangements for their materials and supplies, and organized for the westward push as soon as spring weather might afford good working conditions. The iron rails, 57 pounds to the yard, were coming from England. Other material would come in by boat. This necessitated building track within the Chicago area to connect with the Chicago River. Rails were laid from Chicago south to what is now Englewood for a connection with the Northern Indiana Railroad (now the New York Central) which was then building in from the Indiana Line.

During Judge Grant's tenure of office as president, he signed a contract with the Northern Indiana which made possible the present New York Central's ownership and use of vast terminal properties in Chicago. The contract provided, with minor exceptions, for joint ownership and use of all the property of the two railroads between what is now the northern boundary of 65th Street and La Salle Street Station.

This contract was of vital importance to the Northern Indiana, as it allowed that company to purchase in the name of the Rock Island the needed right-of-way to get into the city. Farnam completed the main line from the depot at 22nd Street, Chicago, to the junction with the Northern Indiana early in January 1852. On May 22, the first Northern Indiana passenger train operated into the Chicago depot, and was accorded a great reception.

With a break in the weather in April of 1852, the Farnam crews struck west with the grading and ballasting of the new railroad. The lawsuits, the difficulties of financing, other opposition, were all behind.

By October 1, the 40-mile segment between Chicago and Joliet was almost ready for opening. Some rail had yet to be laid. From Joliet to Morris, approximately 20 miles, less than a mile of grading remained until track-laying could be begun. Only a small section remained to be graded between Morris and Marseilles, and less than four miles had yet to be graded between Marseilles and Peru. In less than six months the builders had thrown up the fill and virtually completed 40 miles of railroad, and had readied for rails all but a little less than 8 miles on the whole 99-mile stretch between Chicago and Peru. It was truly a remarkable building record.

So insistent were the people living along the line between Chicago and Joliet to see the iron horse make its way over this iron road to empire that arrangements were made to run the first train on October 10.

The first of the orders for new locomotives was standing in its Chicago shed. It was a fine new eight-wheeler (American 4-4-0 type) built by the Rogers works. Six new coaches, gaily painted a bright yellow, also were on hand. The locomotive was named *Rocket*, obviously after George Stephenson's engine which, a few years before, had attained a speed of 44 miles an hour on its run between Manchester and Liverpool, England.

Addison R. Gilmore, the Rock Island's first superintendent, went to Farnam and Jervis, and told them of the public clamor.

From all the evidence of that early history Messrs. Farnam and Jervis knew a great deal about railroad building, but apparently very little about good public relations. Indications are that the launching of the first train was miserably planned. While all the rail was in place and some of the right-of-way was dressed, the line was by no means completed. The only station anywhere near ready to open was at Blue Island. The

Mokena depot was barely under construction, and at Joliet there were no facilities to turn the engine.

Evidently little advance notice of the coming of this historic event was circulated. When at 10 a.m. on Sunday, October 10, 1852, the gaily bedecked train was ready to leave the 22nd Street depot, the occasion had caused hardly a ripple in the busy life of Chicagoans. There were no flag-waving crowds at the station. There was no blare of bugles, and the usual firing of guns that had marked similar occasions elsewhere was conspicuously absent.

But at 10 o'clock James Lendabarker, former packet engineer, opened the throttle of the *Rocket*. The slack came out between the yellow coaches which carried a good-sized crowd of the adventurous. Wood sparks from the balloon stack flattened out on the breeze, and another chapter of history was in the making.

Three days later, on October 13, the *Chicago Daily Democrat* paid tribute to the "quiet and efficient" men who held the destinies of this new railroad. The writer commented about the smoothness of the ride "on the portions of it (the railroad) which are already ballasted . . ."

The run to Joliet was accomplished in two hours. Newspaper records indicate that at the various stations along the rails great crowds shouted and cheered as the *Rocket* rattled and bounced on its way. A vast number of people turned out at Joliet to pay tribute to "this unbelievable thing."

The return to Chicago was a back-up movement. But to compensate, Farnam and his associates that night entertained those who'd made the trip at a banquet at the Sherman House.

5 "One wide river for to cross"

Under the contract with Farnam and Sheffield, the railroad was to be operated by the construction organization until it should finally be completed to Rock Island, fully equipped. Until such time service would be inaugurated by the contractors as each portion of the line was ready for operation. The contractors were to retain the earnings and pay the interest on the outstanding first-mortagage bonds.

Regular service between Chicago and Joliet with two passenger trains daily in each direction was begun on October 18, 1852.

The arrival of the railroad at Ottawa touched off a tremendous public celebration and marked the first in a series that were to become memorable events in one community after another. The first train from Chicago pulled to a stop at the Ottawa station on February 14, 1853. In the coaches were many prominent business leaders from Chicago and intermediate points, and of course Henry Farnam was the host en route.

The citizens of Ottawa tendered their visitors a grand reception and a banquet replete with laudatory speeches by local civic leaders and prophetic speeches by the railroad official personnel.

Naturally, news of this progress spread from town to town along the road yet to be built, and excitement increased among the farmers and the businessmen. The people of Rock Island talked of nothing else.

"Figgered out when the rails'll get here?" was a constant question.

"Might be a year yet—that's what I hear."

"More people comin' in all the time. Buyin' up homesites. Gonna be a real boom in the town."

"It'll be a great day when the trains come. An' are them people over in Ioway gettin' excited—man!"

The people in Davenport had a right to be excited. Nine days before the big reception in Ottawa a group of leading citizens, among whom were Antoine Le Claire, Ebenezer Cook, and A. C. Fulton, gained Iowa legislative authorization for the incorporation of a new railroad to be called the Mississippi and Missouri. Its charter provided for the building and operating of a railroad from Davenport to Council Bluffs, and its capitalization was fixed at $6,000,000.

Farnam was identified with the promotion of the Mississippi and Missouri from its very inception, but his partner Sheffield, would not go along with him in the Iowa venture. Sheffield, according to some records, felt that he'd reached the time of life when he wanted to retire from building activities, and planned to do so on the completion of the Chicago and Rock Island.

The building into Ottawa had been accomplished without any serious setback; however, even before the rails had reached that point, trouble was in the making at the neighboring city of La Salle, just to the west.

The line through La Salle had been surveyed to follow the foot of the bluffs along the river. This survey was not to the liking of a group of businessmen who had acquired considerable land back from the river on top of the bluffs. This group had already started a business and residence development, and wanted the railroad built through that area.

When the contractors refused to consider such a route, the citizens' group succeeded in fomenting local dissension and indignation to the point that the builders were frankly told the people of La Salle would use force, if necessary, to get the line of the railroad changed.

The railroad remained adamant, and the city council finally passed an ordinance providing for a $10 fine to be levied on any "healthy male" between the ages of 21 and 50 who would refuse to answer the call to use forcible means against the railroad builders.

This action made it necessary for the officers of the Chicago and Rock Island to go before the legislature and secure a further amendment to the charter to permit the railroad the right to follow its course. With approval of the amendment the laying of rail on the grade along the river was successfully accomplished.

Through service from Chicago to La Salle was established in the latter part of March 1853, and was extended to Peru the following month.

While the rails pushed westward toward the settlement of Bureau, the firm of Sheffield and Farnam contracted with the newly chartered Peoria and Bureau Valley Railroad to build that line. The charter called for the construction of a railroad "from Peoria, Illinois, to a point in Illinois below Indiantown, in the Valley of the Bureau River." A later amendment to the charter provided for terminating the line in the Bureau Valley at any point that would be most advantageous to the company.

The building contract was executed in May.

It was on the 31st of that month that new excitement seethed through the growing city of Davenport. The founders of the Mississippi and Missouri at last were ready to sit around the conference table and elect directors and officers.

William B. Ogden, mayor of Chicago, and one of the original developers of the Galena Union, was on hand along with Farnam and the Rock Island's president, John B. Jervis.

Thomas C. Durant, who had joined the Sheffield and Farnam firm for the construction of the Peoria and Bureau Valley, took an active hand because he already knew that on Sheffield's retirement he would take over full partnership with Farnam in the construction activities of this Iowa line.

John A. Dix, of New York, was elected president of the

Mississippi and Missouri, and Ogden was named vice-president. John E. Henry, of Iowa, was chosen as secretary. The job of treasurer went to A. C. Flagg who was also treasurer of the Rock Island.

Henry Farnam was named chief engineer and Jervis was appointed consulting engineer. The tie-up between the Rock Island and the Mississippi and Missouri was even made more complete when Durant, Farnam, Sheffield, and Ebenezer Cook all were made directors.

It was the general opinion that such strong management and directorate were clearly indicative of the national importance that this new railroad was destined to assume. Everything was in its favor. Men with financial means almost unlimited—men with fine construction and operating background. What if Sheffield would not take an active part in the building? He would be in the background with his financial support. Durant was a younger man, and a powerful one.

The directors had ideas that reached far beyond just a railroad from Davenport to Council Bluffs. To the south was Burlington. To the north through the Cedar Valley was a rich, green land crying for full development.

The board named a committee made up of Ogden, Cook, and another Farnam man, William Walcott, to go out and get right-of-way, secure support of local communities and make recommendations as to the lines that should be built.

The committee didn't take long to get into the country and come back with a report. The committee visited Cedar Rapids, Iowa City, Muscatine, and several other towns and recommended that a branch be built down through Muscatine to the southern or western boundary of Iowa—or to both—and that another line be built to the northern border of the state through Cedar Rapids and the Cedar Valley.

The charter was amended on June 27, to incorporate these proposed routes and in August the Farnam-Durant firm signed the contract for construction.

With a railroad approaching Rock Island from the east, and with a new line getting set to build to the west from

Davenport, there was still that wide river. Well, the way you get over a river is to build a bridge.

Down at Burrows' Store on Front Street, in Davenport one summer morning of 1853 opinion was pretty well divided as to the sanity of certain leading townsmen, "an' them fellers from the East."

"Just plumb crazy," old Lige, the riverman—a little more stooped and a lot more gray than on that June day of 1845 when he'd got so upset—said to his wizened friend Pete. "Bridge across that river. Why, that'll make navigation so all-fired dangerous—"

"Oh, I don't know," Pete said. He stuffed some fresh scrap into his cavernous jaw. "Folks say the only way it'll interfere with navigation, is mebbe the thing'll fall off its stone pilin' an' float down stream."

"That ain't no comfort to me," Lige said. "It's that same gang that's buildin' the railroad from Chicago. Remember what you said that if Jim Grant's mixed up in anything he's bound to make it good. Well, this Farnam outfit—looks to me like they ain't put their stone pilin' over there on the Island for nothin'. An' that'n right down there—" Lige pointed to the piling that had just been erected on the Iowa shore.

"Guess we'll change as times change," Pete said laconically.

The railroad pioneers hadn't erected the pilings "for nothin'." Long before their iron rails had reached Ottawa, in the early part of this year of 1853, Railroad Bridge Company had been incorporated by a special act of the Illinois Legislature for the purpose of enabling the Chicago and Rock Island to reach the Iowa side of the Mississippi. Now that the railroad was well past the halfway mark on its course from Chicago to Rock Island—in this summer of 1853—everything had been set in motion to begin actual construction of the bridge.

The steamboat interests were crying to high heaven. Legal

brains were employed to develop every obstacle that might be thrown in the path of such a ridiculous thing.

Back in the Bureau Valley the people weren't thinking about a bridge. On September 12 the Rock Island's rails came into the town of Bureau. Southward from Bureau the Peoria line was under construction. A summer of good crops was behind for the farmers. They looked to the day when the railroad would be hauling those crops east to the Chicago markets. They dreamed of good prices. They dreamed of expanding their properties and growing more things. The producers down in the Peoria area wouldn't have to depend on the river to ship their stuff and take a depressed price in the season when navigation remained open. They could hold their grain through the winter, then if the price was advantageous they could load it on the steam cars and send it on its way.

⑥ Mississippi holiday

Washington's Birthday in the year 1854 broke cold and clear over the Mississippi towns of Rock Island and Davenport. A stiff wind blew down from the north, and the pale sun glinted yellow on the blue ice in the river.

All during that morning of February 22 the wagons came. The wagons and the carriages, and men on horseback. Their goal was the wooden structure down by the river front over which a sign hung to tell one and all that this was the "passenger house" of the Chicago and Rock Island Rail Road—the first depot in Rock Island City.

The iron rails were in place at the platform. The iron rails had reached the river. The dream of years had been accomplished.

There was good-natured bantering among the men as they called to the Farnam crews. The workmen were putting the finishing touches to the track and the rough station building, readying it for the arrival of the first train from Chicago.

In the crowd were the enthusiastic supporters and also the unbelievers—men like Lige and Pete from Davenport who still did not want to believe that this thing had come to pass. With Lige and Pete was the bearded and lugubrious driver of the Beardstown Stage. And others who wanted to scoff and ridicule, but whose words were very hollow, because they knew they faced the opening of a new era, and they didn't know how to face it.

All during the day the crowds gathered. Rock Island had prepared for the visitors who would come from Chicago. The program for the festivities had been carefully planned. The celebration would be confined to the people from Davenport and Rock Island City and environs. The big, formal celebration would come later, in good summer weather. Joseph Sheffield had already planned for that. He apparently wasn't going to have things go as they had in Chicago on the occasion of the run of the first train. There would be good organization to the Rock Island events, and there would be a top public-relations job done.

Handbills were all over town. Block type at the top proclaimed "Order of the Day," and below were the words, "Railroad Festival." The handbill gave the arrival time of the train as 5 o'clock p.m., "which event will be heralded by the roar of artillery, the sounds of joyful music, and the acclamations of the people."

When that gaily decorated locomotive pulled its train into the station in the gathering dusk of that February evening it was hard to tell whether the artillery or the people made the most noise. The place was bedlam. The local crowds climbed into the cars as the visitors got out. They climbed on the engine and over its cab roof and over the roof of the coaches. The vast majority of them hadn't even seen pictures of such "a contraption," as it was called.

Then came the banquet and the toasts and the speeches. J. J. Beardsley, of Rock Island, officiated as "President of the Day" and pronounced the welcome. N. B. Buford, who had done so much in the days when the commissioners were trying to raise money, took over as toastmaster. The first toast offered was: "To the 22nd of February, 1854, the espousal day of the Mississippi River and the Atlantic Ocean. May no vandal hands ever break the connection."

Another toast was: "To the Projectors of the Chicago and Rock Island Rail Road. Their hearts rejoice in what their eyes behold. What was conceived in weakness is this day brought forth in strength."

There were others and there were the responses. And finally there was Farnam's response. He said speech-making was not part of his contract.

"It is less than one quarter of a century," he said, "and within the memory of most of you that the first locomotive made its appearance in the States. Now more than fourteen thousand miles of iron rails are traversed by the iron horse at almost lightning speed.

"It is less than two years since the first train of cars entered the State of Illinois from the east, then connecting Lake Erie with Chicago. It is less than one year since the first continuous line of road was completed connecting New York with Chicago . . .

"Two years ago there were less than one hundred miles of road in operation in the State of Illinois, and most of that was what is called the 'strap rail.' Now more than twelve hundred miles of rail of the most substantial character is in operation, eight hundred miles of which leads directly to the City of Chicago.

"Today we witness the nuptials of the Atlantic with the Father of Waters. Tomorrow the people of Rock Island can go to New York the entire distance by railroad, and within the space of forty-two hours."

Farnam praised the coöperation of Governor Matteson, of Illinois, and others. But in the record of his speech no mention was made of the one man who had made possible the whole achievement—Judge James Grant.

The evening was finished off with fireworks, and both Rock Island City and Davenport were "illuminated." Local citizens provided lodging for the visitors who, the following morning, were to return to Chicago.

Another chapter in the history of the railroad's march to empire had been written. The first line of rails to span Illinois from Lake Michigan to the Mississippi had become an accomplished fact.

Even as he spoke to the gathering at Rock Island that February night, Henry Farnam was in trouble. He was in trouble in Iowa, although as yet the Mississippi and Missouri Railroad existed only on paper.

Farnam had sent Hiram Price, an Iowa lawyer of much ability, into the counties through which the proposed railroad would pass on its way to Council Bluffs. Price's job was to enlist the aid of the citizens in getting right-of-way and subscribing to Mississippi and Missouri securities.

At Des Moines, Price found a lot of opposition to what the people termed the "Davenport Road." He had found the same things at other points. In great discouragement he had written to Farnam:

"I have called public meetings at different places and succeeded in passing resolutions leaving a county subscription to be applied to either road, as they may deem best." When he said "either road" he meant the Mississippi and Missouri and another projected railroad called by the Iowans at that time the Lyons Road. This latter had made surveys and its agents had beaten Farnam's man into a number of the county seats and other towns with promises that the Lyons Road would be the very first one.

Of the difficulties in Des Moines, Price told Farnam, "A more crazy and unreasonable people I have never seen than a majority of them are. A few are with us, but the current sets strongly, often irresistibly, the other way . . . The counties between this and Iowa City are not able to take one-third of the stock. The wholly taxable property of Iowa, Poweshiek, and Jasper Counties is only eighty thousand dollars; the distance by a straight line through these counties is seventy-eight miles."

Not very promising, to say the least. Even less so after the results of an election held in Polk County (Des Moines) in which the people voted overwhelmingly to support the Lyons Road.

Through the spring of 1854 Farnam and his associates were too busy to worry a great deal about their Iowa venture. They had the finishing touches to put to the 181-mile completed Chicago and Rock Island, and they had a bridge to build across the Mississippi. Once that bridge actually began to shape up, the people of Iowa's interior might be brought around to a different viewpoint. Certainly that should convince them that nothing could stop the Mississippi and Missouri, and so they had better get on the bandwagon.

Hadn't Sheffield and Farnam proved to the world what they could do in the building of this Chicago and Rock Island? That was a job that could be pointed to with great pride.

And Sheffield was determined to tell the world about it. He sent out invitations on May 1, 1854, to stockholders, bondholders, prominent citizens throughout the East, the top journalists of the day, and the leading politicians, to be guests of the railroad at the formal celebration of the opening of the line on June 5.

It took two special trains to accommodate the guests. They departed from the Chicago station at 9 a.m. June 5, and arrived in Rock Island at 4 that afternoon. On the excursion were Millard Fillmore, ex-President of the United States; George Bancroft, famous historian; Charles A. Dana, of the New York Sun; J. H. Sanford and W. C. Prime of the New

York Journal of Commerce; Chicago's Mayor Isaac L. Milliken and the members of the Chicago city council; and a host of others. James F. Babcock, of the *New Haven Palladium,* wrote long articles on the splendors of the territory through which the excursion passed.

Again there was the banquet at Rock Island, and the speeches. Down on the river the steamboats *War Eagle, Galena, Lady Franklin, Sparhawk, Golden Era,* and *Jenny Lind* were at anchor under charter to the railroad. To these boats the party was assigned, and on the morning of June 6, to the accompaniment of blaring bands, gunfire, and the symphony of the steamboat whistles the excursion started up-river with the town of St. Paul its goal.

At each city and town along the way the party staged parades and concerts and visited the things of interest these places had to offer. The excursion reached St. Paul a little ahead of schedule and found the reception there poorly organized. However, the citizens made up for that during the two days the party visited at that point. St. Paul was the seat of the territorial government of Minnesota and boasted a population of 5,000. There was not one mile of railroad in all the territory.

Visits were made to St. Anthony's Falls (now Minneapolis) and to Fort Snelling. Many in the party saw their first Indians, and the writers who were on the trip were at a loss for words to describe accurately the beauty and the promise of this new far-away land.

Local leaders, listening to the tales their visitors told, were inspired to begin to do something about railroads in Minnesota. They were more than convinced now that railroad development meant their economic development, and they couldn't do without this new form of transportation.

The party returned to Rock Island without stops, and then embarked on their special trains for Chicago and the East. The party was an expensive one, but it paid off for the Chicago and Rock Island which, overnight, became the best-known railroad west of the Alleghanies.

7 Steam cars in Iowa

The Chicago and Rock Island Rail Road was turned over to the corporation by the contractors on July 10, 1854, a year and a half earlier than the time specified in the contract. In the beginning Sheffield and Farnam had agreed to build the road, equip it and turn it over to the company for $3,987,688. Provision was made that any additional expenditures made necessary would be added onto the bill.

The final cost was a little under $4,500,000. That was due largely to the fact that the equipment called for in the contract proved to be inadequate to handle the business that developed from the opening of the first section of the road. The contract called originally for 18 locomotives, 12 passenger cars, 150 box cars, and 150 flat cars. Additions had to be made to keep step with increasing traffic, to the extent that on completion of the contract the builders turned over to the company 28 locomotives, 28 passenger cars, 170 box cars, and 170 flat cars, and a variety of other equipment and rolling stock. In addition the management had on order 10 more locomotives and had under consideration a proposal to increase that order by 8.

The line to Peoria was progressing steadily in that summer of 1854, and the town of Bureau indeed was a busy place. Over the main line, east and west the little wood-burners rattled their way with their yellow coaches loaded and with their laden freight cars strung out behind them. Their smoke plumes arched over the prairies, their whistles blasted the triumph of their progress. From their cab windows the bearded men, who not long before had manned the engines of packet boats, leaned forward with their gaze intent on the gleaming rails and the far horizons.

At Rock Island City business was booming. The pilings were in the river for the contemplated bridge. J. M. D. Burrows, of Davenport, the founder of the store that now was called Burrows and Prettyman, pioneer in developing hog, corn, and wheat crops for transportation eastward, described in his memoirs the opening of the railroad as bringing potato buyers into Rock Island together with other produce buyers in droves.

Years later, recalling those days, Mr. Burrows wrote:

"The opening of the Chicago and Rock Island Rail Road rather bewildered me. It revolutionized the mode of doing business. Heretofore a few men at each business point had done the bulk of the business required, and a great deal of money and good credit were necessary . . . When the railroad got into operation, produce men were as thick as potato bugs. If a man could raise two hundred and fifty dollars he could begin business. That amount would buy a carload of wheat. In the morning he would engage a car, have it put where he could load it, and have the farmer put his wheat, barley, or oats, as the case might be, in the car. By three o'clock in the afternoon the car would be loaded and shipped."

These operators, Burrows said, needed no warehouse, had no rent or labor problem. What Burrows experienced, others did too. The railroad was swiftly changing the whole economy. Old established merchants sensed trouble.

And the bridge project was in trouble, too. It wasn't enough that the money situation in Iowa threatened at that very moment to doom the dreams of Farnam and the Mississippi and Missouri. The United States Government was very busy in an effort to prove, in the courts, that the Rock Island, in condemning land across the Island from the mainland to bridge the river to Davenport, had taken possession of property that was being reserved by the United States for military installations.

The Government sought an injunction on these grounds, and also on the contention that the bridge would be a hazard to navigation. But while the case was being contested in the courts the builders did not stop. They were going to reach Davenport with that structure or they would die in the attempt.

And just to prove that they meant business they had a cornerstone ceremony in Davenport on September 1 that year. They had speeches, and bands marched and played, and flags waved. And the steamboat people indulged in derisive laughter. It was as if they already knew what their first moves would be as soon as this ridiculous thing took definite shape.

To the accompaniment of great cheers, more banquets and more speeches, Sheffield and Farnam opened the Peoria and Bureau Valley line with an excursion from Chicago on November 7, 1854. It was a fine piece of track through a rich farming area along the Illinois River. The Rock Island, six months before, had taken over the property through the execution of a perpetual lease.

The excursion didn't mean that the Peoria line was ready for official operation by the management. The contractors still had much to do before they would turn it over to the railroad company.

At the annual meeting some six weeks after the Peoria excursion, John Jervis announced that he was ready to retire from the railroad's presidency. Farnam's name was placed in nomination, and he was elected. It was of course additional responsibility for him, inasmuch as his building contracts were crying more and more for his full attention.

The Mississippi and Missouri was frankly getting no place, and the way work on the Mississippi Bridge was progressing it looked as if that structure would have trains operating over it before there was any rail laid in the State of Iowa.

It was now early in the year 1855. Material for the river bridge, the stringers and the trusses, were piling up at Rock Island City. The dream of the Iowa people for rails stretching westward from a connection with the bridge seemed farther and farther from realization.

"Something's wrong somewhere," you would hear someone say to a group in the store, or to a friend in the bank. "Ought to be seeing something by now."

"Away last May," another would say, "almost a year ago, we had a big blowout. Antoine Le Claire turned the first earth."

"And what did we do? We laid one wooden tie to mark the beginning of the Mississippi and Missouri. One wooden tie in the dirt there at 5th and Rock Island Streets."

"It's money," would come the rejoinder. "Farnam's men have been moving heaven and earth to get money, to sell their stocks and bonds. But the money is tight."

Farnam raised enough to get started on construction of the 55-mile stretch to Iowa City. The first rail was spiked on June 29. In July 1855, the Mississippi and Missouri executed a mortgage conveying to certain trustees the "first division" of its railroad from Davenport to Iowa City and Muscatine. The mortgage was to secure the payment of the principal and interest on its bonds issued and limited to an aggregate of $1,000,000.

The town of Muscatine was a busy and growing community. Its civic leaders wanted the railroad from Davenport to reach their city first. Groups of Muscatine businessmen met with Farnam and his associates and insisted that Muscatine have the first train.

Iowa City was the capital of the State. It too had great civic pride, and by now there was a feverish interest in getting the rails of the Mississippi and Missouri main line through Iowa City to Des Moines. Unquestionably when Iowa City leaders learned about the insistence of Muscatine people there developed a certain fear that Farnam might

make the Muscatine line the main route toward the Missouri
River.

Accordingly, Iowa City made an offer to Farnam.

"Get your railroad into our city, put a train into our depot
on or before midnight of December 31, this year (1855),
and you get a $50,000 cash bonus."

That, in substance, was what the Iowa City people said
when they laid the deal on the table.

Available records do not specifically state the exact nature
of the internal strife in the Farnam organization between
Farnam and his partner, Tom Durant. It is evident, however,
that Durant was far from being another Joe Sheffield. Durant
possessed none of the financial acumen and sound business
judgment of Farnam's former partner, and certainly none
of Sheffield's ability at organization. Farnam's son, writing
the memoirs of his father, has made reference to Durant's
bent toward wildcat speculation which, at one time, threatened the very destruction of the firm and the personal fortune of Farnam.

Little wonder then that Farnam, without Sheffield on this
Mississippi and Missouri project, was a good deal like a locomotive without a well-fueled tender. This was made strik-
ingly clear by the sorry progress of construction both to Iowa
City and to Muscatine.

The first rails toward Wilton, some 23 miles away, were
laid out of Davenport in midsummer. A Paterson locomotive
named *Antoine Le Claire* was ferried over the river in July and
assigned to construction train service. Another 4-4-0, the
Muscatine, and a third engine, the *Davenport,* were delivered
to the Iowa side to stand in readiness for service on the first
completed section of track.

Wilton was designated as the junction from which the
Muscatine line would veer to the south and the Iowa City
main line would drive straight ahead.

The drive didn't have much behind it. Construction wasn't
difficult from the viewpoint of terrain, but it took better than
five months to spike the last rail in place at the depot in

Muscatine—a total distance of about 35 miles from Davenport.

Farnam advised the Muscatine people that they would have their first train on November 20, 1855. The city planned for a wild celebration. Handbills went out through the country, and an elaborate program was organized. Muscatine had given liberally in the matter of land and money to get this railroad, and what they got finally wouldn't pass too close an inspection. There were rails on the ties, and there was a good grade. But the line was far from ready for regular operation.

November 20 dawned overcast and rainy. In fact all through the morning the rain came in such torrents that the *Muscatine Journal* of that day reported "the mist, mud, and rain were in much greater abundance than should have been visited upon our heads were our sins mountain-high compared with those of any other city in the land."

Through the mist and the rain and the chill, at 1 o'clock that afternoon the first train ever to operate in the State of Iowa whistled on the curve at the edge of town, and the bellowing exhaust of the locomotives *Muscatine* and *Davenport*, double-heading the six overcrowded coaches, sounded the triumphal entry.

The rain didn't dampen the enthusiasm of the crowd. The newspaper later reported that the town was full of strangers who mingled with the residents in the downpour.

Muscatine's mayor, J. H. Wallace, made the speech of welcome, and a flowery oration it was.

"Eighteen years ago," the mayor said, "the spot on which we stand was known only to that unfortunate race that has melted from our sight as the snow melts under the blaze of the meridian sun. Now, instead of the war-whoop we heard the ear-piercing whistle of the locomotive, and instead of the council fire at which was determined the scheme of some bloody foray, representatives from different states are here assembled, proffering their congratulations at the triumph of mind over matter."

The mayor's address was followed by the response of Mayor

Boone, of Chicago, who said Chicago was proud to take Muscatine into its family.

A vast assault on the gastronomical apparatus of the assembled guests at Muscatine's banquet that night is attested to by the newspaper's account of twelve tables "graced with handsome pyramids of cake" and at least twenty kinds of meat. "There was turkey, quail, chicken, venison, tongue, ham, beef, oysters, chicken salad . . . ," and on and on.

Farnam, in response to a toast, said that all this evidence of joy "at the successful completion of a scheme of improvement" was sufficient recompense for his outlay of labor and means.

Watching all this was William P. Clark, of Iowa City. He had taken no small part in promoting the bonus money to get this railroad into his town. He promised the banquet guests that they would hear from Iowa City at the proper time and in the proper manner.

⑧ The battle for the bonus

Farnam, personally, was hearing a lot from Iowa City, and it wasn't very complimentary. The people were asking why their railroad couldn't be built with the same speed that had marked the progress of the Chicago and Rock Island. Here it was December, the bonus money was waiting, the weather was closing in, and it didn't look much as if the Farnam people would make the grade.

The excitement that had been mounting generally among the Iowa City residents found fervid expression in the arguments of the habitues of Crummy's Tavern, the foremost gathering place of those who sought good cheer and the warmth of the big stove.

Among Crummy's guests that early morning of December 31 were two late converts to the belief that the railroad really was here to stay. They were Mr. Pete Simpson and his river-faring crony, Mr. Elijah Wilks, from the environs of Davenport.

They were huddled over their grog at a table in the back corner and they didn't look very happy about anything. They were, to begin with, dog-tired. Their eyes were red-rimmed and their beards were matted. They'd had little sleep, and presently they would trudge their way back to the scene of what looked like a losing game. They were members of that exhausted track gang who were dead-earnest about winning this bonus.

Lige scratched his chin and shook his head solemnly. "A thousand feet away," he said slowly. "Right at the top of the grade comin' into town."

"The wind an' the cold," Pete said. "Gawd, if it wasn't so cold we'd have a chance."

"Thirty below, feller says," Lige responded. He looked at his toil-worn hands. "Never had nothin' like this on the river."

"It was you who said we could make a lotta money on this deal," Pete accused.

"Drivin'," Lige said. "Drivin' so hard we ain't got good sense."

There was a commotion at the front door. A big man, face purple from the bitter cold, stalked into the tavern, and the frigid Iowa blast was at his back. He was the track gang boss.

"Up an' out," he growled in a savage voice. "Yuh can't lay track sittin' here."

Lige got up. "An' us with four hours sleep," he mumbled.

Pete filed out behind him and a group of others.

This was New Year's Eve—the last day of the battle against weather and time.

All that bitter day the crews drove hard. Great fires were built along the right-of-way. By noon the citizens began to drift to the tavern and other places where they could find shelter to wait for news of the railroad's desperate try.

The hoarse shouts of the gang bosses were swallowed in the wind, and the wind burned the reddened, bearded faces. Foot by foot the ties were laid in place. They were laid on the frozen earth. The men couldn't set them or tamp them properly. But they laid the ties and the rails followed.

Eight hundred feet, six hundred feet, five hundred feet to go.

Now it was dark and the great fires along the fill turned the struggle into an eerie sight. No longer could the townspeople stay in the stores and the tavern. They came down to trackside in ever-growing groups. From somewhere came huge pots of coffee, and steaming mugs were passed up to the men who more and more were dulled by the slow paralysis of exhaustion.

As they stopped to sip the heartening brew they looked ahead. There below them stood the wooden structure that was Iowa City's first depot. If only they could make it. Such a little distance yet, and still time. Still a little time.

The people began to cheer the toilers, to shout encouragement.

Nine o'clock . . . ten o'clock . . . eleven o'clock . . .

Sixty minutes. Ties down at the depot platform. Ties on the hard ground. The rails coming along behind them. No time now to spike these rails in place as they should be. Get them down. Get them on the ties. No time for too much sighting for good alignment. Get the rails down. Just spike them any way so that they'll hold that wheezing teakettle of an engine.

Get that engine moving. The engine would be enough. Yes, the deal had been for a train of cars into that Iowa City station. But there wasn't any train of cars. Bring the engine down.

Minutes now—minutes until the church bells would ring

out the old year and ring in the new. If they could only get that engine moving.

The last rail was down. The crowd who saw the spike driven started to shout. The shouts carried back along the track.

John E. Henry, the red-eyed superintendent, gave the rail a quick glance and decided to take the chance. He waved frantically to the engineer. He could see the engine in the dancing firelight, several hundred feet back. Why didn't the thing move?

Crowds were gathering around the engine. John Henry drove tired legs and ran toward it. Something was wrong. He could see the staring eyes in the dismayed faces.

Henry pushed his way to the cab. Charlie Stickles, the engineer was almost in tears. He was waving at his immobile charge.

"She's froze up. I can't move her."

Now Farnam was in the crowd, and Sam Reed, his chief construction engineer, and other officers.

"Pinch bars," Henry shouted. "We'll push 'er."

The pinch bars were produced as if by magic. Men ganged behind the tank to nudge with their shoulders.

Slowly they felt the first give in the stubborn iron thing. There was that awful moment when the silence was broken only by labored breathing. Then the movement was definite. The engine was in grudging motion.

A hell of a way to make a triumphant entry into the capital of Iowa! But they had to get there. Slowly they gained momentum. Nobody could look at a watch. It was the last desperate try.

Foot by foot, now—yard by yard. The fires at the depot were getting closer. The fancy pointed pilot of the engine swayed with the roughness and the bad alignment of the track.

The shouting gained crescendo. It came from the men and from the residents.

It grew to a deafening din as the Mississippi and Missouri's dead engine reached its goal. So deafening was the shouting that seconds later few in that crowd were aware that over the cold blackness of the Iowa night the bells had begun to ring to mark the passing of the year.

Up in the cab of the locomotive, Charlie Stickles looked vaguely around him. He set his brake, climbed slowly to the ground. He raised an arm as if to steady himself beside his engine, and then collapsed.

His fellow workers carried him unconscious into the station.

Throughout this close call to losing that $50,000 bonus, Charlie Stickles had thought he was to blame.

A few days later, on the evening of January 3, 1856, when Henry Farnam stood before the celebrants who had welcomed the first excursion into Iowa City that afternoon, he couldn't have been very proud. He must have remembered his march to empire through the prairies of Illinois when everything had gone off on schedule, where there had been no last minute hitches—certainly nothing so disgraceful as the record of the building into Muscatine and into this capital city of the State of Iowa.

Engineer Charlie Stickles could never have been held up to blame if the builders had lost that bonus.

⑨ Lincoln and the burning bridge

On the early morning of April 1, 1856, two men stood on the ties near the Illinois side of the first bridge to span the broad reaches of the Mississippi River. Both were gentlemen

of impressive physique. The elder was the president of the
Chicago and Rock Island, the builder who probably would
never forget the New Year's Eve at Iowa City and the banquet that followed.

Henry Farnam's record as chief engineer of the Mississippi
and Missouri might not have been anything to point to with
pride. But here, on this April morning of 1856, he might
find some consolation in his survey of this great bridge which
had been planned under his direction, and which he had
supervised to completion in his capacity as Rock Island's
president.

The man beside him was John F. Tracy, Rock Island's
superintendent. Mr. Tracy was known for his rasping voice,
his quick and exacting eye, his taciturnity, his unloving dis-
position, and his inordinate capacity for work. He had come
from Buffalo, and what little can be learned of his career
before his arrival on the Rock Island indicates that he had
worked for some time with the Erie. Unquestionably, he was
a first-rate operating officer and a hard driver of men. He
asked no questions but took hold of a job and personally
saw to it that the job was successfully accomplished.

He had a job to do this morning—the first test run over
this spidery span. He had his engine and eight cars coupled.

"Might as well give her a try," Farnam said.

Tracy agreed. The bridge was all but complete. The mon-
strosity that steamboat men had ridiculed and which one
scoffer had predicted would not stand of its own weight, not
only was firmly in place, and standing serenely, but was ready
for a test to determine whether it would take the weight
of a train.

It did. The engine crossed almost to Davenport, then
backed up to Rock Island. The bridge engineers watched the
performance, checked every tie and rail, the stress on each of
the six spans. The spans were 250 feet in length with the
exception of a draw or "swing" span. The length of this one
was 285 feet. This, when opened, gave a clear channel for
river traffic 120 feet wide on either side of the pier. There was

a little more than 1,000,000 feet of timber in the structure, 220,000 pounds of cast iron and 400,000 pounds of wrought iron. It was, by and large, a modern miracle if not exactly a thing of beauty.

The Davenport *Democrat* whipped up a lot of local excitement by reporting the testing activity on the bridge. Everyone on both sides of the river was talking about it. People with money invested in the sluggish Mississippi and Missouri, which at the moment was doing only a fair amount of business, built new hopes.

"Once we get the connection through with the East," they said, "you watch her boom. Business will be flourishing."

The official connection was made on April 21. The locomotive *Des Moines* crossed and stopped before a gaping crowd at the Davenport Depot. But it was really the next day that the big party came off.

On April 22 three locomotives coupled to eight passenger cars crossed from Illinois to Iowa and really set off a celebration. The *Democrat* pulled out all the stops, used all the adjectives, and gravely pronounced a new era for all the West. Farnam came in for his share of the praise, as did the firm of Stone and Boomer, of Chicago, the contractors.

Unfortunately, the opening of the new era didn't last long. The day the bridge was announced as officially open, no court action stood in its way. The suit brought by the Government earlier had been finally decided in favor of the bridge. Everything looked bright.

Then, on the night of May 6, only a couple of weeks after the impossible had been accomplished, a steamboat got in the way. And it did a very good job of it.

The boat was the *Effie Afton*, out of St. Louis. It was headed upstream after having cleared the draw span. Suddenly it veered as if out of control, swung back downstream, rammed a pier, and instantly burst into flames. The blaze reached high in the air on this still night—mysteriously high when you considered there was no wind—and ignited a span of the bridge.

Just what desperate measures were taken to get the fire under control have never been clearly defined, but evidently the men involved did an excellent job. The fire spread very little beyond the one span, although there was some damage to other parts of the structure. The pier, of course, was considerably banged up.

This *Effie Afton* was an exceedingly fine boat. Her usual run was on the Ohio River and on the Mississippi between Louisville and New Orleans. There was no apparent reason for its appearance this far north on the river in the night. Even today there is no record of who or what the boat carried, or what its destination might have been.

Tension mounted and the people in the Rock Island and Davenport areas were divided into two camps. Those who wanted the railroad, who took pride in the marvelous accomplishment, were sure that the *Effie Afton* had been loaded with something highly inflammable, and that it had been run into the bridge intentionally. The argument was that had it been drifting out of control it would have drifted with the current in the channel and would not have touched the bridge pier.

"No, sir. Them steamboat people done it deliberately," the rail people said. "They laughed at us, an' they said we couldn't build a bridge that would stand. Well, we built her an' she stood, an' so the next thing was to wreck her. But she won't stay wrecked long."

"Them boat people's gonna bring suit. You watch what I tell you."

The steamboat interests were loud in their denunciation of the bridge. They were righteously indignant. Divine Providence had given them the natural waterway for the transportation of people and goods. Then had come these railroaders with their fancy ideas of changing the Divine course of traffic. They had violated all the laws of Nature to clutter up the river with this fool bridge. Now look at what they'd done. They were responsible for the wreck and destruction of one of the finest boats ever to ply the rivers. The railroads would pay for this. They'd be forced to pay dearly and to remove that awful structure.

The Rock Island wasn't quitting now. Word came to Farnam that a man named Hurd, of St. Louis, one of the owners of the *Effie Afton,* would file suit. Well, the railroad had some good law talent, and a good case, as any reasonable man could see, so the railroad wasn't afraid.

Work went ahead all summer to put the bridge back in operating condition, and this was accomplished on September 8, when trains again were run to the Iowa side.

The steamboat interests filed their suit in the United States Circuit court in Chicago. It was officially designated as *Hurd et al.* vs. *Railroad Bridge Company.* Actually it was the river people against railroads. No attempt was made to disguise the true purposes of the suit. The steamboat interests announced in advance that they would base their case on the prior rights of the steamboats to use river waters and that bridges were a dangerous hindrance to navigation and therefore should for all time be prohibited.

The case came to trial in September 1857, before Judge John MacLean. The railroad's legal staff was comprised of Norman Judd, prominent Chicago attorney and a member of the Rock Island's board; George E. Hubbell, of Davenport; and Abraham Lincoln, of Springfield, Illinois.

Lincoln was named principal attorney for the railroad, and because of what he'd been told about the actions of the *Effie Afton* he wanted to look over the bridge and the river carefully.

It was on September 1, 1857, that he sat on the stringers over the current, and with the help of a 12-year-old boy, Bud Brayton, made a time check of the current flow. He secured and made a study of a report on the river in the Rock Island section made by General Robert E. Lee.

During the trial in Chicago Lincoln made his points dramatically on behalf of the bridge. He declared that by no stretch of the imagination could a steamboat, out of control, get so far out of the current as to be able to hit the pier that brought about the fire.

Judge MacLean, in his charge to the jury, said that the whole case simmered down to the one point—was the bridge a material obstruction to navigation?

The jury couldn't agree and was discharged. The case was set down for another trial, but later the action was dismissed by the Hurd interests.

But the bridge still wasn't free from the activities of its opponents. In May, 1858, following the Chicago trial, James Ward, the leader of the steamboat people in St. Louis, brought suit in the United States District Court in Iowa.

Ward prayed the court to find the bridge a nuisance, to prevent the railroad from further enlarging any piers, and, upon final hearing, to "order, adjudge, and decree that the said bridge was erected in violation of the law . . ." and that "it be abated and removed . . . and said river be restored to its original capacity for all purposes of navigation."

It wasn't until April 3, 1860, that Judge Love rendered his decision upholding the Ward contentions.

In his opinion Judge Love said that if he held for the Rock Island in this instance it would let the bars down for other railroads to build bridges until, within not too long a time, there would be a bridge across the Mississippi every forty or fifty miles. He ordered the piers of the superstructure with all appurtenances lying within the State of Iowa to be removed.

The Supreme Court, to which appeal was made, reversed Judge Love's decision. In the first place, said the Supreme Court, the jurisdiction of the Iowa court extended only to the middle of the Mississippi's main channel. Removal of the piers and structure on the Iowa side would solve nothing in the matter of obstruction. Most of all, if Judge Love's assumption was to be accepted, then no lawful bridge could be built across the Mississippi anywhere; "nor could harbors and rivers be improved; nor could the great facilities of commerce, accomplished by the invention of railroads, be made available where great rivers had to be crossed."

The result was to establish for all time the right to bridge navigable streams.

Several railroads had been holding back, watching for the Supreme Court's decision. When it came, the business of spanning the Mississippi with other railroad bridges suddenly blossomed into a boom.

This was the end of the bridge litigation, but it wasn't the end of trouble. Fires and accidents were frequent for the next several years, too frequent and apparently too well-planned to be just happen-so.

1⓪ Farewell to Farnam

While the Rock Island was going through its bridge troubles, Farnam was experiencing both personal and business setbacks in connection with the Mississippi and Missouri.

The year 1857 was a panic year. In Davenport the banking firm of Cook and Sargent went to the wall. So did the big mercantile enterprise of Burrows and Prettyman. Mills collapsed and many businesses went into the hands of creditors. Farnam's partner, Tom Durant, was heavily involved in speculations, and the firm of Farnam and Durant came close to ruin.

On August 29, 1857, Farnam wrote to an associate in New York:

"I thought a week ago that I was a rich man; I now find the concern (his contracting firm) so involved that we cannot possibly go on, and the firm must make an assignment tonight or Monday. The loss of property is nothing, if I was only sure that I had enough for the support of my dear wife and family; to lose everything now is rather more than I can bear."

Farnam was saved through the activities of his friends in the East.

It wasn't exactly Farnam's fault that the building of the Mississippi and Missouri had bogged down after its entrance into Iowa City. The general business depression and the tightness of money brought construction work almost to an end.

And to make matters a little tougher for the Mississippi and Missouri, the citizens and settlers along the route to Des Moines were building a fire under state and local authorities for the forfeit of land grants that had been made to encourage the rapid building of the line.

The grants resulting from an act of Congress approved May 15, 1856, called for alternate sections designated by odd numbers, six sections in width on each side of the line, to be owned by the railroad and to be developed for settlement. In the event settlers on these lands claimed possession, an indemnity feature was provided to extend the railroad grants 15 to 20 miles on each side of the right-of-way and outside the regular land-grant limits.

The Federal Government didn't assign this land directly to the railroad, but to the State, which, in turn, by legislative action, granted the property to the railroad. This arrangement gave the people the opportunity to put terrific pressure on the members of the legislature to have the railroads routed via their towns and completed by certain dates, otherwise the railroads would forfeit their claims to the land.

Because the Mississippi and Missouri was so far behind in its construction, the citizens of Des Moines and the territory between that city and Council Bluffs raised a clamor for the cancellation of the railroad's charter west of Des Moines.

This was the situation in Iowa as the war clouds gathered over the nation. The boom of cannon fire at Fort Sumter, and the subsequent roll of the war drums North and South, turned the attention of the people to the grim crisis that faced the nation.

Farnam had completed in September, 1858, the extension of the Muscatine branch from Muscatine to Washington, Iowa, and the main line from Iowa City to Grinnell reached the latter point in 1862.

The end of the track came for Henry Farnam in June, 1863. He stepped out of the presidency of the Rock Island, a well-built, well-operated, and prosperous railroad. His building of the Mississippi and Missouri, in marked contrast to his record on the Rock Island, had in eight years reached only a little beyond Brooklyn on its way to Kellogg—still far short of Des Moines.

Charles W. Durant, of New York, became the Rock Island's fourth president, and John Tracy was elevated to the position of vice-president and superintendent. Tracy was doing an excellent job of operating the Rock Island.

Gross income on the Rock Island had increased from $1,242,906 shown in the first full year of operation after the contractors had turned the road over to the company (July 11, 1854 to June 30, 1855), to $1,529,141 for the period from April 1, 1862, to March 31, 1863.

Two years later, for the period from April 1, 1864, to March 31, 1865, this gross had risen to $3,359,290.

But for the Mississippi and Missouri from almost the date of the first operation of a train the story was sad indeed.

The story was so grim that in October, 1865, the Mississippi and Missouri president, John A. Dix, addressed a circular to the stock- and bondholders in which he gave the sorry picture. He pointed out that the company's earnings for the first six months after the road was accepted from the contractors—55 miles from Davenport to Iowa City, and 12 miles of branch from Wilton to Muscatine—amounted to $184,193. This had enabled the company to pay the interest on its bonds and to pay a 4 percent dividend to its stockholders. From then on the rising bonded debt and declining income clearly indicated eventual collapse.

Dix, in his letter, said that while gross earnings for the fiscal year ending June 30, 1860, were $207,688, the net before fixed charges for the year was but $97,889, while the annual interest on the bonded debt amounted to $145,300.

The situation during the war years didn't improve. In fact, it got worse. Under pressure to speed up construction or lose its land grants, the company disposed of its land grant bonds at 60 percent of par, "thus adding enormously to the aggregate of its debt."

Dix concluded, "your company is therefore driven to the necessity of selling the road or reorganizing on a basis which will furnish the means of constructing 40 miles of road and extending it to Des Moines, the Capital of Iowa, and deferring to a future time the payment of existing liabilities."

On October 20, 1865, the holders of Mississippi and Missouri securities met in New York to consider the recommendation of the president that the road be sold to the Chicago and Rock Island Rail Road Company for $5,500,000 unless $1,500,000 could be raised immediately to complete the line to Des Moines. The security-holders voted for the sale.

An agreement was entered into whereby the Mississippi and Missouri would act immediately to have all mortgages upon its property speedily foreclosed, and the Chicago and Rock Island Rail Road Company would incorporate in Iowa a company which would purchase the Mississippi and Missouri. A bond issue of $9,000,000 due in 25 years, and bearing interest at 7 percent, would be secured by a new mortgage on all the consolidated property between Chicago and Des Moines. The money thus raised would pay the $5,500,000 purchase price of the Mississippi and Missouri, pay off the then existing mortgage on the Chicago and Rock Island in the amount of $1,400,000 and the bonds of the Bridge Company which stood at $600,000. Further, the Chicago and Rock Island would take over the operation of the Mississippi and Missouri on December 1, 1865.

The Chicago, Rock Island and Pacific Railroad Company in Iowa, referred to as Pacific No. 1, was incorporated under the general laws of the state June 12, 1866, "for the purpose of purchasing, acquiring, and owning the railroad now built by the Mississippi and Missouri Rail Road Company, together with all and singular the railway lands used and occupied for right-of-way . . . and all personal property, rights and privileges and franchises granted to or acquired by said Mississippi and Missouri Rail Road Company at any time heretofore and also all the lands granted by Act of Congress of May 15, 1856, to the State of Iowa, and by the State of Iowa granted said Mississippi and Missouri Rail Road Company, and when so acquired to maintain and operate the said railroad . . .

"And also for the purpose of building, maintaining and operating a railroad from Kellogg, the west terminus of the constructed railroad of the Mississippi and Missouri Rail Road Company to the City of Des Moines, in the State of Iowa."

The Mississippi and Missouri passed into the hands of the new company on July 9 by a foreclosure sale at the Court House in Davenport.

The consolidation of the Chicago and Rock Island in Illinois and of the Chicago, Rock Island and Pacific Railroad Company in Iowa was effected August 20, 1866, by articles filed in both states in accordance with the laws, and the Chicago, Rock Island and Pacific Railroad Company (Pacific No. 2) came into being.

⑪ Late arrival at the Missouri

For John F. Tracy, indefatigable concentration on efficient operation, singleness of purpose, and straightforward drive from the day he went to work for Henry Farnam as assistant superintendent in Chicago in 1854, finally paid off.

In August 1866, upon the consolidation of the lines in Illinois and Iowa, Tracy was elected president. The passing of time hadn't mellowed him. He had no family and his friends were very few. His face was a little more lined and he was gray at the temples, but he was unchanged in other respects. He only needed one quick look at a problem to be able to determine what course to take.

One of his first problems was the necessity for immediate steps to get this railroad into Des Moines and on to Council Bluffs. The Iowa people were anything but friendly, and while Tracy didn't much care whether anybody liked him personally, he was greatly concerned that they should like his railroad.

Tracy put the line into Des Moines on September 9, 1867, and operated the first passenger train to the Des Moines station for the edification of the populace.

But the populace wasn't much impressed. In the first place, a line known as the Des Moines Valley Rail Road had completed building from Keokuk, down on the Mississippi, into the capital city, and had operated a very famous excursion into Des Moines on August 29, 1866. In the second place, there was so much dissension among Des Moines people over the fact that it had taken more than 12 years to get the Davenport-Council Bluffs road this far that they couldn't whip themselves into a lather of excitement when the Rock Island engine finally whistled into town. Somewhere along the line the City of Des Moines had posted a $10,000 bonus to help speed things along, but the builders never made the bonus date, so the money was never paid.

It didn't take long, however, for the citizens of Des Moines and the Polk County area to realize the value of having, at last, a through main line right into Chicago. Tracy saw to that. He left no stone unturned to give Iowa the best operation possible. He won friends the hard way—but only as far as Des Moines.

What about that stretch between the capital and Council Bluffs?

Tracy and his associates hit on a bright idea. They'd win friends there, too. They needed some quick cash to the tune of something over four million dollars to do the job.

Without giving any prior notice to the public—and in those days they were not required by law to do so—the railroad management issued 49,000 shares of new capital stock with a par value of $4,900,000. The sale of these securities, after paying all expenses, put more than $4,800,000 in the treasury. Council Bluffs would have its railroad in record time. The machinery was set up for a rush job to completion.

A very large monkey wrench was suddenly tossed to stop the machinery before it could really get started. The monkey wrench came in the form of a whole series of lawsuits.

Just about the time Tracy and the Rock Island directors got set to float their new stock issue, a group of astute gentlemen interested in speculation both in Chicago and New York were quietly engaged in engineering a corner on Rock Island securities which would give them control of the railroad. It would have been a nice deal on which to ride had not Mr. Tracy's unannounced stock sale caused an overnight upset.

The speculating gentlemen claimed to have lost their shirts and numerous other articles of apparel and forthwith went to the courts.

The legality of the entire proceedings in the Rock Island's acquisition of the Mississippi and Missouri and the issuance of the new stock was questioned.

Court actions against the Rock Island were brought in Eastern districts, and in almost all instances the courts held against the railroad. Some judges even issued injunctions restraining the Rock Island from spending any money realized from the sale of the new stock.

There was a way to meet this unprecedented action. Tracy and the directors met it by throwing themselves on the mercy of the Iowa legislature and appealing to the lawmakers to determine the legality of the railroad's actions.

All that was needed was a good strong law, so the Iowa legislators gave the railroad one. The law demanded the completion of the road to Council Bluffs, recognized the validity of the consolidation of August, 1866, re-granted to the consolidated company the lands granted to the state by the Act of May 15, 1856, and reserved to the State the power to regulate charges for the transportation of persons and goods. It ratified the issue and sale of the questioned stock, and postponed the election of a board of directors for one year.

The speculators might have questioned the validity of the act, and in some legal circles it was felt that the law would not stand up. But, if the opponents made too much ado about it they stood to lose more than what had already gone down the drain. The kicker in the law was the land-grant part, and the lands so granted equaled one-half the value of the whole railroad. The law said that if the Council Bluffs extension wasn't completed by June 1, 1869, the road would forfeit any further claims to all that valuable land. And nobody could complete a railroad within that short a time with the building funds tied up in lawsuits.

The Rock Island won out, and on May 11, 1869, the last rail was spiked down on the bluffs overlooking the Missouri River.

While the final touches were being made to the line into Council Bluffs, the people of Chicago were being treated to a new "wonder of the world." Rock Island's big and recently completed station at the corner of Van Buren and La Salle Streets daily entertained large crowds who came to view a most unusual locomotive.

Since the first engine steamed out to Joliet in 1852, it was not uncommon for locomotives to be gaily painted and to be adorned with brightly polished brass. The one that stood in the Chicago station that May of 1869 was all silver. Its boiler jacket was of German silver and many of the engine's decorations and appurtenances were silvered. Named *America*, the locomotive had been built by the Grant Works, of Paterson, New Jersey, for the Universal Exposition in Paris in 1867. It had attracted so much attention that Allen Manvel, Tracy's purchasing agent, had prevailed upon Tracy to buy it for operation over the Rock Island.

Tracy decided a good time to induct the *America* into service would be with the completion of the Council Bluffs extension.

The silver engine, coupled with four other engines and a long string of crowded coaches, came to a stop at the depot on Pearl Street in the early afternoon of May 12. According to the Council Bluffs *Nonpareil* of May 15, 1869, the arrival of the Rock Island excursion touched off quite a party.

"Train whistles shrieked," the paper reported, "and for a few minutes the earth shook with the reverberations of music and the cannon, that told in numbers not only that Council Bluffs was jubilant, but that there were thirty-eight States in the Union that looked with pride upon the completion of one of the grand tributaries to the great artery that is to bring to our doors the wealth of Ormus . . ."

It is doubtful that any of the writer's audience had any idea as to who or what Ormus might be, but from all accounts of the happenings on that May 12 they had a wealth of fun right at home. Mayor D. C. Bloomer welcomed the guests, led the parade, and got extremely wet during a shower.

Rock Island was very busy regaining friends in Iowa.

PART TWO

The Links and the Forge

1869-1883

12 John Tracy—review and resolve

John F. Tracy, on that night of May 12, 1869, drank no cup of triumph. The last dim purple faded from the western sky and the river picked up the blurred reflections of the scattered lights of Omaha. The gunfire, the blaring bands, the oratory, and the wild acclaim that had marked the welcome for the Rock Island to Council Bluffs long had been stilled. In the eating houses and in the taverns men talked about the new railroad. The oil lamps burned in the editorial offices of the *Nonpareil* while pens scratched out the words that would record this history.

Whatever the scribes would say could in no way bring solace to the big and silent man who headed what in time was to become Iowa's greatest railroad system. To John Tracy it was not great tonight. Not that he himself was in any way to blame for the long series of failures that had marked the shaky progress of the road from Davenport to Council Bluffs. He had set out with grim determination on that day when he had taken the job as president of the Rock Island lines in Illinois and the newly acquired mileage of the Mississippi and Missouri in Iowa, to complete what his predecessors had failed so miserably to do.

From Des Moines to Council Bluffs now stretched the lonesome, curving miles of iron. It was a through main line, under one management, connecting the Missouri with Chicago and serving the important cities of Des Moines, Davenport, Rock Island, Moline, La Salle, Ottawa, and Joliet in between. Should not the realization of this fact have been cause for rejoicing in the heart of John Tracy?

That might well have been, save for one thing. He was two years and five months late. There it was in the newspapers spread out before him. The story of Promontory Point was still on the front pages, and the editorial columns were lavish in their commendations and in their praise.

It had happened two days before. It had come over the telegraph on May 10, from Promontory Point, Utah. It was the story of the completion of the Union Pacific—the joining of the Union Pacific and the Central Pacific with the driving of the golden spike that made at last an unbroken line of railroad from Omaha to the western sea. Now it would be possible for passengers and goods to travel by rail across the whole width of the North American continent from the Atlantic to the Pacific. The dream that in the late 1840's took form in the efforts of Asa Whitney and others to promote a Pacific railroad now had become a reality.

For John Tracy, and for the many who had built their hopes in the Mississippi and Missouri, the whole thing was nothing short of irony. The one railroad that had started out of Davenport with such high promise, that had turned the first wheels over Iowa soil, that had been built up as the railroad that would reach Council Bluffs long before the first earth would be scratched for the building of the Union Pacific, to-night found itself with no part in either the profit or the glory.

In John Tracy's mind the picture moved in sharp review.

Two years and five months before, another road that had started out of Cedar Rapids in 1860, four years after the Mississippi and Missouri had reached Iowa City, had laid its rails into Council Bluffs to become the official connection of the Union Pacific to the East. That road had been organized as the Cedar Rapids and Missouri River and had come under lease to the Galena and Chicago Union (predecessor of the Chicago and Northwestern) in 1862.

The newspapers, in their summary of the Union Pacific's progress, told of the close links between the men who had been responsible for the Cedar Rapids and Missouri River, and the men who had laid the iron across the high plains and over the forbidding mountains. A mighty achievement, indeed, accomplished by mighty men.

Who were they? Here is where the irony bit deeper. Their names in the black type read like the official roster of the Chicago and Rock Island, the Peoria and Bureau Valley, and the Mississippi and Missouri in their beginnings.

"President of the Union Pacific, General John A. Dix, could not attend the driving of the golden spike, but in his stead Dr. Thomas Clark Durant, vice-president and general manager, stood with bowed head, and General Grenville M. Dodge, chief engineer . . ."

Dix, Durant, Dodge, Samuel B. Reed, Peter A. Dey, William B. Ogden—all their names were prominent on the lips of men who spoke in awe of this historic achievement.

"Monumental," one newspaper writer put it, "when it is realized that in 1867, when the Cedar Rapids and Missouri River Railroad reached Council Bluffs, the Union Pacific had constructed less than 300 miles of its line, and now just two years later, its whole length of more than 1,000 miles is ready for traffic."

Dix, editorially, was designated as a man of outstanding business acumen, and with a firm administrative grasp of this great railroad project. Durant was lauded as a driving force, a man of vision who could make reality of what seemed the impossible.

The smile on Tracy's bearded face was crooked.

It was this same John A. Dix who, in the year 1853, was elected to the presidency of the Mississippi and Missouri, and who, almost three years later, on the night of January 3, 1856, stood before an audience in Iowa City to acknowledge the plaudits of the citizens on the occasion of the first train into the then capital of the State.

It was Dix who that night apologized for the delays that had marked the building of the Mississippi and Missouri over these 55 miles from Davenport, and who promised that from here on every effort would be made to have the railroad into Des Moines by the end of the year.

It was Peter A. Dey who, with his assistant, Grenville M. Dodge, located the Peoria and Bureau Valley line and then proceeded to Davenport to be assigned by Dix to make the survey of the Mississippi and Missouri to Council Bluffs. Their instructions were, on reaching Council Bluffs, to cross the Missouri, stake out a location for a bridge, then go westward into the Nebraska Territory to develop a location for a railroad to the far West. That was in 1853.

Dodge's recommendation, after his location job had been completed, was to build the Mississippi and Missouri from both ends—westward from Davenport and eastward from Council Bluffs. He pointed out in his report that materials and supplies for the west end could be brought up the Missouri by boat. It was Dodge's opinion that the whole line could be ready for traffic in 1859.

Whether or not John A. Dix considered Dodge's recommendations, or turned them over to Thomas C. Durant and Henry Farnam, the Mississippi and Missouri contractors, no one now living will ever know. It is a matter of record that, in 1857, Dodge visited the New York offices of President Dix to urge a new survey of that portion of the line between Des Moines and Council Bluffs with a view to eliminating some of the grades and curves. Dix, despite his acumen, apparently evidenced no interest.

Whatever the administrative grasp of John Dix, whatever the driving force of Tom Durant, whatever the engineering genius of Henry Farnam, their dismal performance for the people of Iowa who had placed their hopes and their fortunes in the Mississippi and Missouri was in marked contrast to what the editorial writers were to say about them in May of 1869.

Certainly, from the very beginning these men, together with William B. Ogden, first mayor of Chicago, first vice-president of the Mississippi and Missouri, were thinking of more than a railroad from Davenport to Council Bluffs. That would only be the first segment. Sooner or later Congress would act on the Pacific Railroad—Congress would pass a bill that would make possible a railroad to the coast of California. And when that happened, the Mississippi and Missouri would be bringing the materials and supplies into Omaha—the rails and the timbers and the iron for the bridges.

Congress passed the bill and President Abraham Lincoln's signature made it into law on July 1, 1862. Among the names of the incorporators were Ogden and Farnam. The bill provided that commissioners be named for each of the several States, and that these commissioners take subscriptions for the stock.

The commissioners called a meeting in Chicago in September 1862. Its purpose was to create interest in the Union Pacific so that the stock sale might be given added impetus. Prominent in the meeting were Thomas Clark Durant, William B. Ogden, and Samuel R. Curtis, associate of Ogden, and the man who a few years later was to push the Cedar Rapids and Missouri River into Council Bluffs.

Out of the meeting was formed what was called the Association for the Organization of the Union Pacific Railroad. Ogden, the vice-president of the Mississippi and Missouri, was elected president. He was at the same time serving as president of the Chicago and Northwestern Railway Company, and was a director of the Galena and Chicago Union. He had had behind him by that time a long career in real estate and railroad promotion and speculation and had made a great deal of money, at least on paper. He was now actively engaged in bringing about the merger of the Galena and Chicago Union with the Chicago and Northwestern, and he had his eye on that railroad that was building out of Cedar Rapids westward.

Since Ogden's main interest seemed to be the creation of a great Northwestern system it is little wonder that he had long ago lost interest in the Mississippi and Missouri and its ultimate fate.

If Ogden had lost interest, had he also influenced Durant to look upon the Mississippi and Missouri as a lost cause? It will be remembered that Ogden was on the Mississippi and Missouri committee that had traveled the route from Davenport up the Cedar Valley to Cedar Rapids in 1853 and had brought about the amendment to the Mississippi and Missouri charter to provide for a branch to Cedar Rapids—a line that the Mississippi and Missouri and its successor, the Rock Island, never built.

It was September 1862, and the Mississippi and Missouri was bogged down at Marengo, Iowa. Its rails ended against a mound of dirt and a pile of ties just 84 miles west of Davenport and 232 miles short of its Missouri River goal. It had been more than six years since John Dix had stood before the people of Iowa City and pledged to do his best to get the line to Des Moines by the end of 1856. In that six-year period the Mississippi and Missouri had built just 30 miles west of Iowa City, and beyond the pile of ties at tracks' end stretched 91 empty miles to Des Moines.

It was this same John A. Dix who in October, 1863, after the completion of the Union Pacific corporate structure and the election of directors, was chosen president of this great new railroad company.

Thomas Clark Durant, co-builder of the Mississippi and Missouri, member of its board, member of the directorate of the Chicago and Rock Island, was elected vice-president and general manager of the Union Pacific. Durant had subscribed heavily to Union Pacific stock—reputedly more than a million of his own funds—and now he was on fire. This driving force, this speculating genius who had emerged from medical college at twenty, and who had spurned a slow dollar when he saw how his family turned the dollar faster in grain and stocks and bonds, was on fire.

Already he had sent Peter Dey and Grenville Dodge over the high plains and into the Rockies to find the best location for the railroad to the Pacific. He had, along with Ogden, sold the Union Pacific down the line to every friend and associate he had. His enthusiasm was contagious.

What had happened to his enthusiasm for the Mississippi

and Missouri? Apparently nobody knew, nor did anyone care. John Dix was about to throw in the sponge on that property anyway. Farnam was out of the picture, both on the Mississippi and Missouri and on the Chicago and Rock Island. Durant's brother, Charles W., was heading up the Rock Island management. Charles would help out the Mississippi and Missouri.

What about getting that railroad to Council Bluffs? The Union Pacific would need the connection from the very start. The Union Pacific would have to get its rails, its locomotives and cars, its construction material in from Chicago and the east.

What about it? Ogden's associate, Curtis, was pushing a railroad to Council Bluffs. No, it wasn't the Mississippi and Missouri. The Mississippi and Missouri had gotten as far as Brooklyn, and would reach Grinnell in another year if everything went all right. But the railroad was in bad shape physically and financially, while this Cedar Rapids and Missouri River Line that Ogden was behind—well, it was being built economically; it was under lease to the Galena Union, another one of Ogden's pets; and, together with the Northwestern, there would be a through line from Chicago to Council Bluffs. True, the Mississippi and Missouri had a bona fide contract with the Union Pacific that would make it the official eastern connection, but the contract had a string attached. It depended upon the Mississippi and Missouri reaching Council Bluffs in time to bring in the things the Union Pacific would need as its building progressed.

Building of the Union Pacific began in August of 1865 after so much delay that it had both Dix and Durant in a sweat. Dix, in fact, was in a sweat on two counts.

First, the Mississippi and Missouri debt had mounted to the point where it was something more than staggering. Its rails were now at Kellogg, still 40 miles short of Des Moines. The company had in operation, including the Muscatine-Washington line, 183 miles of railroad. It had taken 10 years to complete this mileage as compared to the 23 months it had taken

Sheffield and Farnam to build the same amount of mileage from Chicago to Rock Island. It had issued $9,525,000 in bonds, $7,000,000 of which, bearing 7 percent interest, were outstanding. That made the bond issue per mile $40,000. Sheffield's record on the Rock Island had shown a total cost for building and equipping 181 miles of main line of $25,000 per mile.

Second, if Dix and Durant didn't get something started shortly on the Union Pacific the investing public might become hard to handle, and it was certainly evident that neither of these stalwart gentlemen could afford to have people taking too close a look at their record on the Mississippi and Missouri. Dix knew that shortly he would have to send his letter to the Mississippi and Missouri stockholders and suggest a foreclosure sale. Already Durant's brother, Charles, currently president of the Rock Island, had loaned the Mississippi and Missouri a half million in cash to get that Council Bluffs construction under way, and nothing much had happened.

The headache on the Union Pacific was centered in Durant's attempts to get a contractor to build the road. He could find no takers, although he had tried every well-known firm with sufficient means to do the job. Finally, he did a little master-minding and came up with the idea of taking on a Des Moines politician by the name of H. M. Hoxie, who had done some contracting, and forming a dummy company which he and some of his associates would finance. What Durant actually started, and what brought about his eventual downfall in the infamous Credit Mobilier does not concern this record.

What Dix and Durant had done, or what they had failed to do in their obligations to the stock- and bondholders of the Mississippi and Missouri, certainly is in marked contrast to their performance in the organization and completion of the Union Pacific.

Durant's last connection with the Rock Island system followed John Tracy's move to complete the Iowa Line by issuing that 49,000 shares of new common that had resulted in so many court actions and had caused so much more delay.

Following the action of the Iowa legislature which put an end to the injunctions against use of the money that had been raised by the sale of the questioned stock, Thomas Clark Durant, his brother Charles, and a third member of the Durant family, Clark, all resigned as Rock Island directors.

Had these three been among the "certain parties" who had been seeking in 1867 to get control of the Rock Island? If John Tracy knew the answer he left no record of it. From what can be pieced together from scattered reports in various financial journals, it appears that groups of leading financial interests, rather than individuals, were involved. The implication seems clear that the Durants were heavily involved and may have been the leaders.

The 49,000 shares of new stock were sold in December 1867. The Iowa legislative action to validate the stock occurred on February 11, 1868. On March 26, just a few weeks later, the three Durants resigned from the Rock Island board. They had held these offices for 15 years. Shortly after, Tom Durant filed a suit at Davenport seeking a writ of attachment against the property of the Rock Island railroad. The court disallowed the writ.

Now it was May 1869, and John Tracy's railroad was at the Missouri River. No time to brood over past failures, no time to rankle over the conduct of men who had been his associates, or what they had done to thwart the hopes of Iowa's *first* railroad.

John Tracy had learned a lot about business ethics, or rather the complete lack of them. He had learned about the ruthless drive of men like Tom Durant. He had learned about speculation. The next big move would be his.

13 High line to Leavenworth

The Rock Island railroad, in that mid-year of 1869, stood on the threshold of a vast expansion. John Tracy already had begun a series of long-range plans, and he was cracking the whip. He had important irons in the fire—much too important to spend time brooding about the mistakes and mismanagement of his Mississippi and Missouri predecessors. Of one thing he was sure—no competitor, no group of speculators, would ever again get the jump on him in tapping fertile territory and increasing his railroad's traffic sources.

With the Council Bluffs line behind him, he found himself involved in three new major projects and a number of smaller ones. First, he was about to get a new bridge across the Mississippi, and the United States Government was going to build it. Second, there was a beautifully fertile territory west of Washington, Iowa, the end of his line from Muscatine, and the time looked ripe for building a railroad to Leavenworth, Kansas, just across the Missouri River. Third, some very quiet and secretive plans were in the making, which, if Henry H. Porter, of Chicago, one of Rock Island's new directors, could work the matter out, would bring the Chicago and Northwestern under Rock Island control.

Back in June of 1866 a bill was passed by Congress authorizing the Secretary of War to relocate the line of the railroad across Rock Island so that there would be no interference with the re-establishment of an arsenal on the Island, a project that was begun by the Government in 1862. The act of June 27,

1866, besides providing for grants of necessary land for right-of-way, also authorized the erection of a new bridge which would be a double-decked affair. Rail traffic would use one level; wagon traffic would use another.

Then, on March 2, 1867, a bill was approved calling for the erection of a bridge at Rock Island and providing "that the ownership of said bridge shall be and remain in the United States, and the Rock Island and Pacific Railroad Company shall have the right-of-way over said bridge for all purposes of transit across the Island and River upon the condition that the said company shall, before any money is expended by the Government, agree to pay and shall secure to the United States, first, half the cost of said bridge; and second, half the expense of keeping said bridge in repair; and upon guaranteeing said conditions to the satisfaction of the Secretary of War, by contract, or otherwise, the said Company shall have full use of said bridge for purposes of transit, but without any claim to ownership thereof."

This looked like a pretty stiff deal—half the cost of the whole job, but no claim to ownership.

Just who might have done the job of lobbying on the bill as it stood, and just who might have pressed for the new resolution in the Congress that was approved on July 20, 1868, does not appear in the record. But that resolution made the deal a better one for the railroad in that it provided that the Government would build the bridge, but the railroad would pay for only half the cost of the *superstructure* over the main channel. The railroad would have to build its own bridge from the mainland across the Island, and would have to pay half the cost of keeping the Government bridge in repair. A further provision called for the removal of the old bridge "within six months after the new bridge is ready for use," and for removal of the original tracks laid across the Island.

John Tracy signed his name to an agreement with the Government, guaranteeing the railroad's fulfillment of the terms of the act, and then and there was able to dispel from his mind any further worries about lawsuits and sabotage. Once the

Government got into the picture, the railroad would never again be liable for any alleged damage to boats on the river, or to cargo delayed by reason of interference with navigation.

John Tracy worked very closely with Army Engineer Lt. W. P. Buller who finally submitted three plans for the new bridge to the Secretary of War. The first called for a double-tracked railroad deck with a deck for wagon traffic above the railroad. The total estimated cost was $1,234,525. Buller's second plan provided for a single track on the railroad portion with the wagon level above the tracks, at approximately $978,085. Plan No. 3 got the total cost down to $934,291, and provided for a single track level for the railroad, below which the wagon traffic level would be built. The last proposal was adopted despite the fact that the Army engineers recommended the double-track plan. The contention on the part of the Government was that the bill which authorized the bridge allowed an expenditure of no more than $1,000,000.

Work on the new bridge got under way finally about the middle of 1869 after Congress on March 3 appropriated $500,-000 for the work to begin.

It was in this month of June, 1869, that Tracy and the Rock Island directors reached their decision to push westward from Washington, Iowa.

The Mississippi and Missouri had extended the line to Washington, from Muscatine, 11 years before, and Washington had been the scene of the one greatly successful first train celebration in all of the Mississippi and Missouri's hectic history. That train, drawn by a new locomotive named *Washington*, arrived with 13 cars and 700 passengers on September 1, 1858.

The business interests of Washington were glad to have their town remain, over the ensuing years, the end of track. Fortune smiled on the community as it became the center of a vast trading territory. People with produce to ship had to bring it to Washington to get it on the railroad, and that meant that these people with cash derived from what they had to sell bought the things they needed from Washington merchants.

But the growing settlement of the land to the west and the southwest made it increasingly necessary to give thought to extending the railroad at last.

As early as 1860 promoters of railroad expansion had an eye on building a line to connect Fort Leavenworth, Kansas, with that other great Army post at Fort Des Moines. In that year, on January 4, the Platte County and Fort Des Moines Railroad Company was incorporated in the state of Missouri, "to construct a railroad from a point on the Missouri River in Platte County, Missouri, on the most eligible and practicable route to a point on the line dividing the states of Missouri and Iowa, in the direction of old Fort Des Moines, Iowa."

This project apparently reposed on paper until February 12, 1864, when the Missouri legislature approved a special act to change the name of the line to Platte City and Fort Des Moines Railroad Company. Provision was made that the railroad should start within one mile of the city of Weston and run through Platte County, passing within not more than three miles of Platte City. Another change in name by special act of the Missouri legislature in July 1867 made it the Leavenworth and Des Moines Railway Company.

Indications are that during these years of changing the corporate names, one after another, the promoters built nothing in the way of a rail line. They probably made surveys, and some grading may have been done at one point or another.

Thus, on March 3, 1869, with the Rock Island behind the incorporators to get something concrete started, the Missouri legislature approved a change in the corporate title to Chicago and Southwestern Railway Company (of Missouri). The new charter specified that the western terminus of the line be at a point on the Missouri River opposite, or nearly opposite the city of Leavenworth, Kansas, and authorized the building of a branch line in the direction of Ottumwa, Iowa.

With the breaking of ground, and the beginning of construction at Stillings Junction, Missouri, opposite Leavenworth, the civic leaders of Leavenworth began negotiations with the Rock Island to induce Tracy to construct a single line, under unified management, from Washington, Iowa, to their city.

At a meeting of the Rock Island directors, a special committee made up of members of the board was named to visit Leavenworth and make a complete survey of the possibilities. Certainly, if a line such as the Leavenworth people proposed had strong economic value the Rock Island wanted to know about it.

The committee visited Leavenworth in June and came back with a report which recommended that "a new company should be incorporated in Iowa, with power to construct and operate a railway from Washington, on the Oskaloosa Branch to a point on the boundary line between the states of Iowa and Missouri, at which it could connect with the railway of the Chicago and Southwestern of Missouri; that these companies should be consolidated; that the consolidated company should issue a series of bonds having a par value of $5,000,000 or $20,000 per mile for the road to be constructed . . ."

Under the recommendation the bonds would be secured by a first mortgage on the company's property, and the Rock Island would guarantee payment of both principal and interest. The bonds, the committee said, should contain a clause which "should secure to the guarantor the right of subrogation as to all principal and interest it should pay in the performance of its contract of guaranty, with the right to demand the foreclosure of the mortgage and the sale of the property subject to the rights of the holders of the bonds secured by the same mortgage, and that the Chicago, Rock Island and Pacific Railroad Company should receive and hold a majority of the capital stock of the consolidated company."

The Rock Island directors accepted and approved the committee's report promptly, and the work of constructing the Leavenworth line gained momentum.

Meanwhile, the promoters of the company in Missouri secured a charter from the legislature in that state for the

Chicago and South Western Railway Company in Iowa. The purpose was to bring Atchison, Kansas, into the picture by providing for the construction of a railroad from the east bank of the Missouri, opposite Atchison, to a junction with the Leavenworth line. This was to be commonly called the Atchison Branch, and in time it was to become an expensive headache to the Rock Island.

With work of construction on the Leavenworth line progressing eastward from Stillings Junction, on the Missouri River, and westward from Washington, Iowa, and with the contract calling for completion of the whole line by November 1, 1871, Tracy could now devote most of his attention to the scheme that had been hatching for control of the Chicago and Northwestern.

14 1,000 miles of railroad

John Tracy, through some pretty bitter experiences, had come to be wary of many of his associates. Henry H. Porter, however, was one man Tracy trusted above all others.

Porter, a New England Yankee, who had first seen the light of day at Machias, Washington County, Maine, was a product of a hard school. He had experienced, in the first 15 years of his life, a comfortable home and seemed destined to enjoy the advantages that could be provided by a family of considerable means. His father was a lawyer, highly intellectual, but probably not very practical from the business viewpoint.

At the age of 15, Porter found himself suddenly on his own, due to his father's financial reverses. He had to forego a formal education and strike out to find a job. He was 17 when he landed in Chicago in 1852. A year later he went on the payroll of the Galena and Chicago Union as a clerk at $400 a year.

Porter early demonstrated to his superiors an enormous capacity for detail, a good head for figures, a pleasant manner with the road's patrons. The result was that he was made paymaster, claim agent, and general ticket agent. He held these three jobs concurrently until, in 1860, he went over to the Michigan Southern and Northern Indiana, predecessor of the New York Central, as station agent at Chicago. Three years later he became general superintendent of the Michigan Southern and Northern Indiana's entire line between Chicago, Toledo, and Detroit.

About the time that Tracy took over as president of the Rock Island, Porter formed a partnership with Jesse Spalding, famous Chicago lumber merchant, and besides acquiring vast interests in timber lands, he explored the possibilities of the northern iron ore deposits and acquired a share of iron ore holdings. He became a director of the First National Bank of Chicago in 1867, and it was in that year that his close association with John Tracy began.

Tracy brought him into the Rock Island directorate in June 1869, a move by which Tracy sought to develop the ideas he had about the Chicago and Northwestern. Tracy felt that a consolidation of the Rock Island and the Northwestern would result in an extremely sound system. The merger would bring about reduction in overhead and operating costs, a more conservative policy on the opening of new territory, and, above all, would eliminate duplication of services in competitive areas.

Porter's connections with investors and strong financial interests were widespread. He knew what groups held large blocks of the common stocks of both the Rock Island and the Northwestern. He was completely sold on the merger idea and he talked with Eastern interests to bring them into the consolidation plan.

The Union Pacific elected Porter a director in 1870, and on June 2 of that year Porter, along with Tracy, W. L. Scott, and Milton Courtright of the Rock Island, became directors of the Northwestern.

Tracy was elected president of the Northwestern on the following day, June 3, while retaining the presidency of the Rock Island system. This move placed him in the position of controlling the operation of more miles of railroad than any other railroad chief executive of that period. He turned over to Porter all the details of attempting to consummate the merger, and devoted his attention to that big construction project across Iowa to Leavenworth.

Construction of this mileage proceeded at a steady pace. All through the fall and winter of 1870 and the spring of 1871, the rails advanced. The demand for transportation through the territory was so great that, as each section of the line was ready for trains, operations were begun on a construction company basis.

As the month of September approached, Tracy began to lay plans for a great excursion train from Chicago to Leavenworth. The engineers had told him to set his sights on a date in the last week of the month, and they would make the date definite within two or three weeks of the finish. That was good enough for Tracy.

His one worry was the bridge over the Missouri River from Stillings Junction into the city. A group of Leavenworth business interests had, in 1869, formed a company to build a bridge. General W. W. Wright was chief engineer and the contract went to the American Bridge Company. Construction was begun on July 26, 1869. The Rock Island was not a partner in the enterprise.

The high hopes of the builders and the bridge company for completion of the structure in time to carry the first train across from the Missouri side were dashed in June of 1870 when a serious accident upset the time-table.

A section of the bridge columns fell over and struck a barge on which was loaded some of the valuable machinery and equipment necessary for the project. The barge sank forthwith, taking the machinery down with it.

Considerable time was spent in trying to get the machinery out of the river, and after long delay this effort was given up and new machinery and equipment had to be ordered before construction could continue.

On receipt of word that the whole line between Washington and Stillings Junction would be open by September 20, John Tracy set the date for the first excursion to Leavenworth to depart from Chicago on the morning of September 26.

He had the mechanical forces groom the silver engine, *America,* for the trip, and the car department assembled the finest equipment the road owned. Invitations were speedily dispatched to a list of prominent citizens both in Chicago and in the cities on the Eastern Seaboard. Ulysses S. Grant, President of the United States, and Mrs. Grant readily accepted the railroad's invitation, and a special parlor car was provided for their use.

Another distinguished guest aboard the train on its departure from Chicago's depot was one of the builders of the Illinois Central, General P. G. T. Beauregard, late of the Army of the Confederacy.

The coincidence of President Grant and his former arch antagonist in the Civil War being aboard the excursion train is credited to the work of Colonel Daniel R. Anthony, the managing director of the famous Planters Hotel, of Leavenworth. Anthony was an intimate friend of both generals and a diligent worker toward healing up the wounds left by the defeat of the South.

The city of Leavenworth had, prior to the Civil War, attracted many settlers from various parts of the old South, and prominent Southerners had built the Planters Hotel. It was considered one of the finest in the West and had long ago gained fame for its elegant appointments and its fine hospitality. Colonel Anthony left nothing undone to make the celebration at Leavenworth something long to be remembered, and it was his hope that the whole affair would kindle a better feeling between those segments of the population that still rankled under sectional bitterness.

The departure of the excursion on the morning of September 26 from the Rock Island's imposing station, then called the Union Passenger Depot, was a holiday occasion. Thousands of Chicagoans crowded the concourse to see the celebrities board the cars. President and Mrs. Grant, delayed enroute from Cincinnati, boarded the special at suburban Washington Heights.

If the excursion's guests were impressed by the tremendous crowds that greeted the train at every station along the route, they were completely overwhelmed by the turnout at Leavenworth on their arrival at the Planters Hotel. Newspapers of the day recorded it as the greatest and most elaborate celebration ever held.

Welcoming speeches, the booming of cannon, the color of a gigantic parade all preceded a banquet the like of which had never before been seen. General Grant saw the troops at Fort Leavenworth in review, and committees of citizens left nothing undone to provide a vast variety of entertainment for the excursionists.

From Leavenworth the train was taken to Council Bluffs, and then headed eastward over that line toward Chicago. A correspondent of the Chicago *Tribune* wired his paper on September 29:

> "At 12 o'clock today the head of the famous engine, *America*, which has drawn the excursion train on its whole route from Chicago, was turned eastward over the Rock Island Railroad, toward home, where the party expects to arrive early Friday (September 30) morning.
>
> "The excursion has been, in some respects a most remarkable one, because on this train two men who directed the contending armies at Pittsburgh Landing and Manassas Junction, where the fate of the Nation trembled in the balance, clasped hands for the first time, and in friendship.

"The party will have traveled over 1,500 miles by railroad, controlled by one company, and without changing either engines or cars. They have been served with both beds and meals on the train during the whole trip.

"At a called meeting in the Ladies' Car this P.M., resolutions were passed expressing the extreme appreciation of the excursionists in regards the perfection of the railroad's appointments, track, equipment, service, etc., and particularly their gratitude to President Winston (Frederick H. Winston, president of the Chicago and South Western and the builder of the Leavenworth line) for the protection, consideration and 'never to be forgotten' pleasures afforded them."

John Tracy felt pretty good about the whole thing. On October 10 the railroad would be exactly 19 years old. From its inauspicious beginning with that little train of cars on October 10, 1852, it had now become one of the biggest systems west of Chicago under one management. With its main line from Chicago to Council Bluffs and its new main line from Washington, Iowa, to Leavenworth, Tracy commanded just a little short of 1,000 miles of well-ballasted railroad, with motive power and equipment second to none.

Revenues were on a continual increase. Industry was developing rapidly in the growing cities all along the railroad. In Iowa, especially, Tracy saw the opportunity for continued expansion. This rich agricultural area needed more and more transportation. Good sound branch lines would provide the answer.

Tracy looked to the nineteenth birthday with great anticipation. He didn't know it at that moment, but he was looking straight at disaster.

15 Fire!

On Saturday afternoon, October 7, 1871, John Tracy sat back
in his creaking swivel chair in the Chicago general offices. He
had spread out before him several newspaper pages on which
were line-cut reproductions of his elegant Chicago passenger
depot.

"Looks like everybody's writing us up," he mumbled. "Says
here we've got the most beautiful passenger depot in America." A blunt finger tapped a news page.

The heavy man across from him grinned quietly. His name
was Hugh Riddle and he was Tracy's general superintendent.
Tracy had brought him from the Erie in November of 1869.
Like Judge Grant, the Rock Island's first president, Riddle
had started his career in Bedford, New Hampshire, as a school
teacher, and then had studied engineering. He had served on
construction crews with the Erie from 1846 until 1852 when
he'd gone to the Canandaigua and Niagara Falls Railroad for
a year. In 1853 he returned to the Erie as chief engineer,
became division superintendent in 1855, and general superintendent in 1865.

"That station isn't what you've got on your mind," Riddle
said.

"You did a good job, Hugh, with that excursion," Tracy
said. "The way you handled those people—well, you did a
good job." Coming from Tracy that was high praise. Tracy
had never been given to compliments.

"The trip did us a lot of good," Riddle admitted. "We're

still getting letters. Hard to answer them all, right off, but the way people express themselves about the train and the railroad—"

"We've got a good railroad," Tracy broke in. "We'll have a greater one." He gazed for a long moment at Riddle's broad face. The day had been unseasonably warm and through the open windows a slight, dry, southwest wind blew softly to stir the air in the room.

"I've got a new job for you coming up, Hugh," Tracy said, shifting his weight in his chair.

Riddle's brows lifted.

"I need you closer to me," Tracy continued. "With some new branch lines proposed in Iowa you can assume new details. So beginning October 16, you'll be promoted to vice-president. You'll keep your title as general superintendent, too, but you'll have more responsibility—more authority."

Tracy offered a hard hand. Riddle clasped it warmly.

"It's been a long day," Tracy said as he stood up. "I'm tired."

"We both need rest," Riddle said. "And—my thanks."

The fire came in the night. The clang of bells on the fire-wagons, racing over cobbled streets, awoke Tracy. The fire had started near the corner of Van Buren and South Clinton streets, just a half mile west of the depot and across the Chicago River.

Weeks without rain, now with that southwest wind blowing, Chicago's stage was set for tragedy.

Tracy went to the depot and there he found a worried Riddle. They gathered what information they could as to the extent of the fire. The sky to the west was bright yellow and deep orange, and the smoke was suffocating. Van Buren Street was filled with the surging crowds trying to get closer to the scene.

A messenger came through the mob to advise Tracy that the whole area between Halstead Street and the river appeared doomed, but that the fire department hoped to keep the blaze from spreading east of the river or north of Adams Street.

The area where the intensity of the blaze increased with each passing hour was an industrial section with lumber yards, coal yards, elevators, and mills, and almost all of them had their own pumping facilities to draw water directly from the river to pump into the flames.

Tracy and Riddle, after an all-night vigil, left the offices on Sunday morning. They had been assured that all danger was over. There weren't very many buildings left standing between Van Buren and Adams on the west side of the river, but the fire had been brought under control.

Sunday turned into a pleasant, warm day and the wind carried off the smoke haze that through the early morning had hung over the lower part of town. Tired fire-fighting crews sought rest after the hideous night.

Then, almost without warning, after many people had gone to bed that Sunday night, it happened. It happened around 9:30 at Jefferson and DeKoven Streets, just a short distance from where Saturday night's fire had started.

Much has been written about Mrs. O'Leary's cow and her contribution to the fire. Whether fact or legend, it was at the place where Mrs. O'Leary lived that the blaze had its origin, and Mrs. O'Leary's house quickly went up in flames to add impetus to the fire. The residents, hearing the alarms again being sounded, followed by the clatter of the fire wagons, thought little about it. Probably just a flare-up from the fire of the night before, confined to some local area where the embers had not been extinguished.

The spread of the flames was phenomenal. By midnight all hope of holding the fire under control was doomed. Yellow tongues of flames licked through buildings in the Loop, and fanned out with the increasing southwest wind.

In the path of this destruction was John Tracy's beautiful passenger depot. The flames enveloped it and gutted it. It was leveled along with the general offices and the out-freight depot. Other Rock Island losses were "three sleeping coaches, eight passenger coaches, five baggage and mail cars, and six freight cars."

Warren G. Purdy, then cashier in the local office, is credited with having saved many of the corporate records. Purdy, on duty that Sunday night, locked everything in the way of papers and files in the vaults before the fire got into the Loop. These records included deeds, contracts, board minutes, and all other things of an official nature. Engineering data, maps, surveys, and many matters of such kind were all destroyed.

The railroad's loss was estimated at $300,000, with insurance covering slightly less than $50,000 of that amount. Traffic was in a snarl, and it would be weeks before such important commodities as lumber and merchandise would move from the Chicago area, or into it.

While the loss was a blow to the Rock Island, the road's strong financial position made it possible for Tracy to meet the emergency in his stride. He called in the architects and engineers, and before the last ember had burned out plans were under way for the erection of an even greater depot at Van Buren and La Salle.

16 The great train robbery

The year 1873 was a year of crisis for John F. Tracy in the pursuit of his plans for the merger of the Rock Island and the Chicago and Northwestern. He made frequent trips to New York to talk with Eastern financiers. He began speculating heavily on his own account, and he urged Henry Porter to renew his efforts to wrap up the merger project.

Meanwhile, the new Union Passenger Station (now known as the La Salle Street Station) was completed. Tracy's drive in getting this new structure ready for a public opening was an incentive to many business leaders of Chicago in the trying days of reconstruction. The effects of the great fire had been far-reaching. Almost a third of the city's population had been left homeless—more than 100,000 people—and the failure of insurance companies to pay out on the property loss had greatly retarded rebuilding. It was estimated that of the total property loss incurred—$196,000,000—only $50,000,000 in insurance had been collectible.

The Rock Island annual report for 1873 described the new depot "as of the same dimensions and occupying the same site as that destroyed by the late fire." The report went on to say, "Some changes in the style of the building and interior arrangements add much to the beauty and convenience, and it may truly be said to be the finest depot building in the West, and second to none in the Country for elegance of design and adaptation for the use intended."

The dedication took place with a notable ceremony that lasted two days. No expense was spared in hiring the best bands for the entertainment of guests. Civic leaders gave themselves over to laudatory orations in which they cited the railroad management for its vision and directness of purpose in transforming the ruins and rubble that the fire had left into something "glorious to behold."

Newspapers reported that the thousands of people who visited the station were inspired by the ingenuity of man to overcome what, only a few months before, had seemed a most hopeless situation. This enterprise, according to the writers, had a profound and far-reaching effect in building up public confidence in an even greater future for Chicago and her citizens.

Where Tracy had succeeded in gaining public acclaim for his new station he faced failure in his consolidation scheme—a failure that struck deep.

Despite all Henry Porter's efforts the merger of the Northwestern could not be accomplished. That system had slumped off on earnings, while the Rock Island continued to gain in financial stability. But the rank and file of Northwestern people and its officers vigorously opposed the plans, and Porter, at last, had to tell Tracy that it was no use.

On June 19, 1873, Tracy had to step down as president of the Northwestern, and for him a dream of empire was over.

Tracy began driving himself harder in the development of new traffic for the Rock Island. The new Government bridge across the Mississippi was now in full operation, and its completion in October 1872 had had a noticeable effect on traffic. Schedules had been stepped up and, as the annual report pointed out, there was "a considerable savings . . . in expense of crossing trains as compared with the old line."

This report accounted for "the completion of the bridge in a most substantial manner, iron superstructure resting on abutments and piers of first-class masonry, the whole erected under the supervision of experienced Government engineers, and it may be justly regarded as among the finest works of its class in America, and an attractive feature to the traveler."

The removal of the old bridge took time and patience, and during the summer of that year it was necessary to rearrange the yard tracks at Rock Island. Additional land was purchased near the east end of the new bridge and three miles of sidetrack was laid.

It was indeed a busy program that the railroad had laid out for itself to rehabilitate its terminal facilities. Industry was expanding all along the line between Rock Island and the area east of Moline. Payrolls increased and new housing proceeded at a satisfactory pace to take care of the influx of new residents.

Prior to the great fire at Chicago, Tracy had seen the railroad's revenues climb to the then record-breaking figure of $6,028,287 for the year ending March 31, 1871. He and his associates had been fearful that, as a result of the fire and its effect on traffic, there would be a sharp decline. But the decline had been small indeed. Revenues for the year ending March 31, 1872, dipped to $5,900,000 and then resumed their steady climb. At the end of the fiscal year, March 31, 1873, they stood at $6,419,231.

Thus, as midsummer of 1873 approached, everything was in splendid shape with the Rock Island. The railroad was enjoying prosperity such as few railroads of that period could boast of. Both freight and passenger traffic were heavy. Mail and express revenues provided a steady source of income.

About the time Tracy was finding that his dream of acquiring financial control and consolidation of the Northwestern was shattered, a rather cunning and observant gentleman of questionable character was taking more than a curious interest in the prosperous Rock Island. His associates were particularly concerned with certain packages that were being handled in the express cars aboard Rock Island passenger trains. Information obtained in devious ways indicated that on certain days these shipments amounted to many thousands of dollars.

The gentleman from Missouri, Jesse James by name, was an earnest believer in the doctrine that institutions entrusted with funds should share the wealth. A very convincing way of enforcing such a program was at gun-point.

Mr. James, and his brother Frank, and others of his bearded and unwashed band, had gained considerable reputation around northern Missouri for their sporadic banditry, striking mostly at small banking institutions, vanishing into the hills with their loot.

Jesse's interest in the Rock Island increased when his agents reported that it would be much simpler to hold up and loot a train than to take their chances with solidly planted institutions such as banks and stores. Jesse had visions of lonely places where trains had to pass in the night—no citizens around to observe the plan of attack or to follow him and his riders as they made off with their takings.

That stretch of the Rock Island between Council Bluffs and Des Moines had some very lonely segments of track. Jesse and his men scouted it and found everything in their favor a short distance from the small town of Adair, Iowa. There were many curves and grades, and near the summit of one of these hills, just beyond a curve, would be a pretty good place to try their luck.

Just how the James band got their information on money shipments by express has never been determined, but there have been many references to "inside" plants.

Word reached Jesse about a shipment of $75,000 that would move out of Council Bluffs in train No. 2's express car on the afternoon of July 21. Having picked the spot for the holdup, the James band proceeded to set the stage. They carefully loosened a length of rail on the right-hand side of the track to an engine running east. They removed some of the spikes and disconnected the rail from the next one ahead. They then fixed a rope around the rail so that, from their hiding place in the bushes, they could begin moving the rail outward toward the tie ends. They figured that the engineer, puffing up the grade, would see the phenomenon and bring his engine to a halt.

With everything in readiness the James boys waited out of sight. They heard the exhaust of the locomotive as it labored up the grade, and hard fingers tightened on the rope. The engine came in sight with its oil headlight flickering. It straightened on the short tangent toward the top of the grade and the rail started to move.

Inch by inch the pull on the rope brought the rail out of line.

In the cab of the locomotive Engineer Rafferty saw the rail and yelled to his fireman. There were no air brakes in those days for quick emergency. There were only hand brakes which were applied by members of the train crew when the engineer whistled for them.

Engineer Rafferty made two quick moves. With one hand he whistled for brakes and with the other he reversed his locomotive. He could do nothing else. The stack belched smoke and fire with the reversal of the valve gear. The wheels slid. But the long, pointed pilot and the engine plunged down the fill on the right-hand side and turned over.

Engineer Rafferty died in his cab and his fireman was critically injured.

The James boys cared little about that. They didn't have to spare a man now to guard the engine crew.

Guns barked. And as the passengers rushed to the exits they were lined up beside the track. Two of the band made quick work of the express car, then stood guard while the others went through the passengers and collected jewelry and cash.

Within an incredibly short period the whole thing was over. The passengers were left trembling and gaping. The sound of horses moving into the brush told them of the bandits' departure.

The express-car haul amounted to $3,000. Since there were 200 passengers, the jewelry and money loot was estimated at about $3,000 more. The $75,000 that had been the James goal had been held over to move on a later train, a last-minute switch. Had there been an inside man on the job to inform Jesse James of this movement, the switch had been made too late for word to be sent to the bandits.

The James gang annoyed the Rock Island at other times, but the affair near Adair that July night set a new pattern for the Western bad men. It was the West's first holdup of a railroad train, and it was to be duplicated many times thereafter in various parts of the Western country. It had been quick and simple, with virtually no risk of being caught in the act or being chased by a sheriff's posse without first having the opportunity for a long getaway. In the case of the Adair robbery it took hours for a crew member to walk to a telegraph office and call for help.

17 Sumptuous meals on wheels

Following the Adair robbery, Hugh Riddle took all possible precautions to prevent a recurrence. He overhauled the police methods then in use on the railroad by placing armed guards on certain vulnerable trains and by arming train and engine crews as well as express messengers.

Riddle, whose capacity for detail and whose drive for accomplishment were equally as great as John Tracy's, little by little found himself taking on more and more of Tracy's functions. Riddle knew of Tracy's stock speculations, and sometimes it worried him. Not for any effect those activities of Tracy's might have on the solidity of the Rock Island but the effect they were having on the man himself.

Tracy was showing signs of wear. The years of driving himself day and night were beginning to tell. He was more lined, more gruff, more withdrawn into the hard shell he had built around himself.

He left to Riddle the business of branch-line expansion. Out in Iowa the Rock Island had taken over the Des Moines, Indianola, and Missouri Railroad Company which had been incorporated back in 1870 and which had built 21 miles of track from Des Moines to Indianola to open up a rich farming belt. The road had been built by B. F. Allen, a contractor, and a director of the Rock Island, and the Rock Island had advanced $179,300 to aid in the construction. Leased to the Rock Island, the road had failed to pay interest on its bonds and a suit for foreclosure had been filed.

While these proceedings were pending the Indianola Company conveyed its road to the Iowa Southern and Missouri Northern Railroad Company, subject to the mortgage and lease to the Rock Island. There followed a court action in Iowa in which the proceedings were challenged. The suit was settled in August, 1876, when the court upheld the foreclosure. The Rock Island purchased the property and conveyed its equity to the Iowa Southern and Minnesota Northern.

Another line now operated by Riddle was the Des Moines, Winterset and Southwestern which had been incorporated in 1871 to build a line from Summerset, on the Indianola branch, to Winterset, in Madison County.

In order to tap what appeared to be a coming industrial section in the Chicago area, Riddle investigated the holdings of a company that had planned a line from South Chicago "in a westerly direction." The capital stock and the right-of-way on which it was proposed to build this road were owned by the Calumet and Chicago Canal and Dock Company. Riddle negotiated a deal in 1874 and the Rock Island acquired the right-of-way and built the South Chicago branch, extending from South Englewood to the harbor of South Chicago—seven and a half miles of railroad that in the years to come was to prove one of the system's most valuable acquisitions.

The middle 1870's saw an ever-increasing demand for better and more convenient passenger schedules and service, and one of the phases of long-distance travel that irritated the passengers was the necessity for meal stops. It was the general practice to lay out a schedule so that at the accepted time of day for dinner and supper the trains would arrive at some central point where restaurant facilities at the depot were provided. There a stop would be made for twenty minutes to a half an hour, and the passengers who had failed to provide themselves with a box lunch before leaving home would pile off and rush the lunch counters.

The food served wasn't too good, and there were many complaints. Railroads in the east had begun to experiment with what they called restaurant cars, and Riddle believed that the Rock Island might get the jump on the Western lines by doing some experimenting now.

Tracy was not against the idea when Riddle brought it up. Tracy liked to feel that his railroad was the best in the United States and that it stood above all else for progress. Accordingly, the Rock Island's general passenger agent, A. M. Smith, was assigned to investigate the possibilities.

On the basis of Smith's report and recommendations after looking over some of the restaurant-car equipment on the Eastern roads, the Rock Island ordered four restaurant cars of its own design from the builders.

They were beautiful to behold, inside and out. Rich paneling filled the space between the windows, brass hanging lamps were provided for oil illumination, and benches with curved backs were provided for seating. The exterior was done in forest green and beneath the windows at the center of the car hand-painted decorations around a splendid cornucopia gave colorful promise of the elegance one would find inside.

Smith bought the best quality in table linens. He handpicked the men to man these cars. It was a radical departure from anything yet offered the traveler in the West, and the Rock Island was going to take full advantage of the innovation. Not only would there be the most superb food prepared by the best of chefs, but there would be fine wines and liquors available at reasonable prices.

Plans were laid to launch this new service early in May of 1877. Tracy would play host to an invited group of prominent people to feast on the food and drink. Members of the press would be included.

John Tracy never gave the party. He knew, in his silent heart, that he stood on the threshold of disaster. He saw it coming. Hugh Riddle saw it coming and could do nothing about it. Tracy, early in the year, was worth a million dollars on paper. He had been lured into a pool operation in stock speculation by a group of his New York associates. On the morning of April 11 he was summoned to New York. The pool was in trouble. There might be a way of working out of it. Tracy didn't know.

April 13 was his tragic day. His financial house collapsed. He lost more than $600,000—every cent he had, everything he had worked for and had contrived to make.

On the following day, his face drawn and his cheeks sunken —visibly a physical and mental wreck—he submitted his resignation as Rock Island's president.

Then Tracy, without a backward look, turned over to Hugh Riddle a system which had grown from 452 miles when he had become president, to 1,003 miles of sound, prosperous, and vigorous railroad. He had seen gross revenues grow from $3,574,000 as of March 31, 1867—his first year—to $7,854,000 at the end of his tenth year in office. He had given unsparingly of his great genius and his indomitable courage, and now it was Hugh Riddle's turn to carry on.

18 On to Kansas City

Hugh Riddle was 55 years old when he assumed the presidency of the Rock Island. Even then he was designated in biographical sketches as "a conspicuous character in railroad history . . . of unswerving integrity, stern but always just." He was exceedingly conscious of the importance of good public relations and of the necessity to keep officers and employees informed of every move designed to further the progress of the railroad. This was evidenced in the meticulous care with which he prepared his annual reports. Long ago he had taken over this chore for John Tracy, and the informative nature of those reports had attracted widespread attention.

The dining-car service was launched under his direction. Overnight it became vastly popular with the railroad's patrons. Officers of competing lines watched the experiment with tongue in cheek. Some thought it would never work. Others grudgingly admitted that sooner or later they would have to follow suit.

General Passenger Agent Smith, at Riddle's direction, assumed the duties of dining car superintendent. He appointed Frank M. Stewart as the first steward. The dining-car policy was set forth in a letter of instructions from Smith to Stewart which said:

"You will have entire charge of the car and help, and will be held directly responsible for the reputation of the car. You will feed no dead-heads (officers and employees traveling on passes) other than provided for as below.

"The price of meals will be 75¢; children, at your discretion, half price. You will understand that no liquor (by the drink) is to be retailed on the car when on the road or when laying over at either end. Our packages are so small and cheap that anyone wanting to buy liquor must buy the bottle or flask, and you will not, under any circumstances, sell liquor to trainmen.

"You will dead-head Mr. Riddle, Kimball, Manvel, and Royce; and anyone bearing a request from Mr. Riddle, Kimball, or Manvel for free meals will be honored.

"Butter, eggs, milk, cream, vegetables, and anything that is needed in the car, that we do not send from here, you will purchase, having, so far as possible, bills made, and present same to Mr. Stearns for payment. We will send you from here tenderloins, fish, hams, bacon, oysters and groceries, liquor and cigars, and anything else that you find you need.

"Your pay will be $75 per month; cook, $65; waiters, $20. You will enclose your report of each day's trip on No. 2 of the same day, enclosing report and money in U.S. envelope, and send it by express.

"I have an ice box made to send your meats, etc., in before you are out of meats, so telegraph me and I will always send the box on No. 1. When the box is received, empty and return it on the next train. A waybill will be sent with everything, which sign and return at once. All other meats like mutton, pork chops, sausage, etc., you will buy in your own market.

"Trainmen and others attached to the train only will be fed for 35¢, you using your own discretion about feeding them; a good fair meal will be served, but not made up of quail, plover, etc. If at any time the trainmen or express or mail officials demur to the substantial meal that you give them, inform them that it is their privilege to eat somewhere else, the cars are not run for their benefit. You will see that your help keep neat, clean and tidy. You will find that the range needs a good deal of attention; the soot and ashes accumulate quickly around the oven which will prevent its heating quick. We have an extra key to the meat box. We will send you, in the *Australia* (the name of one of the four diners) when it comes, the last of the week, some wines."

With the four palace dining cars, the *Australia, Overland, Oriental,* and *Occidental,* the Rock Island's passenger equipment was second to none. The road owned 15 sleeping cars, the first of which had been acquired in 1863. These cars were ornate and highly comfortable in their accommodations.

With the inauguration of the dining-car service, Riddle assigned to the Western Bank Note and Engraving Company the job of making up the menu. The engravers etched an ornate steel plate such as they would prepare for stock and bond issues and from this plate was struck the menu covers. The inside was printed. The dinner and supper menus were most elaborate. Wild game in season appeared in great variety on the 75-cent meal which was complete from soups and appetizers to fancy desserts. The meals consisted of seven courses and the passenger could order all he could consume.

Everitte St. John, advertising agent, created the slogan

The Great Rock Island Route, in the early 1870's, and it was about the time of the launching of the diners that this slogan came into use in all the railroad's publicity and advertising.

Certainly Hugh Riddle drove hard to live up to the slogan. He became the first in the line of Rock Island chief executives to give serious thought to industrial development on the railroad. Having come from the East, where the importance of locating plants and factories on the line, from which additional traffic could be derived, had been fully demonstrated, Riddle realized that such a program of development on the Rock Island was greatly needed.

Until Riddle had developed the idea and built the South Chicago Branch, the railroad's industrial facilities brought about by its own efforts consisted mainly of stockyards at various cattle-shipping points, and a few "grain houses." These were storage facilities, but not grain elevators. The elevator was to come into being at a later date.

Hugh Riddle's feeling about industrial development may be summed up in his written opinion of the South Chicago area.

"The growing importance of this new town," he said, "manifested in the various manufacturing enterprises started, the improvement of the harbor, the grading of streets, and erection of new buildings, give promise of a large business at no distant day.

"Already several large deposits of lumber have been made on its docks. Iron works have been established; new and extensive mills projected; and the attention of the capitalist, as well as the manufacturer, has been attracted to South Chicago, likely soon to become one of the most important and busy of Chicago's many suburban towns. Believing that the time will soon come when the possession of this branch will prove of great value to the company, your managers felt justified in incurring the comparatively small outlay necessary to secure a permanent location to this promising suburb and its harbor."

In his annual report after his first year as president (the report of 1877) Riddle said, of South Chicago, "an addition of nearly three miles of track has been made to the South Chicago Branch road to reach the Joseph H. Brown Steel and Iron Works and the various new lumber yards . . . The growth and development of new enterprises in the vicinity of South Chicago, taken in connection with the traffic already secured, gives assurances that this branch of your railroad will prove a valuable acquisition in the future."

Riddle's interest in South Chicago, great as it was, did not blind him to other possibilities for his system. Ever since the Leavenworth line had been completed Riddle had kept his eye on another Missouri town, which in recent years had given every indication that it would boom into a real metropolis. That was Kansas City.

Connecting with the Rock Island main line at Cameron, Missouri, was the Hannibal and St. Joseph railroad. If the Rock Island could effect a contract with that line, it would be possible to operate into Kansas City.

Accordingly, Riddle entered into negotiations with the Hannibal and St. Joseph, and on December 4, 1879, signed an agreement which gave the Rock Island the right for a term of 25 years "to run its passenger and freight trains from Cameron, Missouri, to Kansas City, together with the right to use jointly the freight depot, tracks, and other facilities of the said Hannibal and St. Joseph Railroad Company in Kansas City."

Under the terms of the contract the Rock Island had to pay the Hannibal and St. Joseph 7 percent interest on one-half of the valuation of the section of the road used and part of the cost of maintenance based on train mileage.

A further contract was made with the Union Passenger Depot Company in Kansas City by which the Rock Island would participate in the use of the passenger terminal facilities on the same basis as the eight other railroads that ran into the station.

Through passenger and freight service between Chicago and Kansas City was inaugurated on January 5, 1880—a big milestone in Riddle's administration.

1⑨ The consolidation of 1880

The rapid growth and the increasing prosperity of the Rock Island Lines during the years of John Tracy's leadership and now under the administration of Hugh Riddle served as inspiration to many promoters and builders, mainly in Iowa, to get into the expanding railroad picture. Some of these schemes were foredoomed to failure and others, while financially weak at the inception, gave promise of future economic soundness.

An example was the first railroad ever to enter the city of Des Moines. It was incorporated in 1853 as the Keokuk, Fort Des Moines and Minnesota Rail Road Company. The purpose, simply stated in the charter, was to construct and operate a railroad from Keokuk, Iowa, to the northern boundary of the state.

Construction was begun in the spring of 1856 after the usual problems of raising sufficient funds had been overcome, and by the following year the railroad, building in a northwesterly line toward Des Moines, reached the town of Bentonsport, 38 miles from its starting point.

The survey for the line was meanwhile extended beyond Des Moines to Fort Dodge, and the company, in March of 1858, through an act of the Iowa Legislature, was granted 468,000 acres of land contiguous to the proposed Des Moines - Fort Dodge route.

The building continued toward the Iowa capital, and by 1861 the road reached Eddyville. There it remained until the close of the Civil War. Meanwhile, the company concentrated on the sale of land north of Des Moines and had little or no trouble in realizing considerable money.

On June 1, 1864, the corporate name was changed to the Des Moines Valley Rail Road Company.

Construction from Eddyville was resumed in 1865 and the last rail into Des Moines was spiked down in August 1866. On the 29th of that month Des Moines saw its first passenger train steam in from the south. The excursion was accorded a great welcome.

This occurred just a few weeks after the Rock Island had taken over the mileage of the Mississippi and Missouri, profiting by all the ill-feeling that had been generated by the Mississippi and Missouri's failure to reach the capital from the east.

The Des Moines Valley railroad ran its construction north from Des Moines to Tara in 1868-70 and secured trackage rights over five miles of the Illinois Central to enter Fort Dodge.

By late in 1873 the net receipts from the sale of the lands granted to the Des Moines Valley totaled $2,587,052. An additional $32,341 represented profit realized from the retirement of land-grant bonds. After paying out $50,130 for the redemption of interest coupons, the company had a net of $2,569,263, all of which went into the construction program.

But despite the land sales, the line, in 1873, was in financial trouble. On October 17, that portion of the road between Keokuk and Des Moines was foreclosed and sold to a purchasing committee representing first-mortgage bondholders. On the same day at Des Moines, in another foreclosure sale, the portion of the line from Des Moines to Fort Dodge was sold to a committee representing first- and second-mortgage and land-grant convertible bondholders.

The Keokuk and Des Moines Railway Company was incorporated January 6, 1874, to acquire "that portion of the Des Moines Valley Rail Road Company between Keokuk and Des Moines." The purchasing committee which had taken over this part of the defunct Des Moines Valley at the foreclosure sale deeded its holdings to the new corporation.

One month later the Des Moines and Fort Dodge Railroad Company was incorporated under Iowa law and the foreclosed property of the Des Moines Valley between these cities was conveyed to the new corporation.

On May 14, 1878, with an eye to the future importance of the Keokuk - Des Moines Territory, Hugh Riddle, on behalf of the Rock Island, entered into an agreement with the Keokuk and Des Moines to lease the line. The contract provided that the Rock Island should acquire a majority of the common and preferred stock of the Keokuk line at 50 cents per share for the common and $1 for the preferred. The Rock Island further agreed to pay 25 percent of the gross earnings to the Keokuk line as rental, with a stipulation that in no case should the annual payments be less than $137,500, this sum representing the expense of maintaining the corporate organization of the Keokuk line.

By the dawn of the year 1880 it was apparent to Hugh Riddle and the directors of the Rock Island that a consolidation of the expanding mileage, including leased lines and lines under separate corporate structure which the Rock Island had financed, should be effected. It would be vastly more economical to bring these properties into one corporate structure, and such a move would result in more efficient operation.

Thus another great milepost in Rock Island history was reached.

The articles of consolidation were filed with the secretary of state of Illinois on June 2, 1880, and with the secretary of state of Iowa on June 3. The corporate name was changed to THE CHICAGO, ROCK ISLAND AND PACIFIC RAILWAY COMPANY, known thereafter in financial circles as Pacific No. 3.

At the time of the consolidation the properties brought into the new structure were as follows:

OWNED LINES

The Chicago, Rock Island and Pacific Railroad Company main line from Chicago to Council Bluffs.

The South Chicago Branch from Englewood to South Chicago.

Washington (Iowa) and Oskaloosa Branches from Wilton to Muscatine and Washington; Oskaloosa to Knoxville.

Main line of the Iowa Southern and Missouri Northern (originally the Chicago and Southwestern) from Washington to Leavenworth.

The Atchison Branch from Edgerton Junction to Winthrop, Missouri, opposite the city of Atchison, Kansas.

The Iowa Southern and Missouri Northern branch lines from Des Moines to Indianola (originally the Des Moines, Indianola and Missouri Railroad); Des Moines to Winterset (formerly Des Moines, Winterset and Southwestern Railroad Company).

The Newton and Monroe Railroad.

Atlantic Southern Railroad, from Atlantic to Griswold.

The Avoca, Macedonia and Southwestern Railroad, from Avoca to Carson.

Atlantic and Audubon Railroad.

LEASED LINES

Peoria and Bureau Valley Railroad, from Bureau Junction (Illinois) to Peoria.

Keokuk and Des Moines Railroad.

The Fort Leavenworth Railroad, extending from the Missouri River Bridge to Leavenworth, Kansas.

Avoca, Harlan and Northern Railroad from Avoca to Harlan, Iowa.

Guthrie and Northwestern Railroad, from Menlo to Guthrie Center, Iowa.

The Keosauqua and Southwestern Railroad, from Mount Zion to Keosauqua, Iowa.

The articles of consolidation provided that the lines involved "merge their capital stocks, corporate and other franchises, rights, privileges and property of every nature and description and create one consolidated corporation to be known by the corporate name of THE CHICAGO, ROCK ISLAND AND PACIFIC RAILWAY COMPANY."

It was further provided that the new company "own, complete, extend, improve, maintain and operate these railroads; use and enjoy all of the corporate and other franchises, rights and privileges, immunities and property which form a part of or are appurtenant to said railroads and . . . construct or acquire by purchase or lease, railroads laterally to any of the several lines consolidated."

The plan provided for the issuance of stock of the consolidated company of the same par value as that issued by the separate companies and outstanding as of June 2, 1880.

A great new system of railroad stood on the threshold of another chapter in its progressive career. Already Riddle had his eye on the future of Kansas. Beyond the high plains was Colorado with its rich gold and silver strikes. Southward was the Oklahoma Territory and the vast empire of Texas. In all that territory there was room for the Rock Island, room for hordes of settlers to take over the treeless prairies and turn the land to the production of grain and livestock.

At the top of Rock Island's official family, as of the consolidation of 1880, were, next to Hugh Riddle, David Dows, of New York, vice-president, representing Eastern financial interests who had heavy holdings in the property; and Ransom R. Cable, of Rock Island, Illinois, second vice-president, who in 1877 had become a director and in 1879 had been appointed by Riddle to the newly created post as assistant to the president.

Ransom Cable was the man to watch. Riddle knew it and the directors knew it. He was aggressive and, in a very large sense, a lone wolf. It was not in his nature to consult with his associates when he saw a move that he thought should be made. He made his decisions quickly, and he carried them out.

Cable was born in Athens County, Ohio, September 23, 1834. His father, a shrewd businessman, had various interests, including coal mining. Young Cable received a good education in school and in business.

He had an uncle in the mining business in the Coal Valley district, south of Rock Island, Illinois. In 1857 Ransom Cable came to Rock Island to visit his relatives, decided he liked the people and the country, and chose to remain. He joined his uncle in that gentleman's various enterprises, including the struggling railroad property that had started out as the Rock Island and Peoria Rail Road Company. It had been chartered in 1855, and its purpose was to build a line from "the City of Rock Island in a southeasterly direction to Peoria."

When young Cable reached the scene the railroad had built 12 miles down into the Coal Valley and it was operating under control of the Coal Valley Mining Company. The mines were doing a profitable business and the owners were inclined to let outside interests do the job of finishing the railroad.

A new company was formed for this purpose in March 1867 under the name of the Peoria and Rock Island Railway Company, and its charter provided for building from Peoria to Rock Island, and extending the line from Peoria to a connection with the St. Louis, Jacksonville and Chicago Railroad in Tazewell County, Illinois. An amendment to the charter in March 1869 gave authority to build a branch to extend to the Mississippi River in the vicinity of Muscatine, Iowa. By prearrangement between the two existing companies, the Peoria and Rock Island was to build from Peoria to connect at Coal Valley with the completed trackage of the Rock Island and Peoria. Surveys were made, rights-of-way were obtained, and most of the grading had been done on the new line when in September of 1869 the two companies consolidated to form the Peoria and Rock Island *Railway* Co. This latter organization completed the railroad and placed it in operation on January 1, 1872.

On August 1, 1874, the property went into receivership, under which it operated until December 12, 1877, when it was bought at a foreclosure sale by Ransom Cable. Cable organized a fourth company under the name of Rock Island and Peoria *Railway* Company and transferred his certificate of purchase as trustee of the first mortgage to that corporation.

Cable's interest in railroads had begun before his departure from his Ohio home. After settling in Rock Island and watching the progress of the Rock Island system, his interest became more and more intense.

During his business progress he branched out to open a real estate and investment firm. Interest rates were from 7 to 10 percent, and because of the ever-expanding business and farm development there was an enormous demand for money. Well-placed loans on good farm land and industrial and residential property, with these high interest rates, made for exceedingly sound and profitable investments.

There seemed to be no limit to Cable's credit. He had developed strong banking connections in the East and appeared to be able to secure large sums of money without the slightest difficulty whenever some new project attracted his attention.

In 1870 he became president of the Rockford, Rock Island and St. Louis Railroad Company, part of which line later was taken over by the Burlington.

Recognized as an outstanding leader in the civic and business life of Rock Island and an important factor in the area's industrial progress and development, Cable was elected to the Rock Island Railroad's Board of Directors on June 4, 1877.

From that time on he was determined to have an active hand in the company's management in a top-level job, and this goal was achieved when the office of assistant to the president was created on June 4, 1879.

Ransom Cable was not cut out to be assistant to anyone. That was apparent right from the start. It caused Riddle no little concern, but Riddle was in no position to say much about it. Cable was a director and a member of the executive committee, and on the board he had many close friends who, to all appearances, had Cable's future in mind.

The job of assistant to the president ended with the consolidation of June 2, 1880. Cable was elected second vice-president, and in this capacity took over the operating and traffic departments.

Riddle, whose aim was industrial development on the line and the greater expansion of terminal facilities, found his next-in-command with no sympathy for that phase of railroading. Riddle, with his eye on the territory west of Missouri, found Cable of the opinion that such an expansion was wholly unnecessary. The big line west of the Missouri was the Union Pacific. Cable felt that a traffic arrangement could be worked out with that road which would redound to the benefit of the Rock Island.

Cable's views apparently had the backing of the majority of the members of the board, including such powerful New York figures as Jay Gould and Sidney Dillon. On June 1, 1881, Cable had his title changed to vice-president and general manager.

At the annual meeting on June 6, 1883, when the business of the election of officers was reached, Hugh Riddle decided he had had enough. He declined re-election to the presidency. He would remain as a member of the board.

Thus the way was cleared for the election of Ransom R. Cable to succeed Riddle. The title of president wasn't enough for Cable. He tacked onto it the words "general manager." He wanted the world to know that he was the whole Rock Island road—the supreme boss.

Riddle could retire with the knowledge that he had done his job well. The system, under his administration, had grown to 1,381 miles. Among important building projects he had fathered was the new line from Davenport along the Mississippi River to Muscatine, thus eliminating Wilton Junction on the route to Leavenworth and Kansas City. This section was completed and opened for traffic in 1881.

Riddle had seen annual revenues climb above the $13,000,-000 mark. From here on it would be Cable's chore.

PART THREE

Beyond the Missouri

1883 - 1901

2⓪ Branching out in Iowa

Cable's first chore, as it eventually turned out, proved to be a sad one indeed for the Rock Island system.

It revolved around that business of expansion west of the Missouri. Several of the Rock Island's competitors had already branched into that territory and were enjoying an increasing amount of traffic eastward to Chicago, and beyond, that the Rock Island couldn't touch. For the Rock Island to consider opening up in Nebraska and Kansas an enormous amount of money for new construction would have to be raised and Cable couldn't see such a project.

He thought the next best thing would be to sit down with officers of the Milwaukee on the east of the Missouri and the Union Pacific on the west and work out a deal.

On December 5, 1883, the three lines came up with what was then called the tripartite agreement. Under the terms of the agreement it was decided "to establish and maintain a closer alliance between said systems" that there might "be secured to each, the friendly assistance and coöperation of all the others in all reasonable and lawful ways, in developing and protecting traffic over through lines composed of portions of the Union Pacific and portions of the railways of one or more of the other parties" thereto; "in reducing the expenses attending such development and protection and the management and operation of their several lines."

It was further declared that "such an alliance can be made most effective and the interests of the public best promoted by an arrangement which will make the railway systems of the other parties substantially a part of the system of the Union Pacific, as to eastbound traffic which would pass through Council Bluffs," and the Union Pacific, "a part of the railway of each of the other parties as to westbound traffic" through Council Bluffs.

The contract incorporated these declared intentions, and the result should have been to extend the Union Pacific right into Chicago over the Milwaukee and Rock Island, and to extend these two roads to each terminus on the Union Pacific's main line and branches.

Up to that point it sounded like a pretty fair proposition for all concerned. But there were a couple of other railroads terminating at Council Bluffs, too. They wanted to get into the act. They were vociferous about it. So, by December 29 the Wabash, St. Louis and Pacific Railway Company and the Chicago and Northwestern Railway Company were made parties to the agreement.

Still another railroad, the Burlington and Missouri River in Nebraska, which was competitive with the Union Pacific at several points, and with the Eastern members of the agreement at Council Bluffs, didn't like the deal at all. It used every means available to it to prevent the contract from becoming effective insofar as performance by the Union Pacific was concerned.

Then the Union Pacific got into financial difficulties, and, before the year 1884 was half over, Ransom Cable had to agree that the only way by which the Rock Island could protect its interests in traffic originating in or destined to the territory beyond the Missouri was to build its own railroad. Certainly, while the Eastern lines tried to live up to the agreement the Union Pacific was not performing in any sense of the word.

While Cable turned over to his law department and his engineering staff the job of working out the possibilities of certain proposals that had been submitted for westward extensions he turned his attention to another Iowa property which should have been, from the very beginning, a part of the Rock Island system.

This was the Burlington, Cedar Rapids and Northern Railway Company.

It will be remembered that when the Mississippi and Missouri was organized in 1853 an amendment was secured to the charter to provide for building a line north through Cedar Rapids and right up the Cedar Valley—a proposal that soon was lost to sight in the bitter struggles the Mississippi and Missouri had in building anything like a railroad at all.

But on October 2, 1865, a group of promoters incorporated, under the laws of Iowa, the Cedar Rapids and St. Paul Railway Company. The purpose was to build a line northwestward from Cedar Rapids through the Cedar Valley. Two years later —October 7, 1867—another project, the Cedar Rapids and Burlington Railroad Company, was incorporated to build and operate a line from Cedar Rapids through Iowa City to Burlington and thence via Keokuk to St. Louis.

Neither of these companies did much more than make surveys, obtain rights-of-way, and grade short stretches of the proposed route.

The two companies got together and on June 30, 1868, formed the Burlington, Cedar Rapids and Minnesota Railway Company. Construction began in earnest in 1869, and by 1873 there was in operation 368 miles of main and branch lines. The main line extended all the way from Burlington through West Liberty, Iowa (where it crossed the Rock Island main line to Omaha), Cedar Rapids, and Cedar Falls to Plymouth just short of the Minnesota boundary.

Branches extended from Linn to Postville, Iowa; from Muscatine to Riverside; and from Vinton westward to Traer.

At last the Cedar Valley had been tapped, but the Burlington, Cedar Rapids and Minnesota defaulted on its bonds, and on May 19, 1875, W. W. Walker was appointed provisional receiver. His tenure of office was ended on the following July 21 when, at the request of the bondholders, General E. F. Winslow was appointed to succeed him.

The reorganization plan for the defunct road provided for the sale of the property under foreclosure of the first mortgage and its purchase by committees appointed for that purpose. The Burlington, Cedar Rapids and Northern Railway Company was formed, and the purchasing committees assigned to this corporation their interests. The deeds were conveyed by the Master Commissioner on June 27, 1876.

Under its new corporate structure the Burlington, Cedar Rapids and Northern, in June 1880, backed the formation of the Cedar Rapids, Iowa Falls and Northwestern Railway, which was a construction and holding company. This company, from 1880 through 1884, built 327 miles of main line, extending from Holland, Iowa, where it connected with the Burlington, Cedar Rapids and Northern main line, to Watertown, South Dakota. It also built branches from Lake Park, Iowa, to Worthington, Minnesota—a distance of 17 miles— and from Dows to Hayfield, Iowa, a distance of 41 miles. The Burlington, Cedar Rapids and Northern, under lease, operated this mileage from the very beginning.

Thus, as of 1885, the Burlington, Cedar Rapids and Northern, with its subsidiaries, controlled and operated approximately 850 miles of substantial railroad with good earning prospects for the future.

Because of the line's growing importance and economic promise, Ransom Cable, with the approval of the Rock Island board, brought about the acquisition of the majority of the capital stock in the Burlington, Cedar Rapids and Northern and thereby assumed complete control.

While he was in the mood for further expansion, Cable took a good look at another line of railroad, called the St. Joseph and Iowa, which was designed to connect with the Rock Island at Altamont, Missouri, and which would provide entrance to the thriving city of St. Joseph. Cable purchased in July 1885 all the capital stock of this road and entered into a traffic agreement, the purpose of which was declared to be "to establish and operate through lines of railway, which shall connect, when the same can be done with reasonable directness, all points on the main line of both parties, treating all railroads with which each party shall have a traffic or running arrangement, or interest, as a part of the line of the party . . . with which it is so related; and to secure the operation of all said lines, as to through traffic, as they should be operated if all were owned by one corporation."

Cable could sit back now and glow with pardonable pride. Only two years in office as president and general manager and he could look at a railroad that crisscrossed the map of Iowa to tap every important industrial and agricultural center—a railroad that more and more was taking shape as one of the great systems of the Nation. The Great Rock Island Route. Yes, that's what they called it, that is what it was known as, both in trade and financial circles.

Well, with things getting ready to start over there in Nebraska and Kansas and beyond, it would be still greater. And he, Ransom R. Cable, would be greater. He liked to feel that greatness. He loved the adulation of his associates.

21 Kansas—a record in building

Once Ransom R. Cable made up his mind to extend his lines west of the Missouri he showed his ability as a gambler, along with his faith in the future of the territory that Hugh Riddle had felt was so important. Cable, on July 4, 1884, laid the groundwork for the expansion by executing a mortgage to the United States Trust Company of New York. In legal language, it was a long and highly involved document. Boiled down to language the layman could understand, the terms of the mortgage were such as to risk the whole system as it stood on that date together with all main and branch lines it might in the future construct, lease, or purchase. You couldn't build 1,500 miles more of railroad without plenty of money and through this mortgage the Rock Island got the money.

Thus, early in the year 1866, things began to happen. The St. Joseph and Iowa Railroad Company, a wholly owned subsidiary of The Chicago, Rock Island and Pacific Railway, completed its line from Altamont to St. Joseph, Missouri, and from St. Joseph to Rushville. Here it made a junction with the Atchison branch to provide a service to that city. The charter of the St. Joseph line was amended to permit it to cross the western boundary of Missouri into Kansas, and the northern boundary into Iowa.

The Chicago, Kansas and Nebraska Railroad Company was incorporated under the general laws of Kansas on December 30, 1885. The charter gave the company the right to build and operate from the town of Larkin, in Atchison County, in a southwesterly direction through Jackson, Shawnee, Waobaunsee, Davis, Morris, Harvey, Marion, Butler, and Sedgwick counties to Wichita. It further provided for the construction of a railroad from a given point in Morris County through Marion, McPherson, and Reno counties to the city of Hutchinson. There were other provisions for building to connect the proposed routes with Atchison and a point opposite St. Joseph. A total of 700 miles of projected line was involved.

This company did no construction, but it acquired valuable franchise rights, some rights-of-way and other property. All its rights and holdings were then conveyed by deed of sale to the Chicago, Kansas and Nebraska *Railway* Company which was incorporated in Kansas in March 1886. Shortly thereafter a company with virtually the same name was incorporated in the state of Nebraska to build from the southwest corner of

Richardson County through Pawnee, Gage, Jefferson, Thayer, Nuckolls, Webster, Adams, Kearney, and Buffalo counties to the city of Kearney. This represented valuable territory in the expansion program.

Ransom Cable had to have a man in charge of this west-ward expansion in whom he could have the utmost faith. In setting up these various companies to obtain franchises, right-of-way, and other properties, it would be impossible for the Rock Island president personally to look after the details, and details annoyed Cable no end.

The man for the job, Cable decided, was Marcus A. Low, then of Trenton, Missouri, division solicitor for the Rock Island. Low had fathered the idea of building west of the Missouri in the first place. Low's fine legal background, his record for accomplishment, his closeness to men in high political office, his ability to get along with people, and his dynamic drive all were factors in Low's character that pleased Cable. That's why Cable had made Low president of the St. Joseph and Iowa line when he'd bought control.

"Here's the map, Mark," Cable said. A stubby finger traced over the lines that the engineers had drawn. "You set up the proper corporate structure, file the necessary papers, and get the contractors. I'm leaving it up to you."

"Just so that I have a free hand," Low said. "That's wide-open country out there, and I've been over a lot of it. I've talked to the governor of Kansas and to many members of the state legislature. We've already made friends in that territory."

"All right," Cable agreed. "Let's see what you can do with it."

Low set up the corporate structure of the Chicago, Kansas and Nebraska Railway Company. He was elected president of this organization. He then caused the sister corporation that had been organized under the laws of Nebraska to be taken into the Kansas company, and he was ready to go.

Like others of his predecessors in Rock Island history, Marcus A. Low was a native New Englander. He was born August 1, 1842, at Guilford, Maine. His parents migrated to

Belvidere, in Boone County, Illinois, when Low was four.

His father was a successful farmer and did very well at Belvidere until he decided to improve the family fortunes by moving to Hamilton, Missouri. Young Low meanwhile had received his public school education at Belvidere, and at the age of 15 was sent to a small academy at Auburn, Maine, to complete his education. This ambition was thwarted by illness which, in 1863, brought about his move to California.

Low took up residence at Folsom City, in that state, and became principal of the schools. At the same time in nearby Sacramento he engaged in the study of law where he continued that pursuit until the fall of 1866. He returned to Belvidere where he became affiliated with Attorney Ira M. Moore. He studied with Moore and the following year was admitted to the bar. Immediately after that he went to Ann Arbor and entered the senior class in the law school of the University of Michigan.

After his family's move to Hamilton, Missouri, Low established himself in that city in the practice of law and made rapid advancement. The Rock Island hired him in 1873 as local attorney. Three years later he was made division solicitor and sent to Trenton, Missouri. He was active in bringing about the Rock Island's control of the St. Joseph and Iowa railroad, of which he was made president, and Cable became very much impressed by the way Low took hold of that property, completed it and put it into operation.

Yes, in Cable's opinion, here was the man to turn loose in the Kansas, Nebraska and Colorado extension of the Rock Island Lines.

Low's first move, after setting up the Chicago, Kansas and Nebraska of Kansas and the Chicago, Kansas and Nebraska of Nebraska, was to establish headquarters at Atchison, Kansas. He later tied these two corporations into one and then brought about the lease of the Chicago, Kansas and Nebraska Railway Company to the St. Joseph and Iowa. In order to get his Western lines started he made a lease agreement with the St. Joseph and Grand Island to connect with that road's tracks in St. Joseph and to use the Missouri River bridge for access to Elwood, Kansas, at the west end of the bridge.

Once he was ready to move, in the middle of 1886, Low lost no time. The grading from Elwood, Kansas, was begun on July 1 in the direction of Horton. The construction gangs, aided by the fair Kansas weather and by ideal terrain, were caught up in a wildly enthusiastic spirit of challenge. They threw up the fill, bridged the streams and had things ready for the tracklayers over the entire 43-mile stretch of that first segment by late September.

The trackmen followed on the first of October and reached Horton before the snow began to drift across the Kansas fields.

Next was Topeka, reached early in 1887, and it was to Topeka that Low moved his offices and the headquarters of his operation. Topeka was the capital of the state. Help from the legislature might be necessary at any moment, and close contact with the political forces of the state was valuable.

Hilon A. Parker, Low's chief engineer, and a man who had made a great reputation in railroad locating and construction work, moved in with Low so that they might work more closely together on this enormous project. Everybody was encouraged by the rapidity with which things were moving, and it was Low's aim to complete all this Kansas and Colorado mileage at the earliest possible date.

Building beyond Caldwell, Kansas, down in the southeast corner of the state, was dependent on an act of Congress since the proposed route would be over Government-owned lands in Oklahoma and Indian Territory. Low had long ago set the machinery in motion for such legislation and had been assured there would be no hitch.

On March 2, 1887, Congress approved the act and thereby was granted the charter right to cross through the Cherokee Strip and Indian Territory into Texas and thence to Galveston. Another line was provided for to extend west and southwest from Liberal, Kansas, across the Indian Territory into Texas and New Mexico with El Paso as the goal.

Under the Chicago, Kansas and Nebraska charter for building through Kansas it was specified that the main line from Topeka through Wichita to Caldwell would pass through a point in Marion County called Lost Springs. From this point the line west toward Hutchinson and Liberal would take off.

On a bright spring day in 1887 a lone ranchman riding the range saw the railroad surveyors driving their stakes down through Marion County. He rode up to the engineers and began to ask questions. The engineers showed him how the route had been laid out on the map.

"You mean you're not building this line through Herington?"

"Herington?" one surveyor asked. "No such place on the map I've got."

"Who's the man in charge?"

"Marcus Low, in Topeka," the rancher was told.

"Where'll I find him?" the rider asked.

"You'll find him at the Copeland Hotel."

The man who entered the Copeland Hotel a few days later was tall, lean, burned from wind and sun, and wore a kind of Van Dyke beard. He was shown to Low's room. He took the chair the builder indicated and pushed back his broad-brimmed white Stetson hat.

"It's about my town," the bearded man said. "The town of Herington. It's not very big now—just a village—but the way you got your railroad routed you're going to miss it."

"Where is it in relation to Lost Springs?" Low asked.

"Seven miles north," the bearded man answered. "Here, let me show you."

He pointed to Low's map. "The way you got your line routed you sort of make an elbow around me down to Lost Springs, and then cut west and south from there. Straighten this line and you hit my town."

"You mean if we build into Herington," Low said, "and then down to Lost Springs—"

"I mean if you build into Herington you can strike straight west from there toward McPherson and Hutchinson, and Lost Springs still will be on the line to Wichita. You route it like

I say and I'll present you with a free deed through Herington for your right-of-way, and through my township."

Low stared at the stranger.

"Just who are you?" Low asked.

"I'm M. D. Herington, and Herington is my town. I own all that land down in that part of Kansas. In fact, I'm the whole thing down there."

"That sounds like the best proposition of any I've heard," Low said.

"I'll even make it better," Herington promised. "I have a little influence with my neighbors. Make it a deal and I'll see that you get every concession possible in the neighboring counties. You'll get fine treatment."

Low made it a deal and he got fine treatment.

By midsummer Herington became a railroad center, and there was laid the foundation for what in time was to become one of the big division points on the Rock Island system.

On south from Herington the ties and rails went down and the border town of Caldwell was reached in December. Caldwell's first train arrived to the usual fanfare, and the frontier town, last outpost of the "white man's country," took on new character. Here the Rock Island paused briefly at the gateway to the Indian domains of Oklahoma.

Meanwhile Low's forces were busy in other directions. One hundred and three miles of railroad was built during that year of 1887 from McFarland, on the southwest line, in a northwesterly direction to Belleville, Kansas. From Herington to Salina 48 miles was constructed, and from Fairbury, Nebraska to Nelson another stretch of 51 miles went into the records.

Following roughly the old Chisholm Trail the construction down into the land of the Indians across the Kansas border progressed through the first half of the following year. Pond Creek was reached on July 15, 1888, and the grading was almost finished beyond to Skeleton and Hennessey.

To the north a line from Horton, Kansas through Fairbury, Nebraska, stretched its lonesome length to Roswell (Colorado Springs) Colorado. Southwestward from Herington, down through Hutchinson and Pratt the rails went into the frontier town of Liberal. Nothing in all railroad construction history had ever before equaled the Rock Island expansion in rapidity.

The entire mileage from Horton, Kansas, to Liberal was placed in service on February 26, 1888, and to Pond Creek on July 15. The first train traversed the 564 miles from Horton to Colorado Springs on November 5. It had taken just two years, four months, and four days to build and place in operation 1,113 miles of railroad.

22 The farmers find a friend

During the early days of extending railroads west from the Mississippi River and later beyond the Missouri, railroad management was ever cognizant of the importance of doing all it could to promote the settlement of the vast lands that offered promise to the farmers.

The Rock Island was among the leaders in this phase of activity. As its lines opened up Iowa, the business of advertising the possibilities of new towns for industry and the agricultural reaches for farm settlement grew steadily. The passenger traffic department was assigned this job of promotion. Special rates were set up for homeseekers and homesteaders.

As early as the year 1856 when the Rock Island was still short by 300 miles from the Kansas border, the road advertised extensively "The Shortest, Quickest and Safest Route" to Kansas and Nebraska. The New England Emigrant Aid

Society located a major outfitting station at Iowa City to help the migratory hordes whose goal was the land west of the Missouri.

When the advertising spoke of the Rock Island being the safe route the inference was that Northern settlers, moving via Iowa City and Council Bluffs, through part of Nebraska to Kansas, ran less risk from attack by Southern sympathizers who, even before the Civil War, had engaged in border skirmishes with their neighbors who felt that the South was wrong.

The population of Kansas, in 1860, was 107,206. After the Civil War, during the period of recovery, the population increased to 257,193. From 1870 to 1880 the growth of population was the greatest in any 10-year period in the state's history, reaching 631,697.

It was during this period that the Mennonites from the Crimea, of Russia, moved into the territory and brought with them the Turkey red hard winter wheat, a new variety that had done well in Russia, and should do exceedingly well in this new land. How well this wheat did is attested to by the fact that in the first year the Mennonites introduced it, 1872, the State produced 2,139,000 bushels, and six years later the yield topped 27,280,000 bushels.

When the first inkling that the Rock Island would open up vast new sections of Kansas was spread among homeseekers in the middle 1880's, the rush for the lands became enormous. Thousands of new settlers rushed in ahead of the railroad, and other thousands followed the course of the building. The big advertising and colonization program paid off.

And now in the year 1889 the boom was on in Oklahoma. The Cherokee Strip was not yet open to settlers but the land to the north and south of it was.

Rock Island's building was proceeding along the Chisholm Trail, long in use by the cattle herds coming northward. Hilon Parker's construction forces learned early that it would be up to them to bring in addition to the railroad a little something in the way of culture to this sparsely peopled land.

There was, for instance, some eight miles south of Caldwell, an outpost that went by the name of Polecat. The builders put up a box car for a station when they reached that point, but the name *Polecat* on the station just didn't do a thing for the railroad.

The name that went on the signboard was Renfrow. Twenty miles further it wasn't so bad. The place was called Pond Creek. That had color and romance to it. The name stayed.

From Pond Creek southward to Skeleton the clang of maul on spike as the rails went down, the shrill of the work-train's wildcat whistle, the chant of the sweating crews played the symphony of progress.

The lay of the land at Skeleton, deep in the Cherokee Strip, gave promise of a good townsite, and Hilon Parker marked it down. The railroad had land from the Government, granted in its charter to build, and a development company such as had already been established at Pond Creek could lay out streets and building sites for business and residence. Yes, Skeleton, too, would be a good point to develop.

The railroad reached Hennessey just beyond the south end of the Cherokee Strip in 1889. The first agent to open the station there, S. R. Overton, left a record of his coming. He told how he had been deputized as U.S. marshal at Topeka and then had proceeded by train to Pond Creek.

Pond Creek was headquarters for "Cannon Ball" Green's stagecoach line.

Agent Overton departed from Pond Creek on July 2. He wrote, "Cannon Ball Green drove the stage drawn by four teams of horses strung out." As Overton put it, the load consisted of "six white men and one lady, and on top of the stage were six negroes." Among the passengers was Dr. Cook, Rock Island surgeon.

The stage overturned the first time near the site of what is now Kremlin, and the second time near Bison. Dr. Cook was the only casualty, suffering a severe sprained ankle, and the lady was "an angel of mercy," because she was the only one aboard with a flask, and its contents revived the doctor.

The first train reached Hennessey in October and Overton

described it as quite an event. With the train came the settlers.

"I delivered household goods from fifteen to twenty merchandise cars a day," Overton wrote, "and checked out goods for Kingfisher, Columbia, Skeleton, and many other inland towns."

A year later the railroad was to finance the settlers by bringing in 12 carloads of seed wheat which was apportioned out in 5- to 20-bushel lots with no cash down—only the promise of the farmer to pay.

The harvest brought in 120,000 bushels, which the railroad bought, and of all settlers who had signed notes for the seed wheat, only three defaulted.

Overton's personal account of what happened in agricultural aid to the new settlers in the Hennessey territory is an isolated incident in a program that was conceived by Marcus Low when he saw the plight of the new settlers back in 1889.

Turning new ground into farm lands under climatic conditions strange to the settler was always a major problem. Beset by drought conditions and a new breed of insect pests, the Oklahoma settler in 1889-90 had to have help. Low's concern for these people moved him from community to community, and he learned that a major cause of failure was the poor quality of the seed wheat. He went to Chicago and told Ransom Cable about it.

This new country had great promise, Low explained, but the farmers were deeply discouraged. They had no money now to buy good seed wheat, and, unless conditions were changed and some help could be provided, these farmers would have to leave the country.

In answer to a question Cable put to him, Low explained that he had been all through the Oklahoma farm country, had made a thorough investigation of crop possibilities, of soil and climate. He had experienced the same difficulties in Kansas as were now prevalent in Oklahoma. And, he said, the land in Oklahoma was every bit as good for wheat as that in Kansas, and, that while the farmers in time might lose a crop or two, they could, with the proper help and encouragement, make their way and prosper.

Low left the meeting in Chicago with a free hand to do whatever he deemed necessary. At Topeka he stopped long enough to make arrangements to secure the best seed wheat Kansas had available from sections where climate and soil were reasonably close to those in Oklahoma.

He prepared the simplest form of promissory note, issued instructions that no endorsement or security would be required, and sent the note forms to each local freight agent in the territory.

Believing in the soundness of personal contact with his patrons, Low went into these towns, appeared before meetings with the farmers, told them what the railroad had decided to do and promised them the very best seed wheat would be brought right to their depots. All they had to do was make their needs known to the agent, sign the note, and go raise a crop. Low acquainted local merchants and other businessmen with the Rock Island's program so that they, too, might be helpful in extending to the farmers needed credit and other aid.

The effect of the program was amazing. It inspired new confidence not only in the farmers but in the businessmen as well. The project got under way in full blast in 1891 after the drought of 1890. Thus was established the principle of a greater agricultural aid program that in years to come was to pay off handsomely in increasing prosperity to the communities, and in ever-growing traffic for the railroad.

23 Outcast in Omaha

Marcus Low's railroad in Nebraska, Kansas, Colorado, and Oklahoma, with its great building record behind it, and its inspirational chapter in agricultural aid fresh on the pages of its history, was in trouble.

Settlement with the parent company, the Chicago, Rock Island and Pacific, had been made by the Chicago, Kansas and Nebraska for the line as far as Pond Creek. The building southward from that point to El Reno was completed in 1889 and the extension to Minco, Indian Territory, was finished early in 1890. This part of the route was completed with $1,143,000 advanced by the Rock Island.

On failure of the Chicago, Kansas and Nebraska to deliver stocks and bonds of its corporation to cover the advanced funds, suit was instituted to bring about foreclosure. On June 3, 1890, the United States Circuit Court for the district of Kansas, in a preliminary decree, found that the Chicago, Kansas and Nebraska had failed to deliver securities to cover its building of 97.5 miles with the money advanced by the Rock Island and ordered the sale of all Chicago, Kansas and Nebraska property, whether in Oklahoma or elsewhere, to settle the claim.

In the middle of the tangle in financial affairs between the parent company and the Chicago, Kansas and Nebraska it was feared that should the suit continue for any length of time, the lands and rights granted under the Congressional Act of

March 19, 1886, and the completion of the lines called for in that bill, might be jeopardized.

Accordingly, pressure was brought to bear on Congress and a new act was approved on July 27, 1890. This legislation granted the Chicago, Kansas and Nebraska the power "to sell and convey to The Chicago, Rock Island and Pacific Railway Company . . . all railway property, rights and franchises . . ." It also authorized the Rock Island to "purchase, hold, maintain and operate the railway heretofore constructed" by the Chicago, Kansas and Nebraska under the provisions of the Act of 1886, and to complete all lines mentioned in that act but not yet built.

The Oklahoma part of the line shortly thereafter was conveyed by deed to the Rock Island on March 10, 1891. On June 10 all the remainder of the Chicago, Kansas and Nebraska property—the lines in Kansas, Nebraska, and Colorado—were conveyed, upon the payment of $1,000,000, to the Chicago, Rock Island and Pacific. The deed of sale was approved by the court on June 17.

Thus passed into history the corporate existence of the Chicago, Kansas and Nebraska. As the line had progressed the Rock Island had taken over the stocks and bonds of the Kansas Company in return for cash advances to underwrite construction.

From the beginning of the building the Rock Island had advanced $29,399,882. Against the collateral provided by the Kansas Company's securities, the Rock Island issued its own bonds in the amount of $25,149,000, all of which were eventually paid off. The Rock Island also received from the Chicago, Kansas and Nebraska $2,643,571 from the proceeds of local aid such as that given by individuals and municipalities to assist in construction. While no collateral had been put up by the Kansas company for the $1,143,692 that was advanced for the Pond Creek to Minco mileage, the Rock Island got the railroad in the final settlement.

While, in the tangled financial manipulations, the Rock Island sustained some loss in dollars, the road certainly saw it offset in the increase in traffic that resulted from new towns and more settlers.

As of July 1, 1891, Ransom Cable found his railroad a great and sprawling web over the heart of the nation's most promising country. It served, together with the lines it controlled such as the Burlington, Cedar Rapids and Northern, eight states and territories. It had entered into an agreement with the Union Pacific for trackage rights from Kansas City, Kansas, to Topeka, thus enabling it to perform through service from Chicago, via its Kansas City route, to its western extremities. It had secured its Colorado mileage through the formation of the Chicago, Rock Island and Colorado Railway Company which had been incorporated January 31, 1888, and which had been merged with the Chicago, Kansas and Nebraska in June of that year. Its Colorado company had made a contract with the Denver and Rio Grande for the use jointly of that company's railroad between Denver, Colorado Springs, and Pueblo. Direct entrance to Denver had been secured through a contract with the Union Pacific, in April of 1889, to use that railroad from Limon Junction, on the main line to Colorado Springs, to the Colorado capital.

As of July 1, 1891, the Rock Island's mileage operated over lines owned, over lines controlled, and by trackage rights was just a little under 4,000.

By this time, too, a major headache had developed in Nebraska—a headache that was to get a lot worse before it got any better.

It concerned Rock Island's route from Chicago to Colorado via St. Joseph, Missouri, and its attempt to get a line through Omaha. The line from St. Joseph through Horton, thence to Jansen, Nebraska, and Fairbury—where it straightened on its Colorado course—was a good 25 miles longer than a direct line through Omaha would have been.

Cable knew even before the service through St. Joseph was inaugurated that this route had been a mistake. The innumerable curves between Columbus Junction, Iowa, and Trenton, Missouri, kept the schedules slow, and the many stiff grades kept the freight trains limited in tonnage. This route was congested with the bulk of Western traffic while the Council Bluffs line was light.

As early as 1887 Cable had begun negotiations with the Union Pacific to use that railroad's bridge for crossing the Missouri from Council Bluffs into Omaha, and Union Pacific tracks and facilities in and through Omaha. With a view to building his own line from Omaha to Fairbury via Jansen, Cable had set up in November of 1889 the Iowa and Nebraska Railway Company. Under a charter amendment obtained in January 1890, the name had been changed to the Iowa and Nebraska Western. This was an Iowa corporation and it had as its immediate purpose the building of a bridge from Council Bluffs to Omaha. Cable had resorted to this method of entering Omaha in the event he could get nowhere with the Union Pacific.

Congress passed a bill authorizing the construction of a bridge. The act was approved February 21, 1890, and provided that the bridge work be started within one year and completed within three years. The Rock Island then filed with the Nebraska secretary of state the necessary papers to give it the status of a domestic corporation.

The management of the Union Pacific, seeing that the Rock Island was determined to get into Omaha, and build beyond that point, and that the Rock Island had already entered into an agreement with the Chicago, Milwaukee and St. Paul to allow that company to use its bridge, began negotiations with both the Rock Island and Milwaukee to use Union Pacific facilities. This included the bridge over the Missouri, the main and passing tracks in Omaha and South Omaha.

The contract was dated May 1, 1890. Under its terms the Rock Island made a deal with the Union Pacific whereby that railroad would use the main line of the Chicago, Kansas and Nebraska for Union Pacific trains between McPherson and Hutchinson, Kansas. At the same time the Union Pacific would allow the Rock Island to use its property between Lincoln and Beatrice, Nebraska.

The Milwaukee began its use of the Union Pacific bridge and tracks into Omaha in July 1890. The Union Pacific began service over the McPherson-Hutchinson segment of the Rock Island just a little ahead of that.

Meanwhile the Rock Island went ahead at top speed with building its railroad from South Omaha to Lincoln, Nebraska. The line was completed in December, just a couple of weeks after the management of the Union Pacific suddenly changed hands.

It was this change of management that made the big headache for Cable. The change came about through the manipulation of Jay Gould and Russell Sage for control of the Union Pacific. The railroad, in 1890, wasn't in any too good shape financially. Gould, like others before and after him, had ideas of gathering under control of one management sufficient railroad properties to set up one gigantic system from the Atlantic to the Pacific. Gould had been a director of the Rock Island, and in his seizure of the Union Pacific one might think that the Rock Island would be given consideration.

Gould replaced Charles Francis Adams, president of the Union Pacific, with another Rock Island director—Sidney Dillon, of New York.

Instead of helping anybody, friend or no friend, Gould and Dillon immediately upon securing Union Pacific control declared the contract with the Rock Island and Milwaukee railroads null and void. They said that the Union Pacific had never had the powers to negotiate and enter into such contracts.

The Rock Island had not as yet entered its engines and cars on Union Pacific property, but the Milwaukee had. The Milwaukee defied Dillon's order to quit using the bridge and terminal. Dillon ordered his men to use force. Milwaukee cars and engines were overturned. Track connections of both the Rock Island and Milwaukee were torn up—the Rock Island's rails suffered at Council Bluffs, South Omaha, Lincoln, and Beatrice. It was mob war, in some instances, and it wrote a dirty page in history.

Cable went before Judge Elmer S. Dundy, in the United States District Court of Nebraska, and pleaded for the validity of the contract. The Milwaukee also filed suit on its own behalf.

The Union Pacific promptly had the case moved to the United States Circuit Court in Omaha. The implication was that the Union Pacific wanted no part of Judge Dundy, who had a reputation for being a contentious gentleman rather than a great legal mind.

The case was heard in May 1891, by Justice David J. Brewer of the United States Supreme Court, sitting as Circuit Court judge. The arguments were elaborate and forceful, projected by the best legal talent on both sides.

Justice Brewer handed down his opinion in July, and entered a decree adjudging the contracts valid in all respects, and ordered their specific performance by all the parties. He allowed an appeal but refused a supersedeas. At the same time Judge Dundy submitted a dissenting opinion upholding practically every contention made by the Union Pacific—an opinion which could result in nothing more than making some Union Pacific official's face awfully red for ever having caused the transfer of the case in the beginning.

The Rock Island began operation of its service between Chicago and Colorado Springs and Denver through the Omaha gateway via Lincoln and Beatrice on August 16, 1891. The next job would be the completion of that stretch of railroad between Lincoln and Jansen, Nebraska, which would eliminate the dip over Union Pacific tracks from Lincoln down to Beatrice.

Cable could now relax, but not for long. Down in the Oklahoma country a war between the settlers and the railroad was on its way.

24 Gunfire on "the strip"

Of all the states in which the Rock Island Lines was destined to become a major part of the transportation economy as it built and grew, none had such a colorful background as that of Oklahoma. And if, in its early history, the Rock Island pioneers thought that they had had troubles with the people of Illinois, with the steamboat interests on the crossing of the Mississippi, with the citizens of Iowa for the failures of the Mississippi and Missouri, and with the Dillon management of the Union Pacific in its fight to validate the contract to use Union Pacific facilities at Omaha, these were minor indeed to what was waiting for them at Pond Creek and at the new town of Enid, on the railroad's Oklahoma extension.

Enid, nee Skeleton, had come by its name after the Rock Island had built its depot in the center of what was hoped would be a townsite development. Again culture had come with the ties and rails. Certainly *Skeleton* wouldn't look very civilized as a name on a railroad station. Enid sounded exceedingly lovely. While there are many stories as to how that name happened to be selected, probably the authentic one is that it was taken from the book, *Idylls of the King,* by some construction engineer who read literature in his spare time.

All of Oklahoma, as it now exists, was originally called Indian Territory. That was its name when the surveys were run down the Chisholm Trail, and Rock Island's subsidiary, the Chicago, Kansas and Nebraska, built southward from Caldwell to Minco.

Congress, on May 2, 1890, made a division of that vast

empire. Under the act Oklahoma Territory was established. This area took in vast agricultural lands from which the various Indian tribes had been removed after the negotiations of new treaties. Roughly the boundary was a line beginning opposite Caney, Kansas, and extending south in an irregular course to the south bank of the South Fork of the Canadian River, near Holdenville; thence west to El Reno, thence straight south along the west border of the Rock Island line to the Oklahoma-Texas boundary. Everything east and south of this line was Indian Territory; north and west was Oklahoma.

Opening of this Oklahoma acreage to settlers had long been advocated by various groups in various sections of the country. The main contention came from Captain David L. Payne, of Kansas. Payne had been an officer of the Union forces during the Civil War, a member of the Kansas legislature, and an employee in the House of Representatives, in Washington, D. C.

There he had heard much private talk by congressmen regarding these "unassigned" lands which, by virtue of the fact that they no longer were property of the Indians, must be public domain and available for homesteading.

Operating on this theory, Payne formed what became known as the Oklahoma Colony. Into the organization was gathered hundreds of men, with families, who were determined to open up that country south of the Kansas border, by force, if necessary. Payne's followers were given the name "boomers," because of the drive in booming the idea of settling the territory.

Payne first assembled his men at Arkansas City, Kansas, for a plunge over the border. His company numbered 600, and these men had with them twice that number of women and children and a large aggregation of covered wagons.

The United States Army, under Colonel Copinger, met Payne at Arkansas City and told him that any move of Payne's people to cross the border would be resisted by armed force.

Payne led his followers westward along the border on the Kansas side to Caldwell, and there was joined by hundreds of others. At the same time Colonel Copinger marched along on the Oklahoma side and when Payne tried to go over the border he was arrested and his followers were dispersed.

The Oklahoma Colony, however, was a determined group. From their first failure in 1880 until 1884 they tried four other forcible entries into the Oklahoma country and each wound up with the Army driving the boomers out.

On his last try Payne, with 500 people and 250 wagons, marched to Stillwater and began to set up his colony. He and his chief aids were arrested and taken to Fort Smith, while the Army escorted the remainder of his followers back across the border to Kansas. The Fort Smith judge deferred a ruling on the Payne case and Payne and his lieutenants were released on bail.

Payne went into the District Court of the United States at Topeka, and the court ruled that he was guilty of no crime. The opinion handed down asserted that these unassigned lands were public lands, and therefore could be settled peaceably by homesteaders.

Payne might have succeeded in bringing the subject to a successful conclusion had it not been for his sudden death at Wellington, Kansas, on November 28, 1884. He had participated the night before in a public meeting as a preliminary to reorganizing his Oklahoma Colony and taking new and forceful action as the result of the Topeka court's ruling. He was buried with a great public ceremony in Wellington.

Less than five years later Congress gave in to the pressures and passed a law setting up the machinery for the opening of certain of the former Indian lands under the Homestead Law. It provided that each opening had to be preceded by a proclamation of the President of the United States which would set the opening date, the area to be settled, and the conditions for acquiring the land. The act was dated March 2, 1889.

Three weeks later, on March 23, the President proclaimed the official opening of what was called the Oklahoma Lands, 1,887,640 acres covering most of what is now the counties of Canadian, Oklahoma, Cleveland, Kingfisher, Logan, and

Payne. The proclamation fixed the opening date at 12 noon, April 22. A total of 11,797 homesteads would be available.

One of the conditions imposed upon the landseekers was that they might assemble at any point on the border of the area to be opened, provided the Indians occupying the adjoining lands were agreeable. No one was to enter the area until the firing of a gun marked the beginning of the race for land. After the gun was fired it would be a veritable horse-race because thousands of the homeseekers prepared for the event by assembling the fastest horses possible. Some even bought race horses to make sure that they'd break out in front of the pack and lead the rush. Thousands of others had to depend on the horses hitched to their covered wagons which provided not only transportation but also living quarters for the families.

Even as now, there were chiselers in those days—men who played the angles, so to speak. These men sneaked into the promised lands under cover of darkness, sought out the lands they wanted, hid in the sagebrush and the creek willows, and after the race for the lands was started, suddenly came out and drove their stakes. To these people was given the name of "sooners."

On that first big opening it was estimated that there were some 30,000 assembled at Arkansas City; between 10,000 and 15,000 at Caldwell, Kansas; 10,000 west of Kingfisher; 10,000 at Purcell; and thousands of others at first one gateway and then another. Those who came by train jammed the Santa Fe, which at the time was the only railroad in Oklahoma traversing the area from north to south. The Rock Island brought capacity loads to the end of track at Pond Creek.

Not everyone in this vast company was a homestead seeker. Hundreds of businessmen had come in from various sections of the country to buy up lots for the establishment of commercial enterprises. The way the Government worked that particular phase of settling was through dividing the land at townsites into business and residential lots. These lots were sold to individuals at very low figures. One stipulation was that one person could buy only one lot. Nothing, however, could prevent a businessman from buying out another individual after he had bought his original lot from the Government.

The settlement that later became Oklahoma City brought in a record number of lot purchasers. They felt that because of the site's location at virtually the geographic center of the territory it would eventually become the capital.

These businessmen didn't find much on their arrival—the Santa Fe railroad station, a few houses, a hastily built post office, and a company of soldiers from Fort Sill who had been sent in to preserve order for the opening of the land.

With 15,000 people rushing in and setting up camps the settlement of Oklahoma City was a nightmare. As soon as one rugged pioneer would leave the lot he staked out to go to the Government office and make the proper settlement someone else would jump the lot and try to hold it.

An attempt to set up a local government failed when the leaders of the new settlement found that there was no legal authority for such a procedure. The Army commander seemed to be the real power, and he and his soldiers had their hands full in an attempt to keep things under control.

This, then, was the established pattern for the settling of the land and the founding of townsites when the President of the United States issued the proclamation to provide for the opening of the Cherokee Strip.

The records are silent as to the identity of the bright intellect in the Rock Island management that laid the groundwork for the skulduggery that, with the coöperation of a group of Indian leaders, would assure the townsite booms at Pond Creek and Enid, with the railroad's depots right in the very center of them and the railroad in absolute control.

Skulduggery it evidently was. But it backfired with a terrific bang. It laid the groundwork for what the old-timers still refer to as the Great Railroad War.

Hoke Smith, of Georgia, Secretary of the Interior, decided in midsummer of 1893 to throw open the Cherokee Strip. This was the section south of the Kansas border extending some 57 miles north and south, and more than 200 miles east and west. Hoke Smith decided to center the townsite development around the railroad stations already erected and in service at Pond Creek and Enid.

White Feather, Cherokee Chief, held out on signing the necessary treaty to make the opening possible until the Government granted him and 66 other tribe leaders the right to select first their allotments—160 acres each for every man, woman, and child in their families. The department agreed and the necessary steps were taken to set the opening of the Strip for high noon on September 16, 1893.

Now the points where townsites would be established had always been kept a deep, dark secret in the Interior Department until the day of the opening. Somewhere this information had leaked out in advance. The Indian leaders knew all about what the Government had in mind at Pond Creek and Enid, and so did the railroad officers. It was soon learned in Washington that Rock Island officers had entered into a deal with the Cherokee tribal chiefs. The deal was that the Indians would file their claims around the railroad property adjacent to the station, and then sell out to the Rock Island for a nominal sum. The railroad then could drive a bargain with the settlers.

Upon learning of this bit of masterminding on the part of the railroad, the Government, on the eve of the opening of the Cherokee Strip, announced that the townsites would, in each instance, be located three miles south of the depots.

The story of the opening of the Cherokee Strip is a great history in itself. From north, east, south, and west the settlers had come—they and their families, their horses and their covered wagons. Again on that September 16, Caldwell to the north and Hennessey to the south were scenes of wild disorder. Thousands were camped in tents along the railroad right-of-way. Other thousands waited for the trains to take them in. Men fought for a position on the boundary lines so that at the firing of a gun they could make a quick break to reach the choicest sections first.

The settlers at Caldwell had their eyes on the townsite at Pond Creek. The riders at Hennessey would dash up the Chisholm Trail for Enid. It was estimated that at the various gateways to the Strip 100,000 people had assembled. At 12 noon that September 16, Pond Creek could boast only of the railroad station, a post office, some railroaders' shacks and a small garrison of troops. The same was true of Enid, 19 miles to the south. It was generally felt that the latter town would develop into *the* town in that territory.

Someone fooling around with a rifle caused the false start at Hennessey. Everybody was set and poised as the hour of noon approached. Then, prematurely, a gun went off at 11:55, and the race was on.

Within a week these two towns had been transformed from mere outposts to teeming cities. But they weren't teeming around the Rock Island stations. Each town was being laid out three miles south of the depot.

Lumber and other building materials had to be hauled in by team and wagon from the station to the townsite. Streets were surveyed and staked out and buildings began going up —mostly rough structures at the start with walls, a roof, and a few windows. Nothing in the way of planned architecture. The walls were unpainted. People lived in tents and wagons and dreamed of the future, of developing a thriving business or putting down the roots for a permanent home.

It was raw, and rough and tough. Guns barked to settle disputes, and no one asked any questions. Saloons and dance halls went up overnight. Then civil government was established and shortly out of chaos came order.

Then became obvious the economic necessity for having a railroad station in the towns. People simply couldn't travel such distances to the Pond Creek and Enid depots. Meeting trains, removing goods from cars, draying it three miles over rough and indifferent roads just didn't make sense.

When the civic leaders in both Enid and Pond Creek met and decided to ask the Rock Island to put their stations right down in the towns, no one suspected trouble. It seemed a reasonable request. Weren't the people of these towns providing a lot of new traffic for the railroad? Weren't they depending on the railroad for service? Committees were appointed to go to Herington, Kansas, and talk to Rock Island officials.

"We'll just tell 'em what we're up against," one merchant blustered.

"What the hell," another chimed in. "It don't make sense for me to have to make three or four round trips a day from my store three miles to that depot to get my stuff, and to ship things out."

The committees were in for a surprise. Those were the days when railroad public relations, with the impetus given by the attitudes of Jim Fiske, Jay Gould, and others like them, consisted of the single-purpose policy of "the public be damned." A far cry from the apparent helpful attitude of the railroad toward its patrons that had been demonstrated just a few years before by Marcus Low.

On the memorable visit of the town leaders of Pond Creek and Enid to present their case to the Rock Island officers, the answer they got was quick.

"No depots," said the railroad. "You got depots north of you three miles. That's what you'll use. We're not spending any money to build new stations at your new townsites."

No sooner had the committees reported back to their respective towns than the Great Railroad War began.

The citizens were incensed. What did the railroad mean? The tracks ran right through the heart of the new towns. Why, the railroad could move their present stations right down to the middle of these teeming, growing cities. But the railroad wouldn't. All right, the citizenry would use direct means.

There was nothing so direct as a slug from a Winchester rifle or a blast from a shotgun shell. Just sort of aimed at a passing train. Not meaning to hit anybody, of course. Just a few shots in the air. Let those railroaders know the people meant business.

That's how it started. It happened that way at both Pond Creek and Enid. But the railroad defied the marksmen. The trains hit these towns wide open, swirling the cinders and dust into a cloud with the speed of their passing.

Pond Creek passed a city ordinance limiting Rock Island trains to eight miles per hour through the town. Enid followed suit.

The crews, on instructions from headquarters, ignored the ordinance. They ran as fast as ever. The gunfire became more serious, the riflemen more in earnest. So much so that passengers were warned before the southbound trains left Enid station to keep down on the floor out of sight of the windows.

The bullets and the buckshot shattered windows and pockmarked the sides of the cars. The enginemen with throttle wide open, would crouch on the cab floor until they were safely by the danger points.

C. O. Royer, a prominent Pond Creek lawyer, was sent to Washington to appeal to Congress. He got nowhere.

Throughout the winter of 1893-94 feeling grew intense. At Pond Creek in May a meeting was held and drastic steps were decided on. City Marshal Charlie Curran said he'd enforce the speed law and arrest the lawbreakers, and there was one way to do it. The women previously had helped their men folk by pouring soft soap from coffeepots onto the rails, but the railroad had put sandboxes on the engine and the sand nullified the soap's deterrent action. So now there was one thing left. These locomotives couldn't run except on rails. You could stop them by taking the railroad away. Just tear up the track, then you can get to the crews and arrest them.

They tore up the track—950 feet of it. Then sent riders in each direction to flag down the trains. There was a northbound stock train of 30 cars swinging up the railroad. The engine crew ignored the riders.

The engine hit the torn-up roadbed and plowed into the dirt. It didn't turn over, but the cattle cars did. They piled up, one on top of another, and broke open. Marshal Curran arrested the crew and the members went to jail. The next day a railroad attorney got them out on bail.

What would be the railroad's move now? Pond Creek didn't

have to wait long. Down from Kansas came a deputy U.S. marshal with 50 men. They were armed to the teeth with Winchesters and revolvers. They arrested 60 of the leaders of Pond Creek and took them to Kingfisher where the sheriff refused to put the prisoners in jail. The men had been arrested without warrants.

The prisoners were marched over to the Kingfisher hotel and were left under one guard at the door while the U.S. marshal went to see about getting the proper warrants. The prisoners soon kidded the guard out of doing anything about their detention, and, led by City Marshal Curran of Pond Creek, they all went out on the town. That night they returned to their hotel prison, much to the surprise of the U.S. deputy. Meanwhile the telegraph wires were kept busy between Kingfisher and Herington, and finally the railroad lawyers instructed the U.S. marshal to take his prisoners back to their home county, secure the necessary warrants, and line them up before a Pond Creek magistrate.

A special train was brought to Kingfisher and two bands with a great parade of citizens accompanied the Pond Creek prisoners to the station. The trial which followed at Pond Creek was a farce, and the whole group was discharged for lack of evidence.

The Rock Island, meanwhile, placed armed guards along the track to prevent any recurrence of the previous episode of tearing up ties and rails. But the burning of bridges followed, and many other acts of violence, until a group of outlaws called the Pitts gang came into the area and held up a train.

For Pond Creek that was the beginning of the end of the Railroad War.

The Pitts gang waved the train to a stop by using a red lantern. The spot was just outside the southern edge of the town. A plucky express messenger surprised the outlaws' plan of attack by whamming away with a Colt .45 and shooting Charlie Pitts, the leader, in the head. The rest of the gang took to their horses and thence to the brush. The Pond Creekers went after them. Capture was effected after a gunfight of several hours and the railroad united with Pond Creek to bring the bandits to justice. The express messenger became a hero.

A short time later, in August 1894, a railroad lawyer called on the mayor of Pond Creek and in a few words told that dignitary that the Rock Island was now ready to build a depot in his town. The mayor took a minute to get over his open-mouthed surprise. Then he sputtered:

"Why in the name of hell did you take so long? You could've done it a long time ago and saved all this trouble."

The attorney said stiffly, "I have no authority to discuss that matter, but if you will kindly drive a stake on our right-of-way showing where you want the depot we will build it just as soon as the material can be moved in."

It was much the same story concurrently at Enid. One act of property destruction after another didn't seem to have any effect. At one point in the war the Enid citizenry moved a four-room house onto the track.

The engineer on a southbound freight train, seeing it from a distance, figured no one would be so stupid as to stay in that house. He got a firmer hold on his cud of tobacco, braced his feet against the bulkhead of the boiler, hooked his Johnson bar on center and latched his throttle out as far as it would go.

It was a sight to behold when he plowed into the structure. The engineer and fireman had got down on the floor to be out of the way of flying timbers. Anyone remembering the old Mack Sennett comedies may have a pretty good idea of what the wreck was like. Timbers filled the air—timbers and splinters, glass fragments and dust. But the Rock Island kept right on going.

The finale came with the sawing of the timbers on the bridge over Boggy Creek. They were sawed under the cover of darkness so that the cut just missed going all the way through. Then the irate mob went back to town square to await results. They left a youngster to watch the bridge.

The results were something to behold. Engine and tank got across, but the bridge buckled under the trailing cars, and the engine and tender were jerked down into the wreckage. Two cars of bright seed-wheat broke open and the wheat spilled over the dry bed of the creek. The lookout made his report at the square and the citizens grabbed bags and baskets and tubs and came down to help themselves to the grain.

The engineer coming up from the depths told the towns-folk:

"Yuh done a damn good job of sawing that trestle."

Enid, too, got its railroad station, right where it wanted it.

25 "The best laid plans..."

Just how much President Ransom Cable had to do with the determination of his officers in Oklahoma to fight their war with the new settlers does not appear in the records of the Rock Island. Cable's annual reports during the years of his administration left much to be desired when it came to details about the company's involved affairs. In the report covering the summer of 1894, when the Great Railroad War came to an end, there is but a brief mention, under the caption New Buildings, that depots were built at Round Pond and South Enid, Oklahoma. Even in capitulation to the demands of the settlers Cable refused to recognize the official townsites of these two communities under the names the Government records gave them. So far as Cable was concerned Pond Creek was three miles north of the real Pond Creek, and Enid was three miles north of the growing city that really was Enid.

That Marcus Low, now general attorney for the Rock Island system at Topeka—and still top man insofar as the lines west of the Missouri were concerned—gave his sanction to the defiance of the settlers at Enid and Pond Creek is a foregone conclusion. Nor in the final analysis was it exactly a reversal of character when compared to what he had done to help the farmers. He was, first and last, a shrewd politician, and not at all averse to turning a fast dollar. The general belief is that he himself was responsible for fostering and furthering the deal with the Indians, and for the loss and destruction that resulted from the antagonism of the townspeople.

Cable, at the annual meeting in June 1898, stepped out of the presidency of the Rock Island to assume the newly created post of chairman of the board. W. G. Purdy, who had come up through the accounting department, and had long served as second vice-president, secretary and treasurer, was elected to succeed Cable as the road's president.

Besides the expansion in Kansas and Oklahoma, during his administration, he had seen the railroad extend into Texas through the creation of the Chicago, Rock Island and Texas Railway Company. This line picked up the rails that had been laid down from Minco to Terral, on the Oklahoma - Texas border. The Texas company was incorporated under the laws of that State in 1892, and was opened for traffic to Fort Worth, July 30, 1893.

Earlier in that year the final dressing had been put on the 52-mile segment of the Omaha - Colorado main line between Lincoln and Jansen, Nebraska, and over it through operations from Chicago to Colorado Springs and Denver had begun, eliminating the use of the Union Pacific between Lincoln and Beatrice and shortening the route by 11 miles.

Because of the development of suburban towns along the Rock Island in the Chicago area, during the Cable regime, a switching line that had been started northward out of Blue Island in 1883 had developed into what today is the suburban line between Gresham Junction and Blue Island, serving the Brainerd - Beverly - Morgan Park District.

In 1894, as the result of a city ordinance, Cable embarked upon one of the great improvement projects of the era—the elevation of the railroad between Sixteenth Street, Chicago, and Englewood. The Lake Shore and Michigan Southern, joint owner of these facilities, would pay half the cost.

Another milestone in Cable's administration was the rebuilding of the Government bridge at Rock Island. As early as 1890 Cable saw that the single-track structure would soon be wholly inadequate. He got help from Congress to authorize a complete remodeling, using steel as well as iron in the structure. When difficulties arose Cable parked himself in Washington and stayed on the job until he got what he wanted.

The work on the bridge moved speedily through the year 1895 and was completed and carrying double-track traffic in December 1896.

Mileage in Iowa was further increased during the late 1880's and the early 1890's through extension of the Burlington, Cedar Rapids and Northern, and through the building of additional branch lines.

When Cable took office in June, 1883, he took over a railroad comprised of 1,381 miles in Illinois, Iowa, Missouri and Kansas. As of that period the rolling stock was made up of 309 locomotives, some of which were wood-burners and others coal-burners (the wood-burners were on their way to retirement); 19 sleeping cars; 127 coaches of all classes; 41 baggage, mail, and express cars; 8 railway postal cars; 6 dining cars; and 2 official cars—a total of 203 in passenger service. The company owned and operated 7,489 freight cars of various classes, of which 4,454 were box cars, 1,021 livestock cars, 1,825 platform and coal cars, and 189 caboose, drover, and other cars.

Virtually all the railroad had been re-laid with steel rails to replace the iron ones—an innovation that John Tracy had introduced back in 1866 with an experiment in Chicago.

As of the end of the fiscal year March 31, 1883, gross revenues totaled $12,189,902.

When Cable left the presidency to Warren Purdy, he turned over a railroad that had expanded into 3,568 miles of lines owned and leased, and that traversed or entered the states of Illinois, Iowa, Missouri, Kansas, Nebraska, and Colorado, and Oklahoma and Indian Territories. The Texas mileage of the Chicago, Rock Island and Texas, totaling 94, was not shown as part of the Rock Island ownership.

Gross revenues had built up to $19,548,583—a rise of almost $2,250,000 over the same period (April 1 to March 31) in 1897, the previous year.

Cable, during his 15 years as president, saw his equipment increase to 564 locomotives, 456 passenger cars of all types, and 16,388 freight cars.

It was a strong and healthy railroad he turned over to Warren G. Purdy, with two exceptions. The property was far behind its competitors in the development of industry along its lines, and it was woefully weak in terminal facilities.

Despite Cable's highly respected business judgment and his highly vaunted vision, he still insisted that his railroad should emphasize more and more "through freight"—loads from and to connections with the Rock Island serving as merely a bridge line over which the traffic could move fast. The railroad should own only such real estate as might be necessary to accommodate shops and yards. Nothing at all for lease to industrial projects or to sell to businesses that might want to build factories or warehouses. It was all right with Cable if the other railroads wanted to go in for that. Let the others have the plants and they could switch the cars to the Rock Island for road movement. That might have been all right if it had worked that way. But it never did, much to the Rock Island's despair in later years.

Another point in Cable's administration not to be overlooked was his tendency to cut corners in construction by leasing all or parts of other lines, or by contracting for trackage rights, when building his own mileage would have been much sounder. Of the 3,568 miles operated on March 31, 1898, only 2,877 was owned. The leased mileage totaled 352.70 and trackage rights extended across 338.05 miles of somebody else's railroad. Rock Island could perform no local service over many miles of these properties and therefore could earn nothing from traffic originating at or destined to points on these lines.

Out of the March 31, 1898, gross of $19,500,000 the company had to pay in rents and for trackage and bridge rights $789,562 for the fiscal year—a very high price, at best, considering the size of the railroad, its earning power, and the territory it served.

Warren G. Purdy had different ideas as to how to run a railroad. That was evident from the very start of his administration. It will be remembered that he had started with the Rock Island under John Tracy. He had begun his career in the financial department, and was local cashier at Chicago in the days of the disastrous fire of 1871. It was he who had raced against the flames to make sure that every corporate record, all stocks and bonds, and all cash were securely locked in the vaults before he left the Loop ahead of the devastation that befell the Chicago station.

Purdy was local treasurer when Hugh Riddle ran the Rock Island, and he admired Riddle's intensity of purpose to speed industrial development. Purdy was well aware of the opposition Riddle had met in this endeavor, and from his position of secretary and treasurer under Ransom Cable he had had many opportunities to see the weaknesses in some of Cable's policies.

The new president resolved to make the Rock Island second to none in *every* department, A long-range improvement program would be the first order of business. The growth in traffic had been steady and strong. But there were some things in the growth of the railroad that had not kept abreast of business increases.

Aside from the faults of inadequate terminal facilities and virtually no industrial development, a portion of the motive power was obsolete. Cable still, after 15 years, had been hanging on to the old wood-burners that should have been retired and scrapped.

2⑥ Enter: the Reid-Moore syndicate

Warren Purdy lost no time in calling in his traffic chiefs, his engineers and others for consultation. Everything that Hugh Riddle, during his term of office, had said about the South Chicago line and its development had come to pass. That branch, with ever-expanding industry along its rails, was a rich source of traffic. But why not more land for dock and terminal facilities?

Purdy's officers agreed with him, and immediately a plan was set up for the acquisition of the necessary property.

Now what about this motive power? Yes, the railroad had some modern locomotives, but not enough. Cable had hung on to outmoded power too long, and engines, on which an attempt at modernization had been made in the road's own shops, were not capable of doing things that the newer power could do.

Taking the system map, Purdy stuck a pencil point on Peoria. Here again the line was woefully weak in terminal facilities—and what was true of Peoria was true of Rock Island, Davenport, Des Moines, Kansas City, Missouri; Armourdale (Kansas City, Kansas); McFarland, Kansas.

Down in Oklahoma new towns were going up in rich agricultural territory off the line. Feeder branches would be profitable.

Purdy dreamed of great things for his railroad. No one knew its strong points and its weaknesses as well as he knew them. There was a healthy surplus in the treasury. The road had never missed a dividend, had never failed to earn a comfortable net. But competition was getting tougher. Other lines were doing progressive things and the Rock Island just had to keep pace.

While Purdy held long conferences with Hilon Parker, his first vice-president and general manager—the same Hilon Parker who under Marcus Low's supervision had made such an admirable record in building the lines west of the Missouri just 10 years ago—a group of gentlemen sat around a board-room table in a Chicago office building with new dreams of empire.

Purdy, like everyone else, had read and heard much about William B. Leeds and his three associates—Daniel G. Reid, called "Czar," and the Moore brothers, William H. and James Hobart. Bill Moore was known as "Judge." Not that he ever sat on a bench but because of his suave and ponderous bearing. He and his brother Jim, a very persuasive gentleman, had already gained considerable notoriety in both financial and political circles for the way they had put together two combines that had formed National Biscuit and Diamond Match.

Bill Leeds, known as the Tin Plate King, and Dan Reid, his companion since boyhood, had joined up with the Moores in putting together a group of tin plate and tin can companies to form American Can.

Collectively this quartet had gained the name of "The Big Four of the Prairies." They were firm believers in and had aptly demonstrated the accuracy of Barnum's theory as to the birth rate of gullible and trusting souls. In the light of their experiences it might be said that they thought Barnum had been slightly on the conservative side. Separately and collectively they could, as one writer put it, "have charmed a bird out of its nest, sucked the eggs, and made the bird like it."

Bill Leeds, through various engineering jobs on the Pennsylvania system, and while a division superintendent at Richmond, Indiana, had long dreamed of being not just a railroad president, but president of the biggest railroad in the world. He got into tin plate in 1890 along with Dan Reid who, as a cashier in a Richmond bank, saw an opportunity to make some real money without too much investment. Together these two bought some shares in the American Tin Plate Company at Elwood, Indiana.

Sometime in 1894 Leeds concluded that the Pennsylvania wasn't going to do very much about elevating him, and his $1,800 a year salary was peanuts compared to what his tin plate holdings were making. He left the railroad and took over as president of the Elwood firm, and Reid went along as treasurer.

Having watched the Moore brothers perform, Leeds and Reid teamed up with them, and conceived the idea of building a lot of small competitive companies into one great big corporation. The Moore brothers had definitely established the feasibility of using little or none of their own money in these schemes, while being very free with other people's cash.

This procedure appealed to Leeds and Reid, and since Judge Moore, early in 1898, was temporarily without funds, he was happy to have the association of these two tin plate manipulators.

They all got together and sent out a feeler to various competitors to see what these people wanted for their stock. When they received enough replies the Big Four held a meeting in Chicago. Each used his persuasiveness to convince the representatives of the various firms that they should all come into the as yet nonexistent big company that the Big Four was about to incorporate.

The build-up by Judge Moore and Leeds carried such conviction that before the meeting was over each manufacturer there had agreed to turn over his company for preferred stock and a bonus of an equal amount of common in the company the Big Four would set up. No cash output by the syndicate was involved. As an example, the La Belle Company, of Wheeling. West Virginia, asked $500,000 for its tin plating plant, which was twice what it cost; the earning capacity of the plant was $70,000 a year. Instead of a half million in cash, as La Belle had expected, its management surrendered the company for $500,000 preferred stock of the as yet unnamed buying corporation, and another $500,000 of that company's common stock.

The Big Four scattered stocks around with a very free hand and kept $10,000,000 of the common stock for themselves for promotion expense. Once the big company was incorporated at a capitalization far in excess of the combined worth of the various component parts that went to make up the whole, the syndicate cashed in and got out with their pockets loaded and their hearts light and gay.

No sooner had Judge Moore and his companions unloaded on tin plate and cans until they began on steel. They used the same methods exactly to get together independent bar mills, and formed National Steel Company. They went after the sheet-steel producers and formed the American Sheet Steel Company. They cornered the hoop manufacturers and came up with the American Steel Hoop Company.

And they had their calculating eyes on railroads for their next big coup. Specifically they had their eyes on Rock Island.

Warren Purdy didn't know it then, but his days were numbered. Purdy, blissfully unaware of the groping tentacles of the Big Four, went on re-laying rail, re-ballasting, and building new stations, permanent bridges, and larger shops and roundhouses.

Under Purdy's drive the Mangum branch from Chickasha, Oklahoma, was begun in 1898; it got as far as Mountain View that year and was completed to Mangum in 1899. Purdy organized the Guthrie and Kingfisher Railway Company in December 1899 to gain entrance to the then capital of Oklahoma Territory. Rock Island advanced the money for construction, and the road was built eastward from Kingfisher to Cashion where it connected with the Santa Fe. This was finished in 1900 and trackage rights from Cashion to Guthrie over the Santa Fe were secured.

Another Oklahoma branch from Enid to Billings, about 27 miles long, was built and put into operation about this time, and by its existence the entrance, years later, into Ponca City oil fields was made possible.

Purdy long had considered the southwest line that ran from Herington to Liberal, Kansas, as of little value unless it was extended, as originally planned, in the direction of El Paso. At a directors' meeting on December 7, 1900, the board gave Purdy the authority to build from Liberal "to a point" on the boundary line between Oklahoma Territory and the State of Texas. Two new companies were set up to provide for building across the Texas Panhandle into New Mexico. Contracts were let, and Liberal overnight became the center of a vast activity. For 12 years the railroad had rested there, and now track gangs, horses, shovels, work equipment all moved in to transform the tranquil town.

Plans were completed for new branch-line extension from Enid to Greenfield Junction in Oklahoma Territory and from a point near the town of Geary to Anadarko, and from Anadarko on the Mangum Branch to Fort Sill and Lawton.

Construction of these projects was under way early in 1901, when, with almost no warning at all, Warren Purdy sensed trouble—deep trouble.

The Reid-Moore Syndicate—the Big Four of the Prairies— was moving into the Rock Island picture.

First there were the rumors in the financial pages, then came the confirmation. Bill Leeds, Czar Reid, Judge Moore, and his brother J. Hobart were buying up Rock Island common on the stock exchange or wherever large blocks could be secured.

At the annual meeting, June 5, 1901, Vice-President and General Manager Hilon Parker was dumped from the Rock Island Board of Directors to make room for Reid, and another member was eased out to make room for Judge Moore. A further change was brought about on July 31, when the tin plate king, Leeds, was elected to the Rock Island directorate.

It was then announced that the Reid-Moore Syndicate had

obtained complete control of the property through the purchase of $20,690,775 of Rock Island common stock, and would take over the management of the property on January 1, 1902. Purdy could stay on until that date, but he would take orders from the syndicate.

Ransom Cable remained as chairman of the board and of the executive committee, but if he had any interest in stemming the tide that was sweeping Purdy under, he gave no evidence of it. Cable was approaching seventy. He was still a big power in his home town of Rock Island in business and finance, and he hoped to remain a power on the railroad, but he had to reckon with Reid-Moore. The syndicate was in the saddle now and Cable would have to go along with the new management if he wanted to stay with the system.

Purdy, on December 31, 1901, gave up the presidency, and William B. Leeds was elected to succeed him. Purdy's resignation gave ill health as his reason for getting out. Thus ended his three years and six months in the administration of Rock Island affairs—a very bright and progressive period in Rock Island's almost 50 years of existence. And thus began the realization of a dream Bill Leeds had long entertained.

Purdy had introduced the high-speed Atlantic type passenger engines for the main-line runs; he had invested in bigger and more powerful Consolidation type freight engines to replace the little 10-wheelers; he had purchased almost 4,000 new box cars of the most modern design and of maximum carrying capacity.

Up in Iowa Purdy had built from Gowrie, a point on the Des Moines and Fort Dodge Railroad, 109 miles to Sibley. It will be recalled that the Des Moines and Fort Dodge came into being back in 1873 when the Des Moines Valley Railroad, which built the line north from Des Moines to Tara, was foreclosed and dismembered. The Rock Island had taken over the Des Moines and Fort Dodge through lease in March 1887. So, when Purdy built the Sibley line in 1900, he had in mind the purchase of the Des Moines and Fort Dodge for incorporation into the system.

This was a bit of unfinished business he could leave in the hands of Tin Plate Leeds, just as he had to leave the hopes and dreams he had long entertained for a stronger and more powerful Midwest system.

Certainly Warren Purdy was leaving the syndicate a well-filled treasury. And even before the ink on Purdy's resignation was quite dry, Leeds and his associates had an eye on the cash box and one hand in the till. Messrs. Leeds and Reid and the Moore boys had great plans for this system. It would be the nucleus of a railroad that would reach from the Atlantic to the Pacific under Mr. Leeds' master hand. It would be the first great transcontinental route extending from ocean to ocean in one unbroken line.

Of course, to accomplish this, a lot of money would be necessary. With Rock Island's treasury, and its common stock as a basis, the syndicate already knew just exactly how it would proceed.

PART FOUR

Pattern for Disaster

1901-1933

27 Big men—big dreams

William B. Leeds took office as president of the Rock Island with the machinery well set up to get things done the syndicate's way. The first step had been to amend the articles of the 1880 consolidation to permit the increase in membership of the executive committee from five to seven. The action had been taken and the amendment approved at a special meeting of the stockholders in October, 1901. Next, at the December 12 meeting of the board, Purdy's resignation as president, and as a member of the board and of the executive committee, had paved the way for Leeds' election to the presidency and James H. Moore's election to the board and his appointment to the executive committee.

At the first meeting of the directors under the Leeds administration, held on January 30, 1902, in the company's New York offices, three more of the directors submitted their resignations. F. H. Griggs, of Davenport, Iowa, long associated with the affairs of the company, dropped out of the running. So did Tracy Dows, prominent New Yorker. The reason for their resignations was not given expressly by themselves, but was graphically set forth in the letter of resignation written by H. R. Bishop and also submitted that same day.

"On account of the great changes," wrote Mr. Bishop, "that have taken place in the ownership of the stock of this company, and the probability that the gentlemen now in control may wish to place on the board of management, directors of their own selection, I tender my resignation as a director to take effect at the convenience of the board of directors."

The syndicate's convenience was right now. George G. McMurtry, F. L. Hine, and F. S. Wheeler, all of New York, immediately were elected to the vacancies.

The executive committee was made up of the entire syndicate quartet—Leeds, Reid, and the Moore brothers—with Cable still chairman, and with Marshall Field and A. G. Flower, survivors of the old board, still holding on.

An outstanding characteristic of the Reid-Moore combine was its ability to move fast. Almost before anyone was aware of what was happening, the syndicate came up with a contract to buy the majority of the outstanding common and preferred stocks of a 600-mile main line of railroad that stretched westward from Memphis, Tennessee, through Little Rock and Oklahoma City to Elk City, Oklahoma Territory. The property, known as the Choctaw, Oklahoma and Gulf Railroad Company, had been incorporated in 1894 by a group of Philadelphia capitalists, to take over some existing lines and to build certain mileage to complete what its predecessors had started.

As of January 1, 1902, the outstanding capital stock of the Rock Island was 599,558 shares at $100 par value. The bonded debt was $12,500,000 in 6 percent mortgage bonds and $58,581,000 in 4 percent general mortgage bonds—a total of $71,081,000, or just a little under $18,000 per mile. A very sound structure, based on business as it was in those days.

The syndicate didn't let it stay that way very long. The board acted on March 27 to call a meeting of the stockholders for the purpose of approving a board resolution to increase the capital stock from the company's authorized 600,000 shares to 750,000 at $100 par value. The resolution provided that the 150,000 additional shares "shall be issued and disposed of for corporate purposes at such times and on such terms and conditions as the Board of Directors or the Executive Committee shall determine."

The Reid-Moore executive committee worked out the details of the purchase of the Choctaw, executed a trust agreement, and, according to procedure in former financial deals, was generous in its treatment of the seller. The Choctaw was capitalized at $16,000,000. The stock was divided into 320,000 shares with a par value of $50. One hundred and twenty thousand shares were 5 percent cumulative preferred stock, all outstanding, and the common shares numbered 200,000, with 196,550 outstanding.

The syndicate agreed to pay $60 a share for all the preferred and $80 a share for the common. To do this $23,000,000 was added to the Rock Island's debt by the issuance of that amount of 4 percent gold bonds. As the stock of the Choctaw came in it was to be pledged with the Central Trust Company in New York which in turn would issue the equivalent in bonds to the Choctaw bankers, Speyer and Company, of Philadelphia. Speyer would then sell the bonds and turn the cash over to the Choctaw owners.

The whole deal was wrapped up by the Rock Island board on May 6, 1902, when the directors approved all agreements pertaining to the purchase. On that same day, by prearrangement, the entire board of the Choctaw, Oklahoma and Gulf resigned, and the Reid-Moore Syndicate elected its own men.

The records do not indicate who, if anyone other than the Choctaw promoters, placed the value of that property at the price the syndicate agreed to pay. Facts indicate that what the Rock Island brought into its expansion program was a very poor property, indeed. It was essentially a coal-carrying road through sparsely settled territory. Its roadbed was in none too good condition, its power was outmoded, its rolling stock was in bad repair, and the history of the predecessor companies that had been brought together to make the Choctaw was one of financial weakness and failure.

On the bright side was the promise of the growing cities of Little Rock and Oklahoma City, and the eventual completion of the railroad into Amarillo, Texas. Its one physical connection with the Rock Island system was at El Reno, Oklahoma, where it crossed the parent road's north-south main line.

Of the properties that went to make up the Choctaw, the

Memphis and Little Rock Railroad Company was the oldest. It came into being on January 11, 1853, by a special act of the Arkansas General Assembly. A group of Memphis business leaders was behind the project and the city of Memphis issued $350,000 of its bonds to spur the builders to quick action.

It took most of the year 1854 to complete the surveys, but by the end of that year construction had begun. The line was completed to Madison, Arkansas, 45 miles west of Memphis, in 1858. At the same time another segment between DeVall's Bluff and North Little Rock was made ready for traffic. That left a 40-mile gap between Madison and DeVall's Bluff, which, with swamps and rivers and other physical conditions to be overcome, was a long way from even being graded. Service between Memphis and Little Rock, however, was begun in 1859, but it was rugged to say the least. The passenger rode the "steam cars" from Memphis to Madison, changed to a stagecoach for the journey to Clarendon, then again changed to river boat from Clarendon to DeVall's Bluff. From there it was back on the railroad again to North Little Rock, and the trip ended with a ferry ride across the river into Little Rock.

The Civil War stopped all efforts to close the center gap in the railroad, and the Confederate Army even confiscated a lot of the railroad that had been laid. After the war, under the leadership of General Robert C. Brinkley, of Memphis, the entire line was finally completed. The engineers had a lot of trouble with high water across some of the territory and had to resort to chains and cables to hold the railroad in place. The 55-pound iron rails weren't heavy enough to hold the ties to the roadbed when the water came up over the fills, and there were many instances where whole sections would float away. The cables and chains were used to anchor the track to the trees.

Through service was established—railroad all the way—in 1871. By 1887 the Memphis and Little Rock, due to financial difficulties, had changed hands and names four different times. In 1898 when the Choctaw bought the property it was known

as the Little Rock and Memphis. The deal was made as part
of an expansion plan which included building west from Little
Rock to the Indian Territory (now Oklahoma) border—a
project of 151 miles, which was completed in 1900.

Over to the west another predecessor of the Choctaw,
Oklahoma and Gulf was a greatly harassed and struggling line
that had been incorporated in 1887 in Minnesota as the Choctaw Coal and Railway Company. This road was built westward from Wister, through the heart of the coal-mining
region, to McAlester for a connection with the Missouri,
Kansas and Texas. Another section was surveyed from El
Reno eastward to and through the townsite of Oklahoma City,
with McAlester as its goal.

The El Reno - Oklahoma City line was set for a formal
opening in April 1889. But, like many other things for which
big plans were laid in that period of the territory's troubled
history, the building of the line ran into difficulty.

When the line originally was surveyed between McAlester
and El Reno a crossing with the Santa Fe's north-south line
was designated on the map at the site where Oklahoma City
would be built. The owners of the proposed railroad com-
plied with all regulations dealing with the crossing of Government lands, and the right-of-way had been carefully staked
out.

The Government set April 22, 1889, as the official opening
of the Oklahoma City townsite. As previously chronicled in
this record, the place became bedlam overnight. Thousands
upon thousands of settlers swarmed in, determined to secure
Government lots, and the carefully placed stakes that marked
the railroad's claims were trampled down or completely removed. The settlers took over, and the Choctaw Coal and
Railway Company was in a helpless situation.

The railroad took what steps it could to reclaim its property.
Its claim was filed in the land office at Guthrie, was approved
and forwarded to Washington. There again it was approved
and the railroad could very well expel from the property the
people who had moved in on it, but by the time the Govern-

ment red tape had completely unwound itself the settlers had erected homes and stores on the right-of-way.

Because Oklahoma City wanted that railroad built and completed, a compromise was finally reached whereby the city paid the settlers for portions of the right-of-way and cleared the land so that eventually the railroad received a 100-foot right-of-way instead of the 200-foot swath it was entitled to. The line was completed into Oklahoma City in February, 1892, and there it remained until the Choctaw, Oklahoma and Gulf took over on a foreclosure.

The Choctaw, Oklahoma and Gulf completed the line between Oklahoma City and McAlester toward the end of 1895, built from El Reno west to Weatherford in 1898, and completed the extension from Weatherford to Elk City in 1901. The further extension westward from Elk City to the Oklahoma -Texas state line was almost ready for operations when the Rock Island bought the Choctaw. In addition to the Memphis to Elk City main line, the acquisition included several important branch lines which the Choctaw had built through subsidiaries and then had purchased to bring the branches into the parent property.

While the Choctaw deal was nearing its consummation the syndicate reached over into Missouri for a distraught and pitifully poor little piece of railroad that, someday, would be an important main line from St. Louis to Kansas City. It was known as the St. Louis, Kansas City and Colorado Railroad Company and it was in the hands of two gentlemen named John Scullin and David R. Francis, receivers.

It had started out, 30 years before, by incorporation in May 1870, as the St. Louis and Fort Scott. A year later it became the Missouri Central Railway Company. Its original purpose was to build from St. Louis to a point in Vernon County, Missouri, opposite Fort Scott, Kansas, an estimated 200 miles. Under these names some survey work was done but nothing was built. Then, in June, 1881, the Central Railway of Missouri was formed and took over the rights and franchises of its predecessors and rigged the charter to permit building from St. Louis to Creve Coeur Lake, thence to Tavern Rock and along the south bank of the Missouri River to a connection with the Missouri Pacific.

Again no construction resulted, and a new company called the St. Louis and Central Missouri Railway was incorporated in June 1883.

Meanwhile, the Forest Park and Central Railroad Company, incorporated in October, 1877, had built a commuter line from Forsythe Junction, in St. Louis, to Creve Coeur. The 16-mile property had started out as a narrow-gauge road and had changed to standard gauge in 1881.

The St. Louis, Kansas City and Colorado Railroad Company was incorporated in December, 1884, and immediately acquired the Forest Park and Central. Two years later, in November, 1886, it also took over the St. Louis and Central Missouri, which still hadn't built anything, but which possessed valuable rights.

The new corporation did little more than maintain and improve the 16 miles of railroad it owned until August, 1887, when the Santa Fe moved in and put up $3,346,000 to complete the line to Belle. The first 39 miles from Creve Coeur to Union went into operation a year later, and another segment of 45 miles from Union to Belle was not completed until 1901.

But long before that date the Santa Fe had had enough. With the railroad still far short of Belle, Missouri, and still more than 200 miles from its Kansas City goal in December, 1899, the Santa Fe sold out to Scullin and Francis for $425,000 —a terrific loss.

So when William B. Leeds, acting for the syndicate-controlled Rock Island, announced the purchase of the St. Louis line from the receivers, he promised that the railroad would be brought to rapid completion. The Reid-Moore board summarily approved issuance of $2,000,000 worth of Rock Island common to buy up all the stocks and bonds of the St. Louis, Kansas City and Colorado held by the receivers, but that was of little matter at the moment.

The next big story was the announcement on June 1, 1902, that the Rock Island had taken over the now 1,289 miles of the Burlington, Cedar Rapids and Northern under a 999-year lease. The Rock Island had long owned that company's controlling stock, but now it would be operated as part of the Rock Island system. Of the increased Rock Island shares, 33,812 were set aside to exchange share for share with holders of the Burlington, Cedar Rapids and Northern stock still outstanding. Through this deal the Rock Island gained entrance into Minnesota and entered into arrangements with the Milwaukee to get into St. Paul and Minneapolis—a through service which was destined to become a reality in November of that year.

Down in the southwest the construction from Liberal through Dalhart, Texas, to Santa Rosa, New Mexico, for a connection with the El Paso and Northeastern, progressed at a rapid rate. By the late summer the Rock Island management was ready to announce plans for through passenger service from Chicago to Los Angeles, via El Paso and Tucson.

The finest of modern equipment was already on order for the inauguration of the Golden State Limited, heralded as the most luxurious train to the Pacific Coast.

The Golden State, its coaches and sleeping cars olive green and gold-striped behind the flashing rods of a high-wheeled Atlantic type locomotive, was launched on its maiden run November 2 as a fitting observance of the railroad's fiftieth birthday.

The Rock Island could claim, on its Golden Anniversary, 6,351 miles of railroad in 13 states, and terminal facilities in Memphis, making up the 14 states that it serves today. Rich and prosperous as it was, however, at the end of 1902 it was already headed, slowly but surely, for disaster.

28 To have and to hold

The Reid-Moore Syndicate, having succeeded in boosting the authorized capitalization from $60,000,000 to $75,000,000, decided that the $20,000,000 in shares it owned still was not enough to make absolutely sure of complete and permanent control of the company. Bill Leeds and Judge Moore could not be sure when some smart shareholder might get hold of enough proxies to stop their free spending and their questionable expansion.

Already, through the former Choctaw, Oklahoma and Gulf owners, they had their fingers on the Lehigh Valley. That property would give them the Eastern seaboard line they needed for one link in the transcontinental chain they hoped to forge. Then there was the Lake Erie and Western that with the Lehigh Valley would form a segment of the New York - to - Chicago part of the empire. Along with the solid Rock Island, the syndicate wanted the Chicago and Alton and the Frisco. Control of these would be followed by acquisition of the Southern Pacific, the most ambitious part of their over-all program.

All this was charted on paper in July, 1902, when the syndicate set up two holding companies of what is called, in financial circles, the superimposed type. The first was the Rock Island Company of New Jersey, incorporated on July 30, and the second was the Chicago, Rock Island and Pacific *Railroad* Company (of Iowa). The first objective was to get hold of all the outstanding stock of the Rock Island railroad without having to put out any money for it, so that forever after the

Big Four of the Prairies would at all times be in complete control of the company's destinies.

[To avoid confusion between the railroad property, the Chicago, Rock Island and Pacific *Railway* Company (Pacific No. 3) of the 1880 consolidation, and the Chicago, Rock Island and Pacific *Railroad* Company (of Iowa), the latter will hereafter be referred to in this record as the Iowa holding company, a corporation which simply existed on paper, as did the Rock Island Company of New Jersey, owning no physical property and operating no railroad.]

Following their procedure of being very generous in their treatment of the sucker as long as it didn't cost them anything, the members of the syndicate set up a package in August, 1902, which they offered to the holders of the solid and heretofore safe dividend-paying shares of the Rock Island Railroad. The package consisted of one share of Rock Island of New Jersey common, $100 par value, one share of Rock Island of New Jersey preferred, par value $70, and $100 worth of 100-year 4 percent collateral bonds of the Iowa holding company—a total of $270 worth of the two holding company securities—for each share of Rock Island common stock offered.

A trust agreement was entered into with the Central Trust Company of New York to receive the offered shares of Rock Island common. The entire capital stock of the Iowa holding company was issued to the New Jersey Company, and the capital stock of the Rock Island Company of New Jersey was issued to the Central Trust Company.

The procedure under the trust agreement was that the common shares of the Rock Island Railroad would serve as collateral for the Iowa holding company's 4 percent bonds. Thus, as each Rock Island shareholder swallowed the syndicate's bait and turned in his shares, the Central Trust Company took them as pledged collateral and in turn issued to the Rock Island stockholder the equivalent in the Iowa holding company's bonds plus common and preferred stock of the New Jersey holding company.

What the Rock Island shareholder neither knew nor realized was that the entire income of these two holding companies would consist solely of the dividends that his surrendered Rock Island Railroad shares would pay, and that the interest he would get on the 4 percent bonds and any dividends he might collect on his Rock Island of New Jersey common and preferred would represent only a portion of the money that those shares earned, and nothing more. In other words, each shareholder who turned in his railroad common bought nothing but a pig in a poke, and a pretty slippery pig at that.

Again the Messrs. Leeds and Reid and the suave Moore brothers demonstrated the infallibility of Mr. Barnum's historic appraisal of the human race. The lure of offering what seemed much for just a little had its immediate results. Rock Island's common stockholders couldn't surrender their shares fast enough. The offering seemed too good to be true—and, of course, it was.

Owners of the railroad's common shares representing holdings totaling $71,353,100, or approximately 95 percent of the outstanding stock, exchanged their holdings for the syndicate's package. The other 5 percent were either sagacious or contrary. That made little or no difference to the syndicate. Through the shares in the vaults of the Central Trust Company the Rock Island Railroad belonged to it, ballast, rail, and good high revenue.

The next move in the syndicate's bid for empire centered on the St. Louis and San Francisco Railroad Company. The syndicate set up a new package to lure Frisco stockholders by working through the Iowa holding company. This package consisted of $60 worth of Rock Island of New Jersey and $60 worth of a new bond issue of the Iowa holding company called the 10-year 5-percent bonds of 1913—a total of $120 in holding company securities for each $100 par value share of Frisco common. The procedure was the same as in the Rock Island exchange scheme—the Frisco shares were deposited with the Central Trust of New York as collateral for the Iowa holding company's bonds.

On May 7, 1903, the two holding companies signed an agreement whereby the Iowa holding company would begin to negotiate for the purchase in the name of the Rock Island Company of New Jersey one-half of the capital stock of the Southern Pacific's lines in Texas. A second agreement specified that the New Jersey company issue the necessary common stock for acquisition of the Frisco shares, and that it then issue all its remaining authorized common and preferred stock to be used in acquiring controlling stock of the Southern Pacific.

Shortly after the formation of the two holding companies the officers and directors of both the Iowa company and the New Jersey company were the same as the officers and directors of the Rock Island Railroad.

Thus, by May of 1903, the Reid-Moore dream of empire became the pattern for disaster—a pattern that in the next few years was to wreak havoc with the railroad that for more than 50 years had grown progressively, had developed soundly and vigorously, and had experienced, in more or less degree, some pretty good management.

By October of 1903, with the Frisco ownership in the hands of the syndicate, B. F. Yoakum, another financial giant in railroad manipulations, came to the Rock Island board to succeed A. R. Flower. In fact, because of Yoakum's personal interest in the Frisco deal, Flower had to resign to make room for him.

Yoakum brought with him the Frisco's vice-president and general manager, Benjamin L. Winchell, who was immediately elected by the Rock Island board to the position of third vice-president. This office had supervision over freight and passenger traffic departments. Winchell's entire previous experience had been in operating capacities on various lines that eventually had gone into the Frisco system, and prior to becoming the Frisco's vice-president and general manager he had been president of the Kansas City, Fort Scott and Memphis, one of the Frisco's principal subsidiaries. He laid no claim to being a financial genius, but when it came to operating a railroad he knew the score.

All during the year 1903 construction on various parts of the Rock Island system continued, and the syndicate's expansion plans moved smoothly. Through the New Jersey holding company, the syndicate had caused to be incorporated another subsidiary called the Rock Island Improvement Company. It was set up under the laws of New Jersey, and its charter granted it the right to engage in almost every conceivable kind of business except such as required the right of eminent domain in the State of New Jersey. Its entire capital stock was acquired by the Rock Island Company of New Jersey.

The primary function of the Improvement Company was to take title to all sorts of property and equipment that the railroad operating company would use, and thereby remove such property and equipment from falling under liens of the railway company's mortgages. The Improvement Company would tap the railroad's treasury for advances to acquire lands, shops, industrial sites, motive power and rolling stock, and for the money advanced issue to the railroad certain bonds.

It must be stated here that through all the complicated manipulations that were to follow virtually every scheme was cooked up in New York where the syndicate maintained its offices. The syndicate was in position to vote virtually all the shares of the railway company, the two holding companies, and the Improvement Company in one breath so that executive committee meetings, board meetings, and annual meetings of stockholders were simply formalities.

As an example, a special meeting of the stockholders was called for March 21, 1904, for the purpose of authorizing an increase of the railway company's bonded debt. The syndicate set the new ceiling at $275,000,000. It specified that this debt would be exclusive of bonds to be issued for the acquisition of additional railways or property which would be secured by the mortgages or pledges of such railways or properties. The vote was taken in just the amount of time it took the secretary to word it properly and place on the minutes the amount of shares voting.

One big reason for the increase in debt was the necessity to peddle enough bonds to place in the railway company's treasury the several million dollars that would have to be advanced to the Improvement Company so that it could buy up property in Cedar Rapids, Peoria, Blue Island, Silvis, Little Rock, and other points, to say nothing of engines and cars of every description.

It was at this time that the burdens of the president's office were having a telling effect on the health of William B. Leeds. The Tin Plate King, who had all his life dreamed of being president of the biggest railroad in the world, found that being president of just a moderate-sized property wasn't at all to his liking. He resigned the presidency on March 26, five days after the 1904 stockholders' special meeting, and Yoakum's man from the Frisco, Ben Winchell, was elected to succeed him.

29 All this and Texas too

Ben Winchell, by virtue of his training and background, believed that a railroad president had to keep in close touch with the property instead of sitting in an office in New York, a thousand miles away from the railroad. In the few months he had been on the Rock Island, Winchell had had an opportunity to travel its far-flung mileage, meet its officers and employees, and get a pretty good picture of what the railroad needed.

It needed a great deal of everything in the way of improved power and rolling stock, better ballast and heavier steel over many sections of it, improved shops and terminal facilities, better bridges and better signaling.

Winchell wasn't much concerned about the ways and means the syndicate had contrived to ring in the Rock Island Improvement Company on the purchasing of rolling stock and other facilities. His concern was getting what he needed.

The Rock Island's Choctaw line across Arkansas and Oklahoma was now completed into the city of Amarillo, Texas, and construction on the 113 miles between Amarillo and Tucumcari, New Mexico, had begun. The building from the Oklahoma State line into Amarillo had first been undertaken by the Choctaw, Oklahoma and Texas Railroad Company, a Texas corporation set up in June, 1901. In November, 1902, the charter had been amended to provide for the extension of the line from Amarillo westward to the Texas - New Mexico border. The Chicago, Rock Island and Gulf Railway Company, another Texas corporation set up by the syndicate, took over the rights, franchises, and property of the Choctaw, Oklahoma and Texas on December 1, 1903, and thereafter completed the line to Amarillo.

The syndicate incorporated on January 26, 1903, the Chicago, Rock Island and Choctaw Railway Company, to build from Tucumcari eastward to connect with the Amarillo extension at the New Mexico - Texas boundary. Contracts were let and most of the grading was completed by midsummer, when work was ordered discontinued. Immediately thereafter this railroad was conveyed by deed to the Chicago, Rock Island and El Paso Railway Company. But the latter company did nothing to further the project.

Meanwhile in December, 1903, the important Texas mileage between Fort Worth and Dallas was placed in operation by the Chicago, Rock Island and Gulf.

Further expansion in Arkansas came in the spring of 1904 at about the time the Rock Island finally secured the last of the outstanding capital stock of the Choctaw, leased the property, and began its operation as part of the Rock Island system. Among the railroads of short mileage that were purchased by the Rock Island were the Searcy and Des Arc Railroad Company, approximately 24 miles long, and the Hazen and Northern Railroad Company which was partially completed between Des Arc and Mesa, Arkansas.

As of the end of the fiscal year, June 30, 1904, the mileage operated in the Rock Island system was shown as 7,258.92. Gross operating revenues for the same period totaled $44,969,491.

It was during 1905 that the Arkansas expansion was pushed to the limit. Thirty-two separate and distinct railroad companies, including the Little Rock and Memphis and the Choctaw, formed, in one way or another, the network of lines that comprises the Rock Island's holdings of today in Arkansas.

The most fascinating story in the railway development of Arkansas is that of the Little Rock - Hot Springs line.

Back in 1874, the Cairo and Fulton, a predecessor of the Missouri Pacific, built southwestward from Little Rock through Malvern, Arkansas, with Texas as its destination. Hot Springs, in 1832, had been made a national reservation by the United States Government and had early become a health resort. Those who sought the benefits of the healing waters of the Springs had to reach the place via stagecoach from the railroad station at Malvern.

The stage trip was one to be long remembered. It was exceedingly rough. But, despite the awful jarring the passengers, many of them in ill health, had to take, the line was a thriving one.

A regular visitor at the Hot Springs resort was Joseph Reynolds, of Chicago, a steamboat operator. He had long been a familiar figure in the river cities, and his sobriquet "Diamond Jo" had been acquired possibly from his display of diamonds on his person and the trademark that gave his steamboat line the same name.

Diamond Jo, after the railroad reached Malvern, became so disgusted with the stage journey that he decided to build a railroad himself. He incorporated in 1870 the Hot Springs Railroad Company. Construction got under way in 1875 and the railroad was ready for service a year later. Starting as a narrow-gauge line, it was converted to standard gauge in 1889.

It became nationally known for the elegance of its equipment, both its motive power and its decorative coaches, and it was a money-maker. It provided, for 25 years, the only rail service into the Springs.

The Choctaw, Oklahoma and Gulf, around the turn of the century, saw an opportunity to create traffic through the Memphis gateway via Little Rock into Hot Springs and acquired the Diamond Jo line. It then built new mileage from Butterfield to Benton to connect with a small line called the Little Rock and Hot Springs Western. The Choctaw leased 26 miles of this company's track to gain the connection with its main line at Little Rock and the service from Memphis was set up.

To further its Arkansas expansion, the Reid-Moore Syndicate incorporated, in 1905, the Rock Island, Arkansas and Louisiana Railroad Company. The general idea was to open up a direct route from Little Rock to New Orleans.

Into this new company was consolidated the Little Rock and Southern, the Arkansas Southern, the Alexandria, Junction City and Shreveport, and the Arkansas Southern Extension Railway. This consolidation resulted in putting together a total of 108 miles of railroad. To supply the missing links that would extend the line entirely from Little Rock to Eunice, Louisiana, it would be necessary to buy 22 miles more and build 200 miles.

The Little Rock and Southern, at the time of consolidation, had done a lot of grading, but had completed no track from Haskell to El Dorado. The Arkansas Southern extended from El Dorado to Winnfield, Louisiana, 98 miles, and the Arkansas Southern Extension Railway was a 10-mile stretch from Winnfield to Packton.

The new construction consisted of 100 miles from Haskell to El Dorado; 45 miles from Tinsman to Crossett; 56 miles from Alexandria to Eunice; and 1 mile of station track at Camden, Arkansas.

While all this was not completed and opened for service until January, 1908, the Rock Island, Louisiana and Arkansas was leased to the Rock Island system for 999 years in January, 1906.

Meanwhile the St. Louis - Kansas City Line, which at the time the Rock Island had taken over had extended from St. Louis only to Bland, Missouri, a distance of 104 miles, was completed and put into operation. The section from Bland to Eldon was opened for traffic in 1903, and from Eldon to Hadsell in 1904. The 33-mile stretch between Hadsell and Kansas City was built by a subsidiary called the Kansas City Rock Island Railway Company which was incorporated for that purpose in 1902. On January 1, 1905, the entire St. Louis, Kansas City and Colorado property was conveyed by deed to the Kansas City Rock Island Company and on the same day this corporation conveyed the St. Louis, Kansas City and Colorado to the Rock Island system.

The St. Louis - Kansas City line, 298.2 miles in length, although not fully completed, had been opened for through traffic on July 1, 1904. Up to June 30 of that year the Rock Island treasury had been tapped for almost $17,000,000 for construction costs. During the following year another $1,711,-891 was expended, which completed the Rock Island's investment in that piece of property.

With the Rock Island solidly established to Dallas, Texas, Winchell saw in 1906 a further chance for a profitable expansion by acquiring a half interest in the Trinity and Brazos Valley Railway Company, the stocks and bonds of which were owned by the Colorado and Southern, a Burlington subsidiary. The Colorado and Southern had bought up the control of the railroad that had been organized in 1902 by a group of Texas citizens whose desire was to establish a short route from Dallas through Houston to Galveston. Rock Island's acquisition of half the property assured its entry into the growing Texas ports.

With operations direct to St. Louis now established, the syndicate, controlling both the Rock Island and Frisco systems, set up on April 9, 1906, the Rock Island - Frisco Terminal Railway Company, which immediately proceeded to provide freight depots and yards and other terminal facilities for the two lines.

While all the expansion in Arkansas and Missouri was taking place, the syndicate management, for some reason never explained in the records, relinquished its lease of the Des Moines and Fort Dodge Railroad, in Iowa, and thereby cut itself off from its own Gowrie-Sibley line. The 70-mile piece of railroad between Des Moines and Gowrie had been operated virtually as part of the Rock Island system ever since 1887, and the important 109-mile line from Gowrie to Sibley had been built as an extension of this property.

As soon as the Des Moines and Fort Dodge lease was dropped, the Minneapolis and St. Louis moved in and took over, and thereafter the Rock Island had to pay for trackage rights to get from Des Moines to its own property at Gowrie. This move not only deprived the Rock Island of ever-increasing revenue on traffic that originated on the Des Moines and Fort Dodge, but increased the Rock Island's operating expenses.

While this major mistake in the syndicate's management —or mismanagement—of the Rock Island was shaping up, the syndicate issued $10,000,000 of Rock Island first and refunding 4 percent bonds to acquire 187,900 shares of the capital stock of the Chicago and Alton Railroad Company. Along with this acquisition went control of the Chicago and Eastern Illinois.

Ransom R. Cable, finding it more and more difficult, due to his health and his advancing age, to travel back and forth to New York for meetings, stepped down from the chairmanship of the Rock Island board and Czar Reid took over that post.

By February, 1906, Bill Leeds gave up on the railroad business and resigned from the executive committee and from the directorate.

During all this time Rock Island Improvement Company went along in great style on money the Rock Island Railroad advanced for Improvement Company operations. The first big deal was the advance by the railroad of $1,815,467 to the Improvement Company for the acquisition of land and erection of shops at Silvis, Illinois. In return the Improvement Company issued $2,700,000 par value of its 4 percent bonds, secured by the property.

This pattern was followed at many other points.

Purchase of equipment by the Improvement Company was another master stroke of syndicate genius. As an example, on January 3, 1905, the Improvement Company entered into an equipment trust agreement with the Bankers Trust Company of New York to acquire certain rolling stock. In the acquisition of this equipment the Improvement Company issued $4,500,000 of its 4½ percent equipment trust bonds, series A, to the Bankers Trust Company and paid $17,136 in cash. The Rock Island Railroad advanced this amount.

Rebates from the builders and from specialties used on the equipment amounted to $73,352. This sum went to the railroad and was carried on the books for the account of the Improvement Company.

The Improvement Company granted to the railroad the right to use the equipment, and for this privilege the railroad had to make all the interest payments on the equipment trust bonds. In addition, the railroad agreed to make cash payments on the equipment, and pay off the equity trust bonds as they matured serially. The deal provided for the conveyance of the equipment to the railroad by the Improvement Company after the last of the bonds had been retired.

Despite the complexity of the Reid-Moore financing and corporate manipulations, President Ben Winchell made some progress out on the railroad. By the end of the fiscal year, June 30, 1909, the Rock Island's operated mileage had grown to 8,026. Winchell's annual reports, a vast improvement over those during the Leeds regime, proudly pointed to a slow but steady improvement in the location of industries along the railroad.

Earnings for the 1909 fiscal year showed an increase in gross from the $44,969,000 when Winchell took over in 1904, to $61,184,886. If Winchell suffered any anxiety over the steadily increasing debt structure against the property he didn't show it.

But by that midsummer of 1909 the syndicate leaders sensed trouble. For six years now they had been paying interest on the 10-year bonds that had been issued as a lure to Frisco stockholders for the acquisition of the Frisco common. And not once in this period had the Frisco common the syndicate held earned one dime in dividends. Of course no dividends could be paid to the former Frisco shareholders on the Rock Island of New Jersey shares that had gone to them along with the Iowa holding company's bonds.

Part of the Chicago and Alton stock and the bonds of that company the syndicate had acquired had been traded for bonds of the Toledo, St. Louis and Western (the Cloverleaf Route). The Cloverleaf was a shaky property; its earnings were depressed, its traffic was light.

All this marked another figure in the pattern for disaster.

30 Broken dream of empire

Ominous clouds shadowed the operations of the Reid-Moore Syndicate in the late summer and the fall of 1909. No one knew better than Judge Moore and Czar Reid how burdensome their acquisition of the Frisco common stock had become. For six years, ever since it had been gathered in by their Iowa holding company with an exchange of holding company bonds and stocks, the Frisco common had failed to pay dividends. Thus the dividends voted on the Rock Island common, reposing in the vaults of the Central Trust Company in New York, not only had to furnish the interest on the 100-year bonds of the Iowa company in the hands of the former Rock Island owners, but had to pay the interest on the shorter term bonds that had been issued to Frisco shareholders.

B. F. Yoakum, one of the cagiest of them all, saw an opportunity to put the squeeze on his associates in the syndicate inner sanctum, and thereby gather in the Frisco for himself. He quietly went about organizing a syndicate of his own. When he knew he had the cash back of him he went before the Rock Island board and laid his cards on the table.

He and his associates would gladly take the Frisco off the hands of the Reid-Moore Syndicate for $37.50 per common share of $100 par value. He would pay $10,852,612 for the whole lot of it. This would leave the syndicate with a nice unhealthy loss—with the problem of retiring the Iowa holding company bonds for which the stock was the collateral.

The syndicate was helpless and Yoakum knew it. Judge Moore and Czar Reid implied an ugly word—blackmail. Yoakum merely told them they could take his offer or leave it. How about the $7,314,660 it would take to retire those short-term collateral bonds? The Rock Island treasury, of course. There was plenty in the cash drawer, and why should the syndicate hesitate to reach into the till and satisfy the bondholders? They'd been reaching into Rock Island's earnings for everything else in their operations.

Ransom R. Cable, at the age of 75, came to the end of his time before the deal could be completed. This grand old man of the Rock Island, still a member of its board, passed away on November 12, 1909. His death came as a blow to those few shareholders who had long held out against the syndicate.

They had always hoped that Cable would live to see the end of the syndicate control and a return to the kind of management that had, for almost 50 years, from the railroad's humble beginning, guided the company's growth conservatively yet progressively.

Cable could recall, in the closing days of his life, a career devoted to high principles. He had not always been right, and no one knew that better than he. He had made mistakes in judgment, but they had been honest mistakes. He could recall Warren Purdy's plea, in the fall of 1901, to strike out and fight the Reid-Moore control, and Purdy's bitter disappointment when Cable had pointed out the hopelessness of it. Purdy then had been an ailing man, but vigorous mentally. And Purdy had not forgiven him. Now Purdy was old and bitter and crippled hopelessly.

Cable could look back over the last seven years and feel that he had done his best in counseling against some of the Reid-Moore projects. The Rock Island Railroad had been his very life, and his love for it was deep. He had hoped for better things for it in its progress. He had given his best toward such an accomplishment.

At the December, 1909, meeting of the Rock Island board the members bowed their heads and voted a resolution to the memory of Ransom R. Cable. They put it on the minutes and in it they said a great man had passed, and that his sage advice and his wise counsel would be sorely missed.

Then they turned around, accepted Yoakum's deal for the Frisco stock, and voted an advance of money from the Rock Island treasury in the amount of $7,314,660 so the Iowa holding company could retire its bonds. In return for the cash the Iowa holding company issued to the Rock Island $7,500,000 par value of 5 percent temporary bonds due September 1, 1913.

With that little matter of business completed, Yoakum resigned from the board and the executive committee of the Rock Island and the holding companies, and Ben Winchell's resignation as president of the Rock Island Railroad was speedily requested and received.

The next order of business was the election of a president, and the man in line for this promotion was the operating vice-president, Henry U. Mudge. Mudge had been brought into the Rock Island picture from the Santa Fe back in 1905, and, under Winchell, had demonstrated a fine ability to spend money right and left in full accord with the syndicate's general policy.

Mudge certainly had a railroader's background, combined with a passion for golf and a bent for sociability. He was a native of Minden, Iowa, where he was born June 9, 1856. A few grades in grammar school comprised his early book-learning and his formal education came as first a water-boy on the Santa Fe, then a station helper, and eventually a tele-graph operator. From 1872, when he first took up his bucket and dipper, to 1896, he rose through the positions of road-master, trainmaster, and division superintendent, to the post of general superintendent. In 1900, E. P. Ripley, Santa Fe's president, made him general manager at Topeka. That's where he was when Winchell brought him to the Rock Island.

From the day of his election to the Rock Island presidency Mudge knew that something drastic would have to be accom-plished if Rock Island's earnings could hope to keep pace with its ever-mounting funded debt. Office detail wasn't much to his liking and he wanted a man in the organization to help him in this respect. That man was over on the Santa Fe.

Mudge asked the board to elect James E. Gorman to the position of first vice-president. This was the freight traffic department. Gorman, on the Santa Fe, was the freight traffic manager. He was known throughout the railroad industry as an affable gentleman with a hearty handshake and an in-numerable number of friends throughout the United States. The fact that Gorman's technical knowledge of down-to-earth railroad operations was merely academic and that his interest in this phase of railroading was something less than passing made little difference to Mudge.

If Gorman could get out and get the business, shake the traffic department into greater production, and give a hand with executive matters, Mudge would look after the acquisition of bigger power and more terminal facilities, and have a little time to improve his golf and throw a party now and then.

His syndicate bosses gave President Mudge a free hand. He spent staggering sums acquiring new property at Little Rock, Memphis, Omaha, and other points; in increasing his locomotive ownership with bigger and better power and in making some improvement to roadbed and bridges. He completed on May 9, 1910, the New Mexico mileage that hooked up Amarillo, Texas, with Tucumcari, New Mexico, thus giving the Choctaw a through route from Memphis to California.

During his administration the major acquisition of additional mileage was the leasing in November of 1913 of the St. Paul and Kansas City Short Line Railroad Company. This company was incorporated February 18, 1911, for the purpose of constructing "or acquiring and maintaining" a line between Allerton and Mason City, Iowa. The real reason for the incorporation was the purchase of existing lines and the construction of such new mileage as might be necessary to provide the shortest possible rail route between the Twin Cities and Kansas City, Missouri.

At the time the Short Line was incorporated the entire mileage between Minneapolis - St. Paul and Des Moines, including short stretches over which trackage rights had been secured, was in full operation. South of Des Moines a nine-mile segment had been constructed to the town of Carlisle. This left a stretch of 67 miles to be built to bring the line from Carlisle to Allerton for a connection with the Rock Island main line into Kansas City.

Mudge let the contracts for this new construction and it was completed partly by contractors' crews and partly by the regular track forces of the Rock Island in 1913. Through passenger and freight service between the Twin Cities and Kansas City was inaugurated on September 14 in that year. The acquisition of the Short Line was accomplished through the advance of more than $11,500,000 by the Rock Island. This money went for the assumption of the Short Line's outstanding obligations, for new construction, and for additions and betterments and for other corporate purposes.

That it was a valuable addition to the Rock Island system was stressed in Mudge's annual report for the fiscal year ending June 30, 1914, when he wrote: "The intermediate connections with your company at Des Moines, Iowa, and at Iowa Falls, afford an excellent outlet for traffic to and from the East and West, as well as the advantage of interchanging traffic with several other trunk-line systems at the above points."

But long before that report was written, the crisis faced by the Reid-Moore Syndicate was acute. Early in 1914, for the first time in the railroad's more than 61 years of history, the board looked at the income account and the balance sheet, and the figures were desperately red. There was no money for dividends.

By March 11, the holders of the Iowa holding company's collateral bonds and the owners of the common and preferred stocks of the Rock Island Company of New Jersey appointed protective committees. With no dividends from the Rock Island common held by the Central Trust Company, the bondholders could receive no interest. The Rock Island common had been pledged as collateral for those bonds, and now that the bonds were in default the Central Trust had to take steps to see that the bondholders were protected.

The news of the impending collapse of the syndicate's operations made headlines. Top financial writers and columnists from coast to coast excoriated the Reid-Moore management. They attacked the syndicate's method of pyramiding the railroad company's debt. Public confidence in the property was shaken to its very depths.

Executives and officers of competing railroads, and members of the railroad industry generally, watched with avid interest. Wherever they gathered they asked the questions:

How long could the sprawling Rock Island last? How long before the century's greatest dream of empire would dismally collapse?

Mudge, grim in his determination to refute the stories in the press, and the backroom gossip and rumors, made note of the attacks in that June 30, 1914, report and set about to justify his railroad's activities.

Mudge set forth a 12-year review of the company's growth and progress from June 30, 1902, to June 30, 1914. He pointed to an increase in operated mileage from 4,094 to 8,328. In 1902, 3,403 miles was owned as compared to 7,407 as of the 1914 date. In 1902, 353 miles was under lease. That had decreased to 272. The trackage rights in 1902 covered 338 miles —in 1914, this mileage was 649. Yards and sidings in 1902 made up 842 miles, and by 1914 had increased to 2,300 miles.

The heaviest rail in 1902 was 80-pound steel on 938 miles, and 70-pound and under on the rest of the system. By 1914 there was 276 miles of 100-pound rail, 143 of 90-pound rail, 1,526 miles of 85-pound steel, and 4,357 miles re-laid with 80-pound rail. That left 3,618 miles still with the 70-pound rail.

The review covered the progress in ties and ballast and bridges. Mudge pointed out that in 1902, 2,018 miles of the railroad was ballasted with either rock, burnt clay, or cinders, and the balance with dirt. As of the 1914 date, rock ballast covered 1,466 miles, burnt clay 681 miles, gravel 2,606 miles, and cinders 686 miles, leaving less than 3,000 miles still with dirt.

Mudge reported that whereas in 1902 there was but 19.61 miles of automatic block signals, in 1914 this facility covered the main lines from Chicago via Kansas City to Herington, Kansas; from Davenport to Omaha and on the northern line from West Liberty to Vinton, Iowa—a total of 1,256 miles.

"In 1902," the review said, "your property was greatly deficient in the matter of terminal facilities and repair shops. Since that time a complete new shop plant has been constructed at Silvis, Illinois, which is equal in capacity and mod-

ern conveniences to any locomotive repair shop in the west
. . . On account of the operation of the 16-hour law on
trainmen and enginemen it was necessary to put in new
terminals, in order to reduce the length of the run, at Manly,
Iowa; El Reno, and Waurika, Oklahoma, and at Pratt and
Liberal, Kansas."

Covering the locomotive situation, Mudge reported that in
1902 the company owned 661 engines with an average tractive
power of 18,015 pounds per locomotive. In 1914 the ownership had grown to 1,678 locomotives with a total tractive
effort of 49,241,511 pounds, or an average of 29,345 pounds
each.

Freight cars had increased in the 12-year period from 19,893
wooden cars to 17,531 steel and steel-underframe cars and
28,143 wooden cars—a total of 45,674. He pointed out that
the average capacity per car had increased from 24.5 tons to
36.9 tons. As to passenger cars, the 1902 ownership was 475
wooden cars of all types. In 1914 there were 346 all-steel pas-
senger-train cars and 817 of wooden structure—a total of 1,163.

Mudge wound up his review by saying, "It will be seen at
a glance that your property not only has been well maintained
but has been greatly improved since 1902 . . . Vigorous efforts have been made by your management to increase the
operating efficiency, the commercial freight train load having
increased from 183 tons in 1902 to 306 tons in 1914 . . . The
large absorption of mileage of light traffic had the effect of
reducing the average operating revenue per mile from $7,288
in 1902 to $6,091 in 1905. Since that time, notwithstanding
the steady decrease in rates, it increased to $8,867 in 1913,
falling back to $8,313 per mile in 1914."

It was a good report up to a point. But improvements and
increased efficiencies weren't enough. Labor costs since the
enactment of the 16-hour law for train and engine crews, and
the 9-hour law for telegraphers, had added greatly to the company's increasing financial burden. Materials and supplies also
had increased. But nothing could compare with the enormous
increase in the company's funded debt.

Prior to the advent of the Reid-Moore Syndicate the debt stood at $67,081,000. As the year 1914 drew to a close it stood at $287,852,370. Annual interest had increased from $3,055,313 to $12,136,425.

The picture was indeed dark and gloomy on that fateful October 8, 1914, when the annual meeting of the stockholders was opened for business in Chicago. The syndicate-controlled board sat glumly at the table. No longer could Reid and Judge Moore cause the 96 percent of the Rock Island common to be voted en bloc as they willed.

In the United States District Court for the Southern District of New York, a suit for foreclosure against the Iowa holding company was being fought. The plaintiffs were the protective committees. Until a decision could be rendered, the railway stock, underlying the holding company bonds, could not be voted by the syndicate.

At the October 14 meeting, Arthur Dryenforth, representing the Central Trust Company, held the proxies. He moved at once for adjournment of the meeting until a date in early November.

When the adjourned meeting was called it was adjourned again, and then again, always until a later date.

Finally, on December 21, 1914, following agreement between the various protective committees of the Iowa company's bondholders, the court ordered the sale of the collateral securities—the $71,353,000 par value of the Rock Island's common stock. The order provided that the stock be sold all at one time to one purchaser.

Special Master Winthrop brought about the sale on December 22, to J. N. Wallace, president of the Central Trust and chairman of the protective committee group. The one and only bid was for $7,135,350—just 10 percent of the par value of the stock.

On January 6, 1915, Judge Mayer, in the Federal court, confirmed the sale. Immediately thereafter the bondholders agreed among themselves to exchange their bonds on the basis of par value of bonds for par value of shares. The protective committee levied a $4 charge per $1,000 in bonds for committee expenses, and succeeded in making the exchange for about 86 percent of the bonds outstanding. To those bond-holders who wanted cash, the committee paid $98.50 for each $1,000 bond.

The New York Federal judge appointed Walter C. Noyes receiver for the Iowa company on January 18, and his action was followed by the U.S. District Court of the Southern District of Iowa, naming Noyes ancillary receiver of all the property and assets of the company within that court's juris-diction.

On February 3, 1915, with the annual meeting still in an adjourned state, Daniel G. Reid, the czar, resigned from the Rock Island board. The handwriting on the wall was large and ominous. The syndicate was breaking up.

Behind the scenes, Charles Hayden, president of the bank-ing house of Hayden, Stone and Company, was setting up the machinery to oust the syndicate from the company's management. So was Bostonian Nathan L. Amster with a committee opposing J. Horace Harding, stockbroker, who was pushing for Hayden.

Judge Moore, however, was as tough a fighter as he was a suave operator. He wasn't going to let things get away from him if he had to move hell on a set of flat-wheeled trucks to prevent it. He had rigged the deal to establish President Wal-lace of the Central Trust Company as chairman of a bond-holders' protective committee that Czar Reid had dreamed up. As much as five months before the court decision which ordered the sale of the bonds of the Iowa holding company, Wallace had advertised for the bonds, asking the holders to deposit them in trust. It was the syndicate's idea, through this device, to get the majority of the bonds in so that it would still be able to control them. What Wallace and the syndicate hadn't foreseen was the smallness in number of holders who would fall for this bait.

Just prior to the court's order, setting the terms for the sale of the Rock Island Railroad's stock to protect the bondholders, the Wallace committee had gathered in only $23,000,-000 of the $75,000,000 bonds outstanding.

It was at this point that Nathan Amster, a minority stockholder, dropped the boom by going to the Circuit Court of Appeals which gave him permission to intervene. The court order then had been held up, and when Amster finally got through with his chore of getting proxies to control future activities of the railway board, he had the syndicate in a squeeze.

With the annual meeting of the railroad's stockholders still in adjournment, the syndicate board met on March 26, 1915, to face the problem of getting money to meet more than $2,500,000 of principal and interest that would mature on April 1.

It was at this session of the inner circle that Judge Moore decided to rig another deal. He told Roberts Walker, his chief counsel, to scout around and find some substantial creditor of the railroad who could be used to throw the Rock Island into receivership. It was Moore's suggestion that Walker find an outside lawyer, draw up a bill of complaint, leave the plaintiff's name blank, and then have the outside lawyer make the proper approach to the creditor. Moore, Walker, and the two or three other syndicate members who were in on the deal pledged themselves to secrecy.

Walker reported back to Moore on March 29 that everything was in order for the presentation of the complaint. All he needed was the nod from Moore. Walker, through Attorney Silas Strawn, had picked as the complainant the American Steel Foundries Company to which the Rock Island owed a bill of $16,000—a sum that could easily have been paid at any time. R. P. Lamont, the president, later testified at the Interstate Commerce Commission investigation of the Reid-Moore scandal, that the attorney who approached him had assured him that this complaint was to be considered a friendly act to the railway company, that it would cost the American Steel Foundries nothing in the way of attorneys' fees and court costs.

The adjourned meeting of the stockholders was called on April 12, at 11 a.m. in Chicago. That it was a bitter and stormy session is attested to by the fact that it continued until 9 o'clock that night.

The syndicate immediately moved for another adjournment, but Nathan Amster and the committee supporting Hayden had the proxies to vote the Moore group down. The vote was more than 2 to 1.

An important order of business was the election of directors to fill the expired terms of Roberts Walker; Edward S. Moore, the son of Judge Moore; John J. Mitchell, Chicago banker who had never attended a meeting since his election; and J. J. Quinlan, financial vice-president of the railway company and president of the New Jersey holding company.

The Amster and Hayden groups moved in with a substitute slate. Amster offered his own name and three others. The so-called Sheldon committee put up Hayden and the names of William J. Matheson and W. Emlen Roosevelt. These directors together with Amster were elected after a bitter fight.

Another deep wedge was driven into the syndicate's front. But Judge Moore still wasn't finished. He sat by serenely, along with Walker, his deposed director, and his son, and said nothing at all about the plans for throwing the company into receivership. That was still a dark secret when that fateful meeting broke up.

Amster rode back from Chicago to New York with Roberts Walker and was given no hint of what was to happen just a little more than a week later.

That Amster suspected something is indicated by the fact that he was amazed that no apparent effort was being made by the directors to get together some $6,000,000 needed to take care of approaching maturities and to tide the company over into the summer. In fact, he set about on his own to get the money, and on April 16 met and conferred with Board Chairman Schumacher and two others. They said they thought highly of the plan by which he proposed to get that money himself. Amster then talked to some Boston bankers and after he had been assured of help, returned to New York to give the board the glad tidings.

Amster arrived in New York on the morning of April 20. He went directly to the Rock Island offices.

"When I got there I was amazed," he later testified. "I could not find anybody there who would say anything. Just a lot of people moving back and forth. I left the office and found on the ticker tape that the Rock Island had been put in the hands of a receiver."

The company's stock which, when the syndicate had taken control in 1901, had been selling as high as $200 a share, took a sharp drop on the market. Over the years the stock had gone down and down until, on March 22 of 1915, it was on the board at 21½. On the day Roberts Walker completed his bill of complaint for use by the American Steel Foundries the stock became suddenly active and was largely dealt in. It jumped from $20 to $39 a share. It then dropped back to $20 on news of the receivership. The total of shares exchanging hands in the 30 days preceding receivership was 1,019,584—more than one and one-third times the total capitalization of the railroad.

Roberts Walker, Moore, and other insiders, fully aware of what they would do to the railroad, unloaded their stock at the top market price—a farewell grab at profits as the dream of empire broke and faded.

31 Easy come, easy go

Judge George A. Carpenter, in the United States District Court for the District of Northern Illinois, heard the trumped-up complaint of the American Steel Foundries and appointed Judge Jacob M. Dickinson and Henry U. Mudge receivers for the Chicago, Rock Island and Pacific Railway Company.

Dickinson, who had once been president of the American Bar Association, Secretary of War in the cabinet of President William Howard Taft, and who had distinguished himself in other public services, was no stooge for Judge Moore or any of his associates. In fact, during the months to come, Judge Dickinson was to give these promoters many sleepless nights. Mudge, on the other hand, was a syndicate tool. Which was one reason why he didn't last very long after that fateful April 20.

The court, unwittingly, saddled Dickinson at the outset, with Roberts Walker, as general counsel for the receivers.

Dickinson immediately got into the tangled affairs in which the syndicate had involved this once-prosperous railroad, and the stench was rank. He knew he would have to work a miracle if he could save the property from the already rising clamor for dismemberment of the system.

Meanwhile, the Interstate Commerce Commission, which had held preliminary hearings in the previous October, at the request of the Committee on Interstate and Foreign Commerce of the House of Representatives, was uncovering more and more of the scandal.

The testimony brought out that it was impossible to determine the profits made by the two Moores, Reid and Leeds, in their various manipulations and their involvements. It was shown that a book surplus claimed on June 30, 1904, of $22,300,000 had dropped to a fictitious $6,100,000 by June 30, 1914. The premise of this fictitious figure was that the syndicate carried as assets a lot of their worthless investments, some of which were in companies that had "no existence, except on paper."

Actually, according to the testimony the Commission brought out, the Rock Island was more than $11,000,000 in the red at the time Mudge prepared his 1914 annual report with its glowing 12-year review.

In questioning Czar Reid on the matter of personal profits, Reid promptly told the Commission that he couldn't say how much he made out of the Rock Island entanglements. "I burn my books at the end of each month," he explained.

The name of L. F. Loree, one-time president of the Baltimore and Ohio, was brought into the testimony. Loree had served as chairman of the syndicate's executive committee for 10 months in 1904. In order to get him into the Rock Island picture the syndicate had offered him a contract for a salary of $75,000 a year for five years, and a payment of $500,000 in cash at the termination of that period. The Frisco was to pay half of the salary and bonus. When at the end of 10 months the syndicate decided it wasn't happy with Loree, Judge Moore and Czar Reid put $450,000 par value of Rock Island bonds in his hands as an inducement to get him to resign. Walker tried to explain this away as an obligation of the company in lieu of the promised half million in cash Loree was supposed to get, but the truth finally was drawn out of him that Reid made the deal to get Loree to resign. Loree testified that Reid had told him it was a question of Loree getting out or other officers walking off the job.

Other startling disclosures the Commission brought out concerning the handy way the syndicate had of dipping into the railroad's treasury at will showed that even the payroll figures as related to the officers were false. As an example Jim Gorman, Mudge's right-hand man, was carried on the payroll at $25,000 a year. He was secretly paid $18,750 a year additional, in advance in one lump sum, making an actual salary of $43,750.

Even the sainted Ransom Cable was shown to have participated in the syndicate's rewards for deals well done. The testimony brought out that Cable was given securities valued at $24,500 from the Rock Island treasury and $85,000 in cash from the treasury of the Burlington, Cedar Rapids and Northern for services in connection with the acquisition of that railroad. All the time he received an annual salary of $32,000 as a member of the board. Bill Leeds, during his term as president, also made it possible for Cable to get $368,300 of Rock Island securities for a cash price of $200,000. Other officials of the railroad—including Robert Mather, in the legal department; H. A. Parker, when he was first vice-president; George Boggs, dummy director and secretary, and syndicate front man; C. H. Warren, one-time assistant to the president and at another time vice-president—together shared in this largess to the extent of more than a million dollars over and above their salaries.

R. A. Jackson, general solicitor for the railroad, besides getting a salary of $50,000 a year, was paid by the syndicate a $10,000 fee for rigging up the incorporation papers that gave birth to the Consolidated Indiana Coal company—another syndicate deal that eventually resulted in heavy losses to the Rock Island treasury. He finally was fired by Reid and given $100,000 to get a job elsewhere.

More than $20,000,000 in losses accrued to the Rock Island in its support of syndicate transactions—including the expenses in incorporating, maintaining, and housing the holding companies; the Frisco and Alton catastrophes; the Trinity and Brazos Valley Railway deal; the Consolidated Indiana and Dering Coal Company manipulations; contributions and gratuities to officers and directors; and various other miscellaneous and unexplained expenditures.

The testimony of officers and directors brought out a firm conviction on their part that it was none of the public's business what they did with the funds of the railroad company so long as rates remained reasonable. The questioning of George Boggs emphasized this highly questionable disregard of the public interest in the following from the transcript:

Q: Do you consider that the directors of a railway company, a public service corporation, have the right to do whatever they please with the money of the railway company?

A: As in their judgment seemed right, yes.

Q: Did it ever occur to you that the money in the treasury of the railway company was the result of taxation of the public in passenger and freight tariffs, and that the public had an interest in funds in the treasury?

A: I don't know that I ever thought of it, particularly.

Q: And that the public had a concern in the funds of the railway company not being dissipated in order that they might be applied to improvements and betterments and to proper purposes?

A: I never considered that they were dissipated.

Q: And did it ever occur to you that in taking money from the treasury of the railway company, a public service corporation, an additional burden was placed upon the passenger and freight traffic in order to make good the loss?

A: No, I never thought of it in that light.

Q: You don't believe it now, do you?

A: No.

F. L. Hine, president of the First National Bank of New York, a syndicate director, acknowledged under questioning that he had never paid much attention to the operations of the Reid-Moore group. Yes, he had attended a few board meetings. Yes, he could recall that some of their strange transactions had been brought up for approval. But, said Mr. Hine, he trusted Moore's judgment. He trusted Reid. He assumed they were men who knew what was best for the company. So he went along with them.

Other directors testified pretty much the same way.

The Commission disclosed the fact that in addition to the $20,000,000 loss the Commission accountants could put their hands on—the result of the railroad treasury being tapped to support the various syndicate enterprises—the railroad had paid out to financial houses some $1,600,000 for commissions, and had suffered discounts of more than $17,700,000 in connection with bond issues.

On July 31, 1915, the Commission issued its report. It sharply criticized the syndicate, the officers, and the directors for gross mismanagement of what had once been a very fine piece of railroad property.

Pointing to the receivership deal, and the sudden turnover of the railroad's common stocks in the open market with the syndicate-rigged receivership imminent, the Commission said:

"It is a forceful commentary on the methods by which a great railway may be manipulated into a receivership when it is noted that the general counsel, after drawing the bill for receivership, sold his stock, and the local counsel, who represented the railway company in the receivership proceedings, owned no stock in the railway company, and that none of those directly participating in the receivership proceedings had any financial interest in the railway company. The real owners of the railway, the stockholders, the security holders, and the directors, except those composing the syndicate and in its confidence, were in ignorance of the receivership application. Mr. Mudge, former president of the railway company, is one of the receivers.

"The general counsel, who planned the receivership in obedience to the will of the syndicate, is now counsel for the receivers.

"The property of the railway company will be called upon for many years to make up the drain upon its resources resulting from transactions outside the proper sphere in which stockholders had the right to suppose their moneys were invested. This record emphasizes the need for railway directors who actually direct. There are too many passive directors who acquiesce in what is being done without knowledge and without investigation. A director of a railroad is a quasi public official who occupies a position of trust. A director who submits blindly to the exploitation of his company is a party to its undoing and he should be held responsible to the same extent as if he had been a principal instead of an accessory before the fact. The greater his prominence the greater his responsibility, and the greater his dereliction . . .

"It should be just as grave an offense for an official of a railway to be faithless to his trust for financial gain as it is for an elected official of the Government to betray his trust for money reward."

There it was—and the stench reeked. Nor did Mudge, Gorman, and other officers escape the invective of editorialists who seized upon the Commission's report.

One of them was reported saying in his defense, "Hell, I just worked here."

The annual meeting of the stockholders was coming up in October. The board met on September 30 to plan for it. Judge Moore would be coming up for re-election as a director. He was still on the executive committee. Others of the old board whose terms would expire included Hine, Ogden Mills, Chairman Schumacher, and James R. McLean.

With the Hayden people in control of the votes, Mudge, who was already out as co-receiver, and George H. Crosby were instructed to cast the majority stockholders' vote at the annual meeting, for Edmund D. Hulbert, vice-president of the Merchants Loan and Savings Bank, Chicago; Charles G. Dawes, president of the Central Trust Company, Chicago; John G. Shedd of Marshall Field and Company; John R. Morron, president of the Atlas Portland Cement Company; Judge Nathaniel French, of Davenport; William B. Thompson, director of the Federal Reserve Bank, New York; and Joel A. Burdick, president of the West Penn Steel Company.

McLean resigned. George McMurtry had died, leaving a vacancy as yet unfilled on the board.

The October annual meeting went as scheduled, and the syndicate was completely out after the vote for the directors was cast. Judge Moore wanted to make a fight of it, but his son Edward talked him out of it.

The board got together on November 5, and that was the end of Mudge. His resignation was accepted as president of the corporation in receivership. Shedd was elected chairman of the board, and the executive committee was made up of Nathan Amster, as chairman; Edward F. Carry, who was elected to the board to succeed Mudge; and Dawes, French, Hayden, Hulbert, and Shedd.

A resolution was passed that hereafter all meetings of the board and the executive committee would be held in Chicago. Another resolution provided that, pending the developments of the receivership and until such time as the board deemed appropriate, the office of president would be held open.

Charlie Hayden was now moving into control and he would pull the strings so far as the corporation was concerned. He would wait to see what luck Judge Dickinson might have in making the property whole.

32 Out of the frying pan

What Judge Jacob Dickinson did to return the Rock Island system whole to the stockholders was almost more than a miracle.

Judge Carpenter, upon the discharge of the receiver, said:

"The able administration of this property by Judge Dickinson . . . has made this extraordinary proceeding possible. This is a reorganization without a sale, the property returning to the original company, and in this the proceeding is historical among receiverships.

"I can't say too strongly how much credit is due to Judge Dickinson and the fine coöperation he has met with from the stockholders. The Rock Island will pay its debts and it has plenty of money with which to pay them."

Judge Dickinson's job was a tough one from the very outset. It was necessary to see what could be salvaged, and one of the first things he turned his attention to was the Rock Island Improvement Company, the stock of which was owned by the holding company, the Rock Island of New Jersey. As will be remembered, this company was formed by the Reid-Moore Syndicate to buy and own property and equipment which would be used by the railroad, but which would not be under the railway's mortgage. When the receiver got into the matter he found the worst tangle of bookkeeping imaginable. The New Jersey company was the last to go into receivership and Dickinson made a deal with the Jersey receiver to take over the Rock Island Improvement Company by acquiring its capital stock on behalf of the Rock Island Railroad. This would give the railroad title to terminal property, buildings, shops, locomotives, and cars for which the railroad was responsible as to payments.

The deal was consummated by the receiver by paying the Jersey holding company $20,000 in cash and returning a demand note held by the railway in the amount of $15,000. For this Dickinson got the entire capital stock of the Rock Island Improvement Company—1,030 shares—and a clear title to everything that the improvement company held in its name. In addition, Dickinson received 250 shares of Rock Island Coal Company, par value $25,000; 125 shares of Galveston Terminal Railway Company, par value $12,500; 30 shares of the capital stock of the Union Terminal Railway Company

of Dallas, par value $3,000; and 31½ shares of the Houston
Belt and Terminal Railway Company, par value $3,125.

Dickinson got permission of the court to enter into litigation against Dan Reid, Judge Moore, his brother J. H. Moore,
and Ogden Mills to make the best recovery he could of the
company's money that had been squandered in some of their
deals. Certain stockholders also sued. A settlement out of
court was approved by which the receiver collected $500,000
in cash and another $5,000,000 which would apply to the
purchase of the new 6 percent preferred stock if and when
issued.

Dickinson's biggest job, however, was the working out of a
plan with the stockholders to keep the company from going
through the wringer. What made it doubly tough and doubly
important to Dickinson was the clamor of the bondholders,
represented by powerful committees, to force a sale.

Rock Island's competitors had a hand in that feature. One
railroad after another sought certain choice sections of the
Rock Island, and would pay a liberal price for the property.
Other sections nobody wanted and these could be abandoned.
Judge Dickinson knew that this could easily happen unless
something could be worked out to keep the property in its
corporate hands and enable it to satisfy all creditors.

The problem was solved when 99 percent of the stockholders and more than 80 percent of the creditors agreed to the
issuance of two new classes of preferred stock on the following basis:

Seven percent preferred in the amount of 294,221.89 shares
at $100 par value would be turned over to the shareholders of
the common. For each share of common held the owner
would be assessed $40 cash, and for this would get four-tenths
of a share of the 7 percent preferred.

New 6 percent preferred in the amount of 251,273 shares
at $100 par would be issued for cash and for other purposes.

When the receiver was discharged at midnight, June 24,
1917, the new capitalization took effect. A total of $29,422,189
realized on the 7 percent preferred went into the treasury.

With this money the company was able to pay off $7,500,-000 of 2-year collateral trust notes; $4,100,000 in loans made by the Central Trust Company and by Hayden, Stone & Co.; $8,500,000 in receiver's certificates; and $11,200,000 to wipe out claims and liabilities and pay all the reorganization costs and expenses.

The company sold for cash $5,000,000 of the 6 percent preferred and issued more than $20,000,000 to the holders of the railway's gold debentures on the basis of 10 shares for each $1,000 bond. Thus on the emergence from the receivership the capital structure of The Chicago, Rock Island and Pacific Railway Company was increased from the original $75,000,000 in common stock to a total capitalization of $129,530,289, including the two classes of preferred.

Many pressing obligations were paid off, many new and important stockholders came into the picture, and, above all, credit was restored so that in the event of necessity the company could now market a goodly amount of new bonds.

With the war in Europe having its effect on the rise in traffic in the United States, which by now had declared war on Germany and its allies, the increasing revenues gave the railroad bright promise once again.

It was into this picture that, on June 22, 1917, the day after the receiver was discharged, James E. Gorman came to assume the presidency of the railroad. Other staff officers of the system had plumed themselves for this honor, and one or two of them had more or less secretly campaigned for the election to the presidency, but Charlie Hayden had made up his mind. The board of directors was more or less under his control in that a majority of them were men of his picking. And Charlie Hayden thought that Gorman, with his vast traffic connections, could do a better job. Hayden also had found that Gorman was good at taking directions, a quality that years later was to lead the Rock Island into more trouble.

In fact, one of Jim Gorman's closest friends over a long period of years and one of his closest associates, quoted Gorman as once saying, "Whatever the boss asks for, that's what he gets. I never say no to the boss." The boss in the first part of Gorman's service as president was Hayden. Later it was to be another New Yorker by the name of E. N. Brown.

In 1917, as the result of new accounting procedures introduced by the Interstate Commerce Commission, the railroad went on a calendar basis in its reporting. Through the new setup the funded debt came into critical focus and the board was able to bring about a reduction of more than $44,000,000. The business of improving terminal facilities at Lonoke (Arkansas), Fort Sill (Oklahoma), Des Moines (Iowa), and Memphis (Tennessee), got prompt attention with an expenditure of more than a million dollars.

Over in Iowa, during the receivership, Judge Dickinson had disaffirmed the Rock Island's lease on the Keokuk and Des Moines Valley Railway Company—a lease which had been in effect since May, 1878. The receiver had stopped all payments and had ordered the road to be operated separately in order to determine just what the proper rental should be. He had been convinced that the price the railroad had been paying was entirely too high.

High or not, Gorman reinstated the lease for its full term at the full original rental, and paid the company what it had been deprived of during the term of receivership. The Rock Island, of course, owned a substantial amount of the Keokuk and Des Moines stocks and bonds, and Gorman felt that the long affiliation should be continued inasmuch as the line was a valuable feeder.

Gorman's job as president ended on July 10, 1918, when the United States Government stepped into the railroad business and, under the guise of war necessity, took over the nation's railway systems. Gorman was appointed federal manager of the Rock Island and certain neighboring roads under the United States Railroad Administration group setup.

The Rock Island board then elected Charles Hayden to serve as president of the corporation.

Before the seizure of the railroads by the Government, however, Gorman had exerted a hand in clearing up the

Rock Island's share in the distraught affairs of the Trinity and Brazos Valley between Fort Worth, Houston, and Galveston (Texas). The Rock Island's contracts as related to this property, and entered into by the Reid-Moore Syndicate, had been disaffirmed by the receiver. Thereupon the Colorado & Southern, with which the contracts for half interest in the line were made, went to the courts. The disaffirmation was thrown out and the railroad was ordered to pay the Colorado and Southern more than $6,600,000 in 6 percent preferred stock, and $176,354 in cash, the amount due on certain bond and note guaranties.

The Rock Island made a deal with the Colorado & Southern to pay, in lieu of preferred stock, 60 percent of the amount in cash. This settlement was agreeable, and the Rock Island raised the funds by selling $4,500,000 3-year 6-percent gold notes. The Colorado & Southern turned over to the Rock Island $4,300,000 Trinity and Brazos Valley first mortgage bonds and $152,000 face amount of capital stock—exactly half of the Texas line's entire bond and stock issue.

Any attempt at detailed accounts of the operation of any railroad during the period when the United States Railroad Administration was in control would serve to confuse rather than enlighten.

As an example the following is a quotation from the railroad's annual report for the year ending 1918:

"In addition to the 30 new locomotives purchased by your directors in 1917, and delivered in May 1918, the Director General of the United States Railroad Administration has allocated to your company 20 road locomotives and 10 switching locomotives at a total cost of approximately $1,132,670. Your directors have protested against this allocation, believing that the additional locomotives were not necessary at this time. At the date our objections were filed . . . 23 Rock Island locomotives, including 15 of the 30 that had just been purchased, were being used on foreign lines, so we felt that it was not fair to the Rock Island to buy new power for it when the power it already had was not being used on its own road. At this time there are approximately 90 idle locomotives on the system, so this protest is even more meritorious now than when it was first made . . .

"The Director General has also allocated to your company 1,000 box cars and 1,000 coal cars at a total cost of approximately $5,610,000. Your directors have protested against this allocation . . . on the ground that the acquisition by the Receiver of 4,000 new box cars and the rebuilding of 3,000 old cars rendered the purchase of new equipment at this time unnecessary . . ."

Hayden, in this report, pointed out that a prime factor in the objection was that the railroad would have to pay about $2,850 per car at inflated wartime prices as compared with $850 a car paid by the Receiver in 1915.

What happened to the protests? The Director General overruled the Rock Island board.

The whole thing turned out to be a blessing in disguise, however. Nor was the end result due to any farsightedness of the bureaucrats who decreed such things.

The new cars were found to be needed because in a large measure the operations under the Government, of the Eastern railroads especially, found tens of thousands of cars backed up at ports, on sidings, loaded with supplies and materials waiting to be shipped. Embargoes were out at terminals all over the Nation, and thousands of other loaded cars stood in passing tracks and spurs along dreary miles of main lines as storage facilities for whatever cargo they were carrying.

Payrolls were increased step by step by a beneficent Government; wages went up on the inflationary spiral; inefficiency was to be found everywhere. Power facilities and rolling stock were subjected to excessive wear and tear as were roadbed, rails, and structures. And all through the period the undermaintenance of these items was a staggering problem.

At the beginning of Federal control Rock Island employees numbered 40,326 and the monthly payroll was $3,500,000. At the end of the Government's control the employees totaled 45,950 and the monthly payroll had grown to almost $6,000,000.

The war with Germany ended on November 11, 1918. It was not, however, until February 29, 1920, that the Government returned the Nation's railroads to private ownership. And a sorry mess of property it was.

Jim Gorman was returned to the presidency of the Rock Island on March 1, 1920. Serious problems faced the railroad's management, prominent among which were negotiations for settlement of all wartime claims between the company and the Government, and a whole new batch of labor negotiations. Under Government operation labor had made great gains both as to wages and working conditions; the railway clerks, as an example, prior to the United States administration had been the smallest and weakest of the organizations. It was now a solid power with a huge membership and strong contracts.

The policy of the Government in raising wages without giving any consideration to upping freight rates and passenger fares gave Gorman great concern.

That the management made considerable progress in getting the railroad back to somewhat reasonable operations after the relinquishment of Government control is shown by the fact that on February 28, 1921—just exactly one year after the management had taken over—the number of employees had been reduced from 45,950 to 34,531. The payroll, however, failed to show a relative cut. This decreased only from $5,800,-000 to $5,100,000 monthly.

Early in 1921 the first oil well was brought in at El Dorado, on the company's Arkansas lines, to mark the beginning of a new boom in traffic, at least in that commodity. By the year's end 3,800,000 barrels had moved by rail with the Rock Island taking almost 90 percent of the tonnage. At the same time, oil became a big factor in the vicinity of Duncan and Walters, Oklahoma, and at Mexia, Texas. This latter strike gave new hope for the eventual success of the Trinity and Brazos Valley venture.

Gross revenues which reached the company's all-time high of $142,000,000 in 1920 dropped off only slightly through the calendar year 1921 when the railroad wound up the year with $139,000,000.

Business continued good the first half of 1922. Then, without warning, 11,000 employees in the shop crafts joined their fellows on all the other railroads and walked off the job on July 1. The strike wasn't directly against the carriers but was brought about by the organization leaders because of dissatisfaction with a decision of the United States Labor Board in which were fixed their wages and working conditions.

The walkout had serious effects on the operation of the railroad and proved disastrous not only to the company but also to the employees for the length of time it lasted. It was, from the outset, a lost cause for the strikers. New men were hired to man the shops and the strikers found themselves shut out. By September most of them were willing to call it quits and come back to work. But those for whom jobs could be found had to fall in behind the new workers insofar as seniority was concerned.

Settlement with the Government was completed on the wartime operations on "all matters arising out of Federal Control." According to Gorman, in his annual report, the items included not only United States Railroad Administration operations for the total period of control but also "the so-called guaranty period of six months" following February 29, 1920.

"Their balance of accounts," the report said, "between the company and the Director General of Railroads, which related only to the Federal Control period, showed that we were indebted to the Government . . . in the sum of approximately $7,900,000. After much negotiation and consideration of our claims for undermaintenance, the Director General agreed to reduce this amount to $2,500,000 and accept in settlement our 8-year 6-percent collateral trust note, due March 1, 1930 . . .

"Under the funding provisions of the Transportation Act,

we were allowed to fund certain of the expenditures made by the Railroad Administration for additions and betterments . . . By conference with the Director General this amount was fixed at $5,500,000, which we borrowed from the Secretary of the Treasury under the provisions of the Transportation Act, giving our 8-year, 6-percent collateral trust notes therefor.

"After much discussion of the amount necessary to make good the Government's guaranty for the six-month period ending August 31, 1920, we agreed to accept approximately $2,000,000 in full settlement of the balance due us . . . With approval of the Interstate Commerce Commission we sold in September, 1922, $5,500,000 first and refunding bonds. The proceeds . . . amounted to $4,673,760.

"On the other side of the ledger we paid in full our notes to the War Finance Corporation, aggregating $10,430,000, covering indebtedness originating during Federal control."

Gorman wound up the year 1922 by celebrating, on October 10, the 70th anniversary of the company's operations. Just why he and his officers picked the 70th year instead of say the 75th, which would have been the Diamond Anniversary, has never been logically explained.

It was a celebration, however, befitting even a centennial. A special train was run from Chicago to Joliet to re-enact the running of the original *Rocket* of October 10, 1852. Fifty-four commercial clubs and employee clubs located at various points on the system took part. One hundred and two memorial trees were planted along the company's line, each with a bronze plaque mounted on a stone to honor past officers and employees who had distinguished themselves in the railroad's service.

"It was a great occasion," Gorman said in his annual report, "and we feel that the celebration helped to cement the friendly feeling which we are inculcating between the company and its employees on the one hand, and its patrons on the other."

33 Under two masters

By the dawn of 1924 conditions on the Rock Island system had progressed to the point where even the most conservative analyst could be highly optimistic of the railroad's future. From every point of view the plan that Receiver Dickinson had evolved to keep the property in the hands of its stockholders seemed highly justified.

But backstage in the inner councils of the management a new chapter in the railroad's drama for survival was taking shape.

Back in 1918 when the Government was running the Nation's rail systems, Charlie Hayden reached over to the Seaboard Air Line, in which he also had a stake, and hired away that line's general manager, Louis C. Fritch. He made Fritch, a man with a long engineering background, the corporation's vice-president and chief engineer. Fritch's duties were to keep an eye on the maintenance problems developed by Government control and to build up the Rock Island's claims against the Government for presentation at such time as the Government should relinquish the property.

While this transaction came about, Jim Gorman's former general manager, Thomas H. Beacom, was acting for the United States Railroad Administration as Federal manager of the Rock Island Lines. Beacom had a long background of operating know-how, having started his career as a brakeman. He had since 1902 worked his way up on the Rock Island through the ranks to positions of trainmaster, superintendent, general superintendent, and assistant general manager.

Beacom was a big, powerful man, almost a head taller than Fritch, and pretty positive in his ideas as to how a railroad should be run.

The conflict between Beacom and Fritch grew apace after the end of Government control. At that time Hayden had Fritch made vice-president in charge of maintenance, construction, and capital expenditures, and President Gorman succeeded in having his man, Beacom, named vice-president and general manager. Fritch nominally reported to Gorman, but more often than not went over Gorman's head directly to Hayden. Definite factions began to form—the Fritch faction and the Beacom faction—and Gorman found himself attempting to act in the role of arbiter.

The conflict got so bad by the middle of March, 1923, that Beacom was fired. Hayden immediately moved Fritch into the job of running the operating department, and Gorman couldn't open his mouth. Beacom went on to become receiver for the Denver and Rio Grande, and to build for himself an enviable name in railroad history in the rehabilitation of that line.

Fritch went on to help Hayden start the prospering Rock Island on the road to doom.

Hayden was now chairman of Rock Island's executive committee in addition to heading up the finance committee. It was the executive committee that cracked the whip.

How Hayden could devote so much time to Rock Island affairs is still somewhat of a mystery. He concurrently was a director in 58 other companies. He collected directorships very much in the same manner as people collect rare coins, or postage stamps, or old prints. He was a man of small stature, a confirmed bachelor, and brilliant when it came to financial affairs. He owned a priceless collection of old jade which filled cabinets in his apartment.

How he used his directorships to good advantage is illustrated by the case of the American Locomotive Company. He was chairman of its finance committee in the mid-twenties when that company faced financial difficulties. It was very necessary to get its plants into production before something serious should happen. Hayden looked at the Rock Island's good cash position and ordered Gorman to buy 65 locomotives which, at that particular time, he needed just about as much as he needed a cavernous hole blown through his right-of-way.

Under the Hayden rule the Rock Island recovered from the 1922 postwar dip in revenues—$125,000,000—to $130,400,000 in 1923. After the preferred dividends were taken care of and fixed charges were met the common had earned $1.22 a share.

A further increase in the gross in 1924 to $130,800,000, coupled with a drop in operating expenses, brought the common stock earnings to $4.36 per share. How could this increased share earning be possible with the gross just a little above the previous year? The answer is found in the maintenance program.

The Hayden-directed policy called for Gorman and Fritch to get that net up to where common dividends would be possible. Lopping off a little here and a little there would do the trick. The Oklahoma line was an example—especially the line between El Reno and Fort Worth. The chief engineer had reported that a lot of critical bridge work was needed. This bigger power that was coming to the railroad couldn't operate in that territory unless some money was spent. Not only did bridges have to be made stronger, but banks had to be widened. There were many other problems.

But you couldn't spend money like that and make a dividend possible. Hayden wanted to see that net operating income boosted.

Over on the Frisco system, at about this time, a very astute group of gentlemen headed by Edward N. Brown, of New York, had been watching the Rock Island operation and had, among themselves, worked out a deal which, if it could be carried through, might very well help to shore up the Frisco's shaky structure.

In his position as Frisco's board chairman and chairman of its executive committee, Brown could look back upon a vivid career that took him from his Barbour County, Alabama, birthplace, through Auburn College, with an engineering degree, a variety of jobs on the National Railways of Mexico, and finally to the presidency of that property in 1901. He left Mexico, in 1914, set up a New York office, developed his banking connections to a high degree and finally moved into the Frisco picture in 1919 to take over active management of the railroad.

Now, possessed with as sharp an eye for a fast dollar as could ever have been claimed by any member of the late Reid-Moore group, the Rock Island to Brown looked exceedingly good. Where he differed from the pirates who first boarded the ship in 1902 was in his vast experience as a practical railroad man. Certainly if he should succeed in getting into the Rock Island management, what happened with Reid-Moore would never happen with him.

Only Brown and the New York bankers who controlled the Frisco were acutely aware of the fact that the common stock of their railroad was, in the middle of 1924, so badly watered that it stood in imminent danger of floating completely out from under them.

Brown's move was to get hold of enough Rock Island stock so that he could move into that picture. Rock Island dividends were needed to put some money behind the Frisco.

The Brown group got hold of 183,000 Rock Island shares in 1925 and with the consent of the Interstate Commerce Commission in 1926 walked into Hayden's little empire and took their seats on Mr. Hayden's board.

What possessed the Commission, designed to protect the public interest, ever to consent to this manipulation is completely beyond the realm of understanding. Commissioner Joseph B. Eastman alone dissented.

Hayden had to provide a place on the executive committee of the Rock Island's board for Brown and his New York banking house associate, Jesse Hirschman. Another associate, J. M. Kurn, of St. Louis, the Frisco's popular president, took his place on the Rock Island finance committee.

Jim Gorman suddenly was faced with the problem of serving two masters, because it wasn't very long until Brown moved Hayden out of the chairmanship of the executive committee and proceeded to do a lion's share toward running the railroad.

Just prior to the advent of the Frisco interests, Gorman had made a friendly deal with the St. Louis - Southwestern (Cotton Belt) owners to acquire a minority stock interest in that railroad. President Gorman saw a chance to make traffic from Texas points through the St. Louis gateway an additional source of Rock Island revenue. Now the Cotton Belt was a very active competitor of the Frisco between St. Louis and the Southwestern territory.

Certainly this alliance between the Rock Island and the Cotton Belt was not to E. N. Brown's liking, and the fact that shortly after the Frisco group moved into the Rock Island management this stock was suddenly sold to the Kansas City Southern Railway at a profit of $2,400,000 is evidence of Brown's master hand. The sale was consummated before the Interstate Commerce Commission, which had held hearings on the proposal, had had time to render a decision on the Rock Island's petition to become active in the Cotton Belt management. Rock Island's stockholders had every reason to believe the Commission would place its stamp of approval on the Cotton Belt deal.

Gorman's 1925 annual report said the stock was purchased from the owner, who was Edwin Gould, without commissions of any kind, and was sold to the purchasers directly without any commissions or charges. He pointed out that the profit would not appear in the 1925 earnings, but would show up in the 1926 surplus account.

Gross revenues in 1926 climbed to $137,900,000, and the management claimed, in the annual report for that year, that "the maintenance is fully up to the standard of roads similarly situated, and the road is in shape to handle a large increase in its traffic without greatly increased expenses."

The mention of maintenance in that document was not without purpose. Vice-President Fritch knew the maintenance was not keeping pace with requirements, and so did the chief engineer. The latter, however, was powerless to make his voice heard. Fritch and Gorman knew what the Hayden-Brown combine wanted the figures to show.

The figures for 1927, from the viewpoint of the banker-controlled inner council, were sublime. The gross hit $140,-000,000, and after all interest and fixed charges and dividends on the preferred stock there was a net of $12,500,000. The common had earned $12.10 a share and the board declared on this a dividend of 5 percent.

The dividends the Brown-controlled Frisco was collecting on its holdings in the Brown-controlled Rock Island certainly were giving the Frisco a beautiful shot in the arm.

34 Dividends or bust

Brown, while sitting high in the saddle in Rock Island management, had his own great dream of empire. It was his desire to merge the Rock Island into the Frisco, under his absolute control. With this in the back of his mind he constantly kept one eye out for every opportunity to do the Frisco a favor if it could put the Frisco in a more advantageous position.

A very excellent chance came in Oklahoma City in 1928.

It will be remembered that the Rock Island's predecessor—the Choctaw—had great difficulty in getting into Oklahoma City at all when the settlers poured in and jumped the right-of-way claims, with the result that some few years later in a settlement that was made the railroad had only a 100-foot right-of-way instead of its original 200-foot grant.

As the city grew through the 1920's, the Rock Island location became a trouble spot. The passenger depot was small and the railroad owned too little ground to make any considerable improvements. Its location was right downtown in the heart of things, and along its narrow strip of property some small plants had located. In the eyes of the civic-minded citizens the whole thing was an eyesore.

The city urged the local railroads to elevate their tracks, and the Santa Fe immediately assented. The Rock Island, under the Hayden-Brown rule, deferred making any pledges, but officers of the company held intermittent conferences with city authorities to determine what, if anything, could be done to get the Rock Island out of the heart of town.

Brown, aboard a special Frisco inspection train, stopped in Oklahoma City early in 1928 and made a call on the civic leaders. The Rock Island location became an urgent subject of discussion and Brown agreed to take a tour of the Rock Island facilities with a view to seeing what could be done.

He agreed with the authorities that the whole thing was "intolerable," and wound up the meeting by saying, "I give you positive assurance that it will be corrected shortly."

Brown told Gorman to send the engineers and operating officers down to Oklahoma City and make a deal. He, in fact, directed what kind of deal should be made. The result was that before the conferences were over the Rock Island was out of its downtown location.

The problem could have been worked out, and the Rock Island's location retained, with an expenditure of about $3,000,000. As it happened, the Rock Island, under Brown's direction, agreed to abandon three-quarters of a mile of main track and sidings in the downtown area, retain the outlying line for industrial purposes, and build six miles of new railroad around the south end of the city to a new station which it would use jointly with the Frisco. The cost would come to more than $2,300,000.

It was in all respects, as time was to prove, a costly mistake for the Rock Island. It resulted in losses in passenger revenues and in a serious dislocation of freight business that took years to recover. It increased the cost of switching on the disconnected lines two to three times.

Despite the glowing accounts in Gorman's annual reports of the progress and the advantage of the new station facilities, the fact remained that the joint passenger station was built in the worst sort of location—out on the south edge of the city with no local transportation, other than taxicabs, to the downtown area. The net result, finally, was to place the Rock Island at a distinct disadvantage.

Meanwhile the Rock Island was adding to its mileage across the Oklahoma and Texas Panhandle through a growing wheat-producing country. It was completing a line between Liberal, Kansas, and Amarillo, Texas, and on the blueprints in the engineering department was projected another short stretch from Dalhart, Texas, on the southwest main line, to Morse, a point on the new 153-mile Liberal - Amarillo link between the Golden State route and the Memphis -Tucumcari line.

On the strength of earning $12.81 a share on the common stock in 1928 the dividends on these shares were upped to 6 percent. It was, on paper, a rosy and prosperous picture. The annual report called attention to the income account. "The outstanding feature," the report said, "is the fact that traffic representing an increase of over $3,500,000 in gross freight revenue was handled with a reduction of over $400,000 in transportation expenses, due principally to economies in operation produced by improvements to facilities, and improved condition of equipment." Attention was called to wage increases in the amount of $1,095,700, "otherwise transportation expenses would have shown a decrease of $1,496,885 under the previous year."

On certain sections of the system there was still much to be done toward building up the roadbed, but this was kept a secret. There would be time to get to these things. The important matter now was to keep that net income on the upgrade. Keep those dividends safe.

The world turned upside down in November of 1929!

The stock market crashed, fortunes were lost overnight, one company after another failed outright!

In the New York offices of Hayden and Brown hardly an eyelid flickered.

The Rock Island was closing out a record-breaking revenue year.

The gross topped $147,721,000. The setback to business generally would be brief. Just a period of readjustment. If the management had to cut corners the cutting would be done all in good time. The thing was to show the world how prosperous this property was. On the strength of the good showing for the year, with the common stock earning $14.04 a share, this was the time to declare a dividend of 7 percent. Why give a thought to conserving the surplus funds, to taking a good long look at that railroad and making sure that it was physically able to withstand any emergency?

The dividend was declared and everybody was happy except the employees. They began to feel the pressure before the year of 1930 had gotten well under way. Business fell off substantially and maintenance was cut to the bone.

Herbert Hoover, President of the United States, appealed to business and industry to bolster the wobbling economy by spending money on plants and equipment.

The Rock Island board approved the expenditure of $34,600,000 for, among other things, 41 new locomotives, 5,000 freight cars, and 19 passenger cars. To offset this, the maintenance of road and equipment again suffered.

The Brown-Hayden combination was aware that the 1930 earnings would fall short of meeting many items of expense. It got permission from the Commission to float an issue of $32,228,000 of 4½-percent 30-year convertible gold bonds. It charged to profit and loss the discount and expense of the bond sales.

The Dalhart - Morse line was completed at a cost of $1,500,-

000 and a new line was under construction between Trenton, Missouri, and Birmingham, Missouri, to straighten out the Chicago - Kansas City main line. The total involved was better than $12,000,000.

Part of the money derived from the convertible bond sales went into this picture.

In order to make those convertibles look good, the board, under Brown's direction and with Hayden's consent, declared its regular dividends on the two issues of preferred stock, and although the common at the year's end had dropped in earnings to $5.56 a share, another dividend of 7 percent was paid. This came out of the profit-and-loss surplus account.

At the annual meeting, in May that year, the controlling powers brought about certain changes in the corporate structure. They upped the authorized capital stock of the company from $140,000,000 to $170,000,000. The increase was all in common stock, and the directors explained that this move was necessary to protect the conversion privilege of the new 30-year convertibles. None of the new stock was issued.

The membership of the board was increased from 13 to 15.

The debt limit on the property of $275,000,000, fixed by the Reid-Moore Syndicate, was wholly repealed with the explanation that since the Interstate Commerce Commission had complete jurisdiction over securities issued by common carriers, this limitation was no longer necessary.

This move was necessary to get the 30-year convertibles issued, since, as of the close of 1929, the funded debt, in the hands of the public, of the Chicago, Rock Island and Pacific Railway Company stood at $263,503,000. The convertibles and an issuance of $900,000 of first and refunding mortgage gold bonds brought the debt up to $296,631,000 as of December 31, 1930. With the addition of the debt on the Burlington, Cedar Rapids and Northern, the Choctaw and the Rock Island, Arkansas and Louisiana, coupled with equipment trusts, the grand total of the funded debt stood at $389,064,-

235. The annual interest that had to be met thus took more than $13,800,000.

That the whole thing put together presented somewhat of a frightening picture, especially in view of the general trend of business all over the Nation, seemed to have no effect on the Brown-Hayden policies. Both Hayden and Brown seemed imbued with the idea that so long as you trimmed all the corners and could find a little money in the surplus account with which to pay dividends, it made little difference what might be happening to the property physically, or what might be happening to the world in general.

Words were cheap, and Gorman and Hayden used them in that 1930 annual report to salve their respective consciences.

"Anticipating the reduction in gross revenues that would inevitably follow a general decline from the remarkable industrial activities of the previous year," the report said, "measures were promptly taken to minimize the effect of the reduced transportation receipts on the net results from operation, by reducing, as far as possible, consistent with proper maintenance and satisfactory service to the public, the operating costs of performing the service . . .

"While substantial reductions were made in maintenance expenditures, the excellent condition in which the property has been maintained for several years last past enabled us to make the reductions without seriously impairing the physical condition of roadway or equipment, and the property is now in adequate condition to handle the expected return of normal traffic."

They talked of substantial reductions in maintenance; they said the property was in shape for a return of normal traffic.

What they didn't tell the unsuspecting stockholders was the scandalous, hush-hush story of the acquisition of 25,000 shares of Frisco stock between October and the early part of December, using $1,752,872 from funds on deposit to the Rock Island's credit in the coffers of the Speyer banking firm in New York.

They didn't tell the stockholders how Edward N. Brown,

without any formal authorization from the executive committee, developed this idea on his own, spoke privately to close associates on the committee, pledged them to secrecy, and told them he was going to get the stock on the New York exchange through Speyer and Company, and when this was accomplished he would bring it before the executive committee and the board.

When the lid blew off much later and the Interstate Commerce Commission investigated Brown's operations and his use of both Frisco and Rock Island money in these undercover deals, Jim Gorman was to testify that, without any thought as to the wisdom of the acquisition, he assured Brown that Brown had his vote and that he would discuss the deal with no one.

The deal was revealed on December 10, 1930, to the Rock Island directors, and before they voted to approve Brown's actions, they engaged in a heated discussion. At least one director threatened to resign should anything like that ever happen again.

Brown took the attitude that if he had mentioned it in the executive committee or to the board before the stock was bought, word of the proposed purchase would have leaked out and the price of the stock would have risen to the point that would have defeated his purpose in getting the shares at a nominal figure. He paid on an average $70 a share, and at the time the board ratified his scheme Frisco stock had dropped to $46 and was still going down.

Brown later told the Commission that he had no personal interest in the transaction. He brought it about because he thought it advantageous to the dream of merger he had so long entertained. There were 183,000 shares of Rock Island in the Frisco investment accounts, and now there were 25,000 shares of Frisco in the Rock Island vaults.

At the end of 1930 anyone with half a brain cell could see that the Frisco was rocking on its heels, and the Rock Island wasn't much better off than the Frisco.

Without a doubt, the million and three-quarters that went

out of the Rock Island treasury for the Frisco purchase could have been put into the property or could have been held to build up a cash reserve; and by the same token that 7 percent cash dividend declared on Rock Island common against an earning of only little more than $5 a share could have been deferred and the cash used as a backlog against what was to come.

Such display of plain horse-sense apparently was too much to expect from the controlling interests.

35 Broke again

Through the first half of 1931 the Rock Island wheezed and rocked and staggered; trailing behind it was its devastating load of debt. January of that year should have been enough, revenue-wise, to indicate to the board of directors that any further dividends were out of the question. The danger signals were obviously ominous.

Apparently the men in control didn't believe in signs. They dipped into the dwindling surplus, slightly enhanced by proceeds from that convertible bond issue, and declared a dividend of 1¼ percent on the common stock.

They declared another dividend of 1 percent on the common, payable June 30, and a 3½ percent dividend on the 7 percent preferred, and a 3 percent dividend on the 6 percent preferred, all payable on the same date. Altogether this took $3,356,637 out of the treasury, and at the same time the gross revenue dropped more than $12,000,000 off the like period for the preceding year.

Where were the voices of Gorman, Vice-President Fritch, and the other executive officers of the property while this piracy went on?

Those voices, for the most part, were either silent or at least ineffectual. The truth is, Jim Gorman was desperately afraid of his job, and he was afraid of Fritch who, for years, seemed to have the inside track with Charlie Hayden, and who could do a beautiful job of yessing E. N. Brown.

Employee relations, which in one annual report after another Gorman had pointed to as being highly harmonious, were by the middle of 1931 anything but that. The employees couldn't understand what was going on, and nobody in the high councils dared tell them. They couldn't understand the layoffs, the talk of salary reductions and wage cuts—and the lust for dividends.

All along the lines of that great system, rolling stock was stored in side-tracks, the paint scaling from the onslaughts of sun and rain. Rust was gathering over the rails that led to closed-down industries. Locomotives were stored on weed-grown spurs at division points.

By mid-October the railroad was going to the banks for time loans. These totaled, by December 31, $8,750,000. And, when the figures were all in for the year the gross revenue was slightly over $99,000,000. The deficit, after taxes and interest, was $386,544, a startling red figure. It was the lowest gross since 1917, and from the steady decline in business during the last half of the year the indications were that things would get a lot worse before there could be any sign of a leveling off.

The management went to the Reconstruction Finance Corporation in the middle of 1932 to borrow money with which to meet maturities. The Interstate Commerce Commission approved borrowing up to $10,000,000. At the same time negotiations with the labor organizations representing virtually all employees on the system resulted in the workers taking a 10 percent cut.

Officers and employees not covered by the agreements suffered greater reductions. Stations were closed down and agents and operators were cut off. Maintenance-of-way forces were slashed right and left. All work was at a standstill, with additions and betterments wiped out of the budget. Those employees remaining in service contributed heavily to a relief fund that had been established in 1930 to assist Rock Island men who could find work nowhere else, and their families.

To complete the dismal picture came the wheat crop failure and the devastating dust-storms in the Southwest. Revenues fell off rapidly. The year ended with $70,700,000, the lowest gross since 1914. The operating losses totaled $9,956,800.

The General American Tank Car Company bought the Rock Island's 1,243 old refrigerator cars for $3,454,454, which put some cash in the treasury, but many times more than that would be needed before the sinking ship could be brought about to face the swelling sea.

If borrowing could do the job the Messrs. Brown and Hayden should have won some sort of award for effort, at least.

They went back to the Commission in the early part of 1933 and made another plea to touch the Reconstruction Finance Corporation for $1,181,872. The Commission was in a considerate mood, and the treasurer dug up securities to cover the loan. Jesse Jones, the famous Texan, who headed up the Government's lending agency, wrote out a check.

But no sooner was this money in the management's hands than they had to go back for $2,536,828 in addition. This brought the total owed to the Reconstruction Finance Corporation up to $13,718,700. Gorman, in his annual report, explained that this took all the company's available collateral.

In May the railroad went back to the Commission with a new plea for borrowing, and a joint session was held with the Reconstruction Finance Corporation. This time it was no good.

This, for the Messrs. Gorman, Hayden, and Brown, was the beginning of the end. They looked at the income account for the first four months of the year and the situation was hopeless. They faced maturities in 1934 of more than $144,000,000, and with borrowing power at an end, so was this management that, with the assist from the Interstate Commerce Commission during better times, rode hell-bent on the pursuance of the fantastic dividend policy that shaped up the new pattern for destruction.

The May meeting of the board brought the resolution to seek protection of the courts.

On June 7, in the District Court of the United States for the Northern District of Illinois, the Rock Island filed a petition before Judge James H. Wilkerson under the newly enacted section 77 of the Bankruptcy Act.

For the second time in 31 years of almost continual bad management, a cycle that had its beginning with the advent of the infamous Reid-Moore Syndicate, the sprawling Rock Island lay desperately ailing in weeds and dust and cinders.

Out of the whole sorry record one thing should have been patently clear, not only to the Interstate Commerce Commission but also to railroad officers and owners everywhere— no railroad could survive Eastern banker management when those in control had no interest in the physical property, the territory, or the people the railroad served—no interest whatever in anything except the dividends that could be derived from their holdings.

PART FIVE

Re-birth
and Regeneration
1933-1952

36 Spring of hope

Judge Wilkerson's order approving the petition for protection of the property under section 77 of the Bankruptcy Act was promptly issued, and the officers of the railroad were instructed to continue its operation.

The directors appointed the firms of Hayden, Stone & Company, and Dillon, Reed & Company, together with the Chase National Bank of New York, to act as reorganization managers. Any plan of reorganization under section 77 would have to have the tentative approval of the Interstate Commerce Commission after a public hearing. The next step would be to submit the plan to the creditors and the stockholders. If two-thirds of the holders of all classes of bonds and stocks gave their written approval, the plan then would need the final approval of the Commission. After action by the Commission on the result of the vote, the Commission then would recommend the plan to the court.

The procedure sounded simple enough, but putting it into effect was quite another thing, as the passage of time was to demonstrate.

The Rock Island, in this period of tribulation, had a good deal of companionship. Several other major lines either had gone under or were about to do so. Included in the list were the Denver and Rio Grande, the Cotton Belt, the Chicago and Northwestern. If misery loved company there was plenty of it around.

Under the provisions of the Bankruptcy Act as it applied to railroads it was necessary for the Commission to approve a panel of names from which the court could make its selection

225

of trustees. This panel, submitted to the Commission by the railroad, naturally contained the name of James E. Gorman.

Whatever else might be said of Gorman and his ability as an administrator, he nevertheless was still an outstanding traffic man. And if the Rock Island was to get out of this mess it would have to have the confidence and the help of shippers everywhere. Gorman had the contacts and the acquaintances, and if there was additional traffic to be had to bring up revenues Gorman appeared to be the one man who could perform.

Despite his many failures in the capacity of the chief executive officer of this forlorn property, Gorman had inaugurated, over the years, certain departmental activities that proved to be very much in the right direction.

It was under Gorman's administration that the industrial development department was set up as a separate unit reporting directly to Gorman, with instructions to go out and locate plants and elevators and warehouses on the system's rails.

Gorman took an active part in the greater expansion of the agriculture department. He authorized special trains equipped with motion pictures, displays, and other material to aid and encourage the farmers served by the railroad to greater crops and a wide diversification of production.

Until 1923 the railroad had had no public relations or employee relations program. Gorman set up this department with a view to the restoration of public confidence in the railroad and a more harmonious relationship between the management and the employees.

He took the leadership in encouraging the national 4-H Club movement and gave the railroad's support to the efforts of youngsters on farms to achieve outstanding results. He proceeded on the theory that this activity along with industrial development would certainly produce more and more traffic on the rails.

Judge Wilkerson got around to the appointment of the trustees on November 22, 1933. He named Gorman, Joseph B. Fleming, a prominent Chicago lawyer, and Frank O. Lowden, the ex-governor of Illinois.

It was now up to these three, who officially assumed their duties under the jurisdiction of the court on December 1, to manage the property.

Protective committees representing the holders of the various classes of bonds not only of the Rock Island proper, but also of its several subsidiaries, were formed. The groups would have a great deal to say about any reorganization plan that might be developed.

From the 1933 gross revenue of $64,848,448, it was plain to be seen that not even the semblance of a plan could be then anticipated. This decrease was almost $6,000,000 below the 1932 revenues, and the deficit amounted to more than $11,000,000.

Gorman, in his annual report for 1933, sounded a hopeful note, however, when he said, "The present capitalization of the company is not large. The funded debt including equipment trust notes is $40,102 per mile; the capital stock is $16,647 per mile; or a total capitalization outstanding in the hands of the public of only $56,749 per mile. It is apparent that, with a moderate increase in traffic, the Rock Island should have no difficulty in earning its present fixed charges." The fixed charges then were more than $14,000,000.

"We are happy to say," he concluded, "that business appears to be improving; and are confident that with the early upturn of prosperity a reorganization plan can be prepared which will meet the approval of all interests."

One big money-saving project that Gorman had hoped to bring about in his anticipation of new financing in 1934 was the unification of the system. This plan had been advanced to bring into the parent company all the subsidiaries. It went before the Interstate Commerce Commission, and that body on August 9 gave its approval but attached a string to the deal. The Commission told the Rock Island that it would have to agree to acquire, at commercial value, in the event the Commission so found, the Wichita Northwestern Railway. This line, about a hundred miles long, connected with the Rock Island's Golden State Route at Pratt, Kansas. It had been a prodigious money-loser for more than 10 years; it owed the Government for loans about $650,000, and was in debt to the State of Kansas for $100,000 in back taxes. Charlie Hayden decided that to accept the indefinite obligation imposed by the Commission's ruling might be detrimental to any reorganization plan whatever. Thus the unification scheme died.

The protective committees of the bondholders, representing the Rock Island, Arkansas and Louisiana; the Choctaw; the St. Paul and Kansas City Short Line, and the Rock Island's 4½ percent convertibles, engaged H. G. Moulton, of New York, a consulting engineer, to make a study of the property and a report. The idea of this was to give some factual basis for a reorganization plan.

Moulton wisely recommended against any reorganization while the property was at low ebb in its depressed earnings. He suggested that a good deal of study be given to the possibility of taking the Choctaw out of the system and arranging for its development by some strong Southeastern or Southern line and an equally strong Western line. He mentioned the possibility that the Louisville and Nashville or the Southern Railway, on the Memphis side, and the Santa Fe, on the west, might be sold on the idea of taking over this part of the Rock Island property. Another recommendation covered the Burlington, Cedar Rapids and Northern. Moulton brought out the possibility of a study of this network with a view to holding part of it to the Rock Island and abandoning large sections of it extending into various Iowa communities.

That the report was superficial at best is indicated by Moulton's summation in which he said that none of the Rock Island's difficulties, either before the 1915 collapse or the present failure, was due to any fault of management, but rather to the general business conditions and the crop failures. He pointed out that if business recovered to the extent that the railroad could gross on an average of $120,000,000 a year it could support its fixed charges of more than $14,000,-000 annually.

Once again there was talk of dismemberment. This, of

course, was not popular with Messrs. Hayden and Brown. They wanted a reorganization plan that would keep the system, as it now stood, completely together.

However, the railroad was still falling apart as the gloomy year 1934 went into history. There was another deficit of $12,100,000 to add to the $11,000,000 of the year before, although the gross showed a slight upturn to $66,000,000 as compared to 1933's $64,900,000.

The Moulton report had pointed out that great sections of the main lines and branch lines needed tie and rail replacements, new ballasting, a lot of work on bridges, and several other necessary remedies if the deterioration was to be brought under control.

Thus, when it was definitely apparent, by the summer of 1935, that the railroad was still far from improving in its earning power, the protective committees, the banking interests, and the Reconstruction Finance Corporation brought pressure to bear on the trustees to get new management. The influence of Jesse Jones on this problem cannot be underestimated. His stake in the Rock Island—the $13,500,000 the road owed the Reconstruction Finance Corporation—was small, but his recommendations carried enormous weight.

Aging Jim Gorman, still president of the now inactive corporate body, still struggling to give his best as a trustee, knew he was finished. Nothing in his jovial bearing indicated his realization of this fact which was so graphically brought home to him when the question of bringing to the railroad a chief executive officer was put before the trustees.

High on the list of prospective candidates—all of whom were known to be outstanding railroad men—was the name of Edward M. Durham, Jr., senior vice-president of the Missouri Pacific system.

Durham, powerful and dynamic, had behind him an outstanding career. Born in Memphis, Tennessee, he graduated from the Memphis Military Academy in 1891 and went on to Lehigh University to obtain his degree in engineering. After service with the War Department in hydrological surveys he joined the engineering staff of the Chicago and North-western in 1899. A year later he went to the Southern Railway and progressed through various engineering capacities to the position of assistant chief engineer for the system. He was appointed chief engineer of the Atlanta, Birmingham and Coast Railway, and executive general agent of the Southern where he served until 1919. In that year he went to the United States Railroad Administration as manager of the Department of Ways and Structures. He became director of the Division of Liquidation, where, in settlements of claims of the various carriers that resulted from Government control of the rail-roads, he made an outstanding record.

The late Louis W. Baldwin, president of the Missouri Pacific, brought Durham to that property as assistant to the president in 1924. Two years later he was elected a vice-president, and in 1927 was made senior vice-president.

Known to his friends as Ned, Durham was rated as a railroader not only with a vast grasp of engineering and operational problems but also with outstanding administrative ability. He had a reputation for knowing how to pick top men for departmental supervision and how to delegate to his staff full authority.

The Rock Island's trustees took the recommendation of the various creditor interests that Durham could do the job if any man could, and the trustees offered Durham the post.

Durham was then 60 years old—sharp and vigorous.

Financially, the Rock Island job had little appeal. But here was a definite challenge. Here was an opportunity to put into practice everything he had ever learned about men and machines, rails and ties and ballast. Here was a railroad in such shape that it either had to show under proper management a turn for the better or it had to perish. And Durham was pretty well convinced in his own mind that there was, at least, a long chance that he could save it.

The patient was in a sorry mess, but if the doctor had nerve—

That's what Ned Durham had plenty of. He told the trustees he was their man. He shook hands with his Missouri Pacific boss, Louie Baldwin, and Baldwin wished him luck.

On a bleak December day in 1935 he headed for Chicago and a new adventure.

37 The long chance

Ned Durham's arrival in Chicago, as later events were to prove, marked the first great turning point in the fretted fortunes of this 84-year-old storm-battered railroad. He strode into the executive offices in La Salle Street Station where 33 years ago William B. Leeds, the tin plate king, arrived in high silk hat and faultless frock coat with a great dream of empire. Stretching out from the train shed below him were the rails that extended the course of empire to the far reaches of the prairie states, to snow-blown Minnesota, the Colorado Rockies and to the sun-washed sands of the Texas gulf shore.

There was the big map on the wall with the black lines denoting the system, transversing the great rich heart of the continent.

Ned Durham looked at the map. It was his railroad now. He felt a deep flush of pride in the opportunity that lay before him. Whatever had gone before was history—good or bad— and to hell with that! He, E. M. Durham, Jr., was now chief executive officer of the Chicago, Rock Island and Pacific Railway under the trustees. If he should be successful in aiding a sound reorganization he stood in line to be president. It was his railroad. It had been great once and, by God, it could be great again.

Durham knew that he would have to get along with a lot of conflicting interests insofar as the reorganization was concerned. Even now, as he turned from the map to sit behind the broad table, a movement was afoot to strip the system of its Louisiana and southern Arkansas lines through a sale to the Louisiana and Arkansas Railroad. Durham knew he would have to move cautiously, but he would have to be firm.

Meanwhile he had to take a thorough look at this property, cover every mile of its lines, inspect its equipment, check the service it performed, listen to shippers and patrons—in other words take inventory as it had never been taken before.

He started out in January of 1936 in blustering, frigid weather. He headed west in the business car that had been provided for him. He talked to trackmen and to trainmen. He sat down with mechanics and master mechanics. He asked pertinent questions and he made sure he got straight answers. He had a way of making his men understand that he wanted their confidence and that he would respect it.

Everywhere he went, over division after division, Durham found the morale of officers and employees shot to pieces. In fact, morale was almost nonexistent. The trainmasters and superintendents, for the most part, were old men—weary and defeated. They were men who had tried their best under increasingly difficult circumstances. They were uncertain and insecure.

The new chief executive officer inspected shops and yards and other facilities. He studied the roadbed. No wonder passenger trains could not make the time.

Rail replacements were badly needed. Ties had to be replaced in vast quantities. Buildings needed paint and repairs.

Durham interspersed his road inspections with quick trips to New York to confer with the creditor interests and with Hayden and Brown. The 1935 earnings were all in, and the figures might have completely discouraged a less courageous man. The gross revenues had not improved, and the deficit had jumped from 1934's $12,100,000 to $15,000,000.

The figures, coupled with what Durham had to report to the protective committees concerning the state of the railroad, certainly were not conducive to optimism. Those groups, however, had confidence that Durham somehow could turn the tide.

By early spring Durham was convinced that before he could do very much toward bringing a turn for the better in the patient's condition, he would have to do something drastic about the whole nervous system—the operating department. It would take a job of major surgery, and the place to begin was at the top.

L. C. Fritch, with the title of operating officer, was not, Durham was definitely convinced, the man for the job. A younger man was needed—one who would have the ability to make one Rock Island dollar do the work of two, whose intestinal fortitude would match or excel that of the chief executive, and who could take the authority that would be delegated to him and do a complete overhaul, not only of the operating department but also of the 8,330 miles of railroad.

Durham talked to the creditor groups, to Jesse Jones, and to the trustees. The names of several outstanding young operating men came under discussion. The one Durham knew the most about was down in Fort Worth, Texas, a 45-year-old dynamo with a big iron jaw, an inexhaustible drive, and a demonstrated ability to get the ultimate in service and performance for every buck in his budget.

This candidate was John D. (for Dow) Farrington, Burlington-trained general manager of the Burlington's Fort Worth and Denver City subsidiary. Right at this particular time Farrington was much in the minds of the big financial groups as a result of the exhaustive report he had only recently completed on the Missouri Pacific and its subsidiaries. The survey had been undertaken for the bondholders of that property, represented by the Prudential Life Insurance Company, which had large holdings.

The Rock Island trustees went after Farrington in May, and Ned Durham called in Operating Officer Fritch to advise him that he was being pensioned. Fritch immediately boarded a train for New York to seek audience with Charlie Hayden. He was not going to take this dismissal by the chief executive officer without a battle.

Hayden quietly explained to Louie Fritch that there was nothing Hayden could do about it.

"This property is in the hands of the trustees," Hayden said. "The chief executive officer under the trustees has full authority. The corporation is inactive. It has, for the time being, no control over the property, its officers, or its assets."

It was at a subsequent meeting between Hayden and Durham that Hayden refuted the long-accepted belief that Fritch was "his man" on the railroad—a very surprising thing to Jim Gorman, who could remember the countless instances from which no other conclusion could be drawn.

Farrington, on the receipt of the offer from the Rock Island trustees, had the normal reaction. Here he was in a good job on a live and progressive property, confronted with another job that could lead to the very top, or that could result in oblivion. He could stay with the sound and vigorous Burlington and rely on the record he had behind him to put him in line eventually for the operating vice-presidency, or he could cast his lot with Ned Durham and the Burlington's sick competitor, and take his chances on making railroad history.

Farrington could look back over his service with the Fort Worth and Denver with justifiable pride. He had rehabilitated the Texas main line, had built important branches. He was in the middle of an area that stood on the threshold of vast development. Who knew what opportunities this new empire held?

These Texans liked Farrington. In four and a half years it was as if he had become an integral part of them. Bankers, oil men, cattle men, industrial chiefs—Farrington talked their language. They wouldn't want to see him go.

But the decision was his and not theirs. The Rock Island,

too, had a stake in Texas. Not a very prominent one right then, to be sure, but with the proper kind of attention to developing that railroad's possibilities, something important could be made of it.

Something important could be made of the whole Rock Island system if a man had a little money to spend. A little money?

Engineer Moulton in his report to the protective committees had estimated that in the event of early reorganization, at least $30,000,000 would be needed to put the Rock Island back on its feet—to take care of emergency requirements and to make up the deferred maintenance of roadway and equipment.

That was a lot of money, but Farrington knew that $30,000,-000 would be but a starter.

Farrington took one last look at his Texas domain and plunged. He accepted the Rock Island offer.

38 First signs of recovery

John Farrington moved into La Salle Street Station on May 16, 1936. To the general office people it was just another day on the calendar—the beginning of the second pay period for the month. It was a hot, sunny day, with high, thin clouds and almost no wind. Just another day in May.

To the Rock Island Railroad, to the far-flung communities it served, to the thousands of its employees on and off line, it was in a very real sense quite a day of destiny. It was a day that was to mark the beginning of a rebuilding and revitalizing program which, in years to come, was to be called by railroad analysts "nothing short of miraculous."

The man with the iron jaw, the piercing blue eyes, and the photographic mind that caught details with sharp clarity was born in St. Paul, Minnesota, January 27, 1891. His father, the financial vice-president of the Great Northern, was a close friend of empire builder James J. Hill. As a youngster John Farrington became steeped in the intricacies of railroading. His eyes were on the far stretches of the Hill main lines even as he went to St. Paul's Central High, and later to St. Paul Academy.

He went as a rawboned youth into the Montana and Idaho country with Great Northern surveying crews and thus got his first taste of the romance and drama of railroad building.

At the age of 19 Farrington left home and cast his lot with the Burlington. If it was in him to make the grade in railroading he wanted to do it on his own. He didn't want his fellow workmen ever to point a finger at him and say that he had "pull." He was assigned to a track gang as a timekeeper. Within a comparatively short time he was an assistant foreman, and by the time he was 21 he was bossing a crew. During the ensuing five years—up to World War I—he served first as roadmaster then as assistant trainmaster and trainmaster.

He entered the Army as a lieutenant, went overseas with an engineering outfit and served with distinction. When, in 1919, with the war behind him, he was mustered out, he held the rank of major. He returned to the Burlington as an assistant superintendent. In 1920 he became superintendent of the Quincy, Omaha and Kansas City line, moved to the St. Joseph Division in the same capacity in 1922, and a year later took over the Aurora Division. In January, 1930, he was promoted to general superintendent, first of the Missouri District and then of the combined Iowa and Missouri Districts. Everywhere he went he set new records in operating economies, in increased efficiency. Thus it was that in November, 1931, he became general manager of the Burlington's Texas lines.

Now here he was in La Salle Street Station, Chicago, poised on the threshold of a whole new career.

Farrington got a general briefing from Ned Durham on all the things that Durham had uncovered and observed. Durham told Farrington that from here on out the details for the development of this property, and its return to the status of a great and important railroad, were in his lap.

"We'll go to the trustees and the court for the things we need," Durham said. "Until these earnings increase we won't have much cash. You see what you can do."

The best way to see what he could do, Farrington reasoned, was to get out on the system and take a close-up view of what he had to work with. A close-up view could be obtained in no better way than from the ground up, and the division inspection cars would get him around.

These cars were, for the most part, old Fords with flanged wheels for rail travel instead of rubber tires. If your railroad was any good you could run the Ford up to 40 or 50 miles an hour on the tangents without too much fear of derailment. If your track was very much below par you had to creep along.

Farrington crept. He loaded in with him the superintendent, the division engineers, the roadmasters, and various other officers. He poked into the weeds and walked over the ballast. He made a close inspection of the rolling stock and the power. When he came to a bridge he wanted to see its timbers and trusses. He never missed a tie or a switch or a signal.

Forlorn men in overalls stood by silently while Farrington walked through shops and roundhouses, asked questions and made notes. Classification yards at the various terminals came under his watchful observation. The farther he went the more grim became the thin line of his mouth, the more determined the jut of his big chin.

Challenge? Farrington hadn't, prior to this tour, guessed at the half of it.

Meanwhile the corporate officers submitted to the Interstate Commerce Commission their proposed plan for reorganization. The plan was designed to protect the holders of all classes of stocks and bonds through a new capitalization and the issuance of new bonds of the income, noncumulative type. Capital stock consisting of two classes of new 4 percent noncumulative preferred and new common would total $206,593,216. The new bonds would amount to $159,000,000, and to this would be added equipment trusts, collateral loans, etc., for a total funded debt of $227,430,578. The proposed total capitalization would be $434,026,797 as compared with the company's present capitalization of $457,698,173. A voting trust would be set up to represent the various security-holders in the management until such time as the earnings returned to the point where interest on the bonds would be paid for two consecutive years.

This plan, filed by E. N. Brown on behalf of the debtor corporation, was set down for immediate hearings, and it was Brown's hope that a plan previously presented by the Rock Island, Arkansas and Louisiana bondholders would thereby lose some of its appeal. The latter plan provided for the elimination of the common stock of the R. I. A. & L. and the purchase of its property by the Louisiana and Arkansas road. Brown wanted no part of this proposal, since the Rock Island, Arkansas and Louisiana common was owned outright by the Rock Island.

Brown now became chairman of the debtor company board, succeeding Charles Hayden whose interest in the reorganization was waning, and whose health was fading.

Brown's reorganization plan had no sooner been made public than committees for the various creditor groups began to lay their plans to fight it.

While all this was transpiring John Farrington found himself facing a new role in railroad operations. He was about to become a master junk dealer with interests in fourteen States —probably the best-mannered, best-dressed junkman in the Country.

Things were beginning to look a little better for the Rock

Island. Freight traffic was showing definite signs of being on the increase by late summer of 1936. If Farrington could make better use of the company's biggest locomotives to get longer and heavier freight movements with a decrease in operating costs he would have to have a railroad that could use these engines. The company owned 65 of the 4-8-4 variety and, with a little modernization of this power, he could show some satisfactory results.

The chief operating officer explained his scrap-drive program to Durham. It was the beginning of what Farrington was to publicize nationally as a program of planned progress. Until the road should show definite signs of steadily increasing earning power, Farrington would have to get money for roadway and structures without much help from borrowing, and the scrap drive was the solution. He had seen from his inspection of the property that millions could be realized from this source. He sent out the word: "Get everything on the system that possibly can be converted to scrap under the hammer and torch. Get everything that can be salvaged in the way of steel and timber sorted and classified so that this material can be put to good use."

This marked the beginning of the rebuilding program. The money derived from the sale of scrap bought more new and second-hand rail. Farrington directed the rail relay program to sections where it was immediately needed. The Bridges & Buildings forces got after the bridges. New and salvaged materials went into the strengthening of these structures and in many instances the replacement of old structures with new.

"Sa-a-ay! Things're happenin'! This new operatin' boss— he's doin' things!"

The men on the line looked at one another and spoke with a new note in their voices. They felt the spark of new life. For the first time in years they began to feel the inner glow of excitement about their railroad and their jobs.

This was the situation early in 1937 when the word went out that streamlined trains were coming to the Rock Island.

Already the Burlington had made headlines by its experiment with this new diesel-powered transportation.

Farrington had it all figured out. Durham concurred heartily.

"I had Rock Island's reputation to overcome," Farrington said later. "It was a very bad reputation as to service—both freight and passenger. Public confidence in the property did not exist. The newspapers continued to print stories about the reorganization plans, and the proposed plans for dismemberment. That didn't help employee morale one bit. Our passenger business was at an all-time low and it seemed to me that a radical departure with the introduction of the streamliner would have the desired effect."

Farrington, in 1937, used cash and equipment trusts to get 6 passenger diesels and 10 diesel switchers. In addition he purchased 20 stainless-steel streamlined passenger cars of various classes.

The name *Rocket* was chosen for these new trains. The Rock Island Rockets. This sounded good to the ear, and putting it into type looked good to the eyes. And what could be more fitting in a name since it was that same name which, in gold letters, decorated the first locomotive ever to pull a train over the railroad—the memorable little 4-4-0 of October 10, 1852.

The first streamlined Rocket was inaugurated on the Chicago-Peoria run. It was a bright and beautiful thing to behold. And it soared into prominence overnight.

What was happening to this dilapidated Rock Island? Why, said the residents along the line, it's hard to remember when we had an on-time schedule, to say nothing of clean and comfortable cars to ride in. Now, look at this!

The people could hardly believe it. In fact there was some question as to the sanity of Messrs. Durham and Farrington. This railroad was broke, and yet here were these guys coming out, in the face of generally declining passenger earnings, with this sort of thing.

From the day the Peoria Rocket first flashed its bright sleek sides through the wash of the morning sunlight over newly reballasted and improved rail on its flight downstate, the passenger revenues of the Rock Island turned upward.

As the year 1937 came to a close Durham could look at Farrington with a satisfied grin and say, "Looks like we're going somewhere, John."

The year closed with a $3,500,000 increase in gross revenues, with freight up $2,700,000 and passenger up $750,000, for a total of $81,643,250. The patient was showing definite signs of life.

The program of planned progress was gaining ground. On the drawing boards were plans for major line relocations that would be started just as soon as funds could be found. It would be necessary to eliminate curves and grades at many points on the Chicago - Kansas City - Tucumcari line. Besides the modernization of motive power and the acquisition of new rolling stock, shops would have to be brought up to date with modern machinery and other facilities. Engine runs were to be lengthened and certain shops on the system could thereby be eliminated.

The laying of 112-pound rail as standard for main lines and the continuation of the bridge program would have to be pushed at a rapid pace. The tie replacement schedule could not be allowed to falter, nor could the reballasting be deferred. More diesels would have to be purchased.

Automatic block signals, which covered less than 1,500 miles of the railroad, were entirely inadequate. Additional mileage of these signals would have to be added along with centralized traffic control.

All these things would be necessary to bring this railroad to the point where it could take its rightful place in its competitive territory.

Could Durham and Farrington make these things come true? Both men realized that anything could happen in the battle to get the corporate structure through its reorganization. The debtor company's plan was still before the Commission. Many objections to it had been filed.

Edward N. Brown was now in complete control of the corporate activities. Charles Hayden had passed away early in 1937, and Brown, now chairman of the board, had put Trustee Jim Gorman in as chairman of the executive committee. Brown naturally was concerned with saving the equity of the preferred and common stockholders in any reorganization plan that might be offered, which meant that he was ready to oppose to the last ditch any and all plans of the creditor groups in which such equity might be drastically reduced or completely eliminated. From the progress made thus far reorganization seemed a long way off.

39 Samson of the Cimarron— a symbol

The 1937 upturn in general business over the Nation, and in the fortunes of the Rock Island, failed to hold through 1938. But despite a drop back to lower earnings, the railroad pursued its policy of re-laying rail and spreading new ballast. The Des Moines Rocket, second of the streamliners, was in service between Chicago and the Iowa capital, and Farrington was turning over in his mind the advisability of inaugurating a new streamliner between Chicago and Colorado to replace the Rocky Mountain Limited. He knew, of course, that he would run into opposition on such a move because the Colorado line, aside from being longer than the Burlington and the Northwestern - Union Pacific routes to Denver, wasn't in too good a physical condition.

More work on the roadway would help a lot. But first, for

immediate consideration, was the southwest line—the Golden State Route. Aside from the curves and grades through Southern Iowa and Missouri between Davenport and Kansas City, there was the granddaddy of all bottlenecks out in Kansas across the Cimarron River.

In the vicinity of that crossing the railroad wandered all over the plains, crooked as a snake on both approaches to the stream. The old bridge was a decadent thing at best and susceptible to the violence of Nature when that country experienced the mad freshets that made the Cimarron a thing to fear.

Farrington, in working out his personnel problems, had carefully evaluated officers on the operating staff, and had made numerous changes. Older men had been retired and replaced with men brought in from the Burlington, the Missouri Pacific, and other lines to take over key posts. He had made some promotions.

For aid on the rebuilding program he had brought into the Rock Island picture a top-flight maintenance man from the Burlington, and had put him in charge of the system maintenance-of-way program. This man was William H. Hillis.

Hillis, a native of Colona, Illinois, had joined the engineering forces of the Burlington in 1906 and had worked up through various capacities to the position of superintendent of construction on the Texas lines where Farrington was then general manager. Hillis was assistant superintendent of the Burlington's La Crosse Division when Farrington brought him to the Rock Island.

Durham agreed with Farrington that the rehabilitation of the southwest main line should not be deferred. Farrington took Hillis with him and the two men made an on-the-ground study of the Cimarron problem. Farrington decided on the course he wanted to follow, but again he was faced with the problem of money.

The only answer was more scrap. It was estimated that the bridge together with the grading and track for the new approaches would cost in the neighborhood of $1,500,000. If another good healthy scrap drive was staged, Farrington was sure he could find the money.

Farrington saw his way clear to get the grading started by late September.

Meanwhile he had under way an $8,000,000 program of locomotive modernization and rebuilding of freight cars. Three hundred miles of main track was being re-laid with new 112-pound rail and with second-hand rail. Fences were being replaced and the paint gangs were going full blast. The drop in traffic might be felt in the number of loads and empties hauled, but, from the ballast up, it was a railroad buzzing with activity. It was a property being readied for plenty of business once this depression had been overcome.

Durham and his new team took the $3,800,000 dip in the 1938 revenues in their stride. The deficit was $11,300,000 as compared with 1937's $9,500,000, but the investment in additions and betterments would result in savings if the railroad could survive the reorganization battles.

Farrington was making his dollars stretch to a remarkable degree. He and Durham convinced the trustees that additional diesel switchers would result in greater operating economies, and thereupon the trustees got the court's permission to acquire 26 more for yard service. This brought the diesel-electric fleet up to 43, including the 6 passenger locomotives. The Rock Island, in 1938, became the first Western railroad to place an order for diesel power in such quantity.

The program of planned progress steamed into 1939 with a wide-open throttle. All eyes were on the Cimarron bridge project. The grading, which had continued through the winter, was pretty well completed by the end of March. Three million cubic yards of earth and gravel had to be moved to make the fill for the long approaches. The project extended approximately from the depot at Kismet, east of the river, to the station at Hayne, to the west.

The distance via the old line was 12 twisting miles. The new line would cover the route in 8.423 miles straight as an arrow.

After completion of the masonry, the deck truss spans—five in all—were swung into place. It was an engineering marvel, 1,269 feet in length, and the superstructure was erected in 85 days.

They called it the Samson of the Cimarron. They opened it for operations on July 8, 1939.

John Farrington could look proudly at the lofty web across the dry flats and the trickle of water that was the unpredictable river, and feel that somehow this structure stood against the blue of the Kansas sky as a symbol of the reborn railroad.

However, Farrington wasn't pausing for anything. He knew his bridge would be there, 95 feet above the stream, long after he was gone. He had taken out 353 degrees of curvature with the building of the new line, and he had eliminated 113 feet of rise and fall. So much for that. Let history record its worth. There were other things to be done.

He had decided to go ahead with a new streamlined Rocky Mountain Rocket. Other railroad men told him he wasn't quite bright. How could he ever equal the time of the Burlington Zephyrs and the Northwestern - Union Pacific City of Denver?

Well, maybe he wouldn't come close to the time, but he'd have a train second to none and he would offer to the public the only main-line hot-shot between Chicago and Colorado Springs. He would split the Rocket at Limon and send half of it to Denver and the other half to the foot of Pikes Peak. Vacationists heading for the Pikes Peak area and the dude ranches beyond would no longer have to change trains at Denver to get to their destination.

Farrington was heartened in his decision by his own experience. Besides the Peoria and Des Moines Rockets, he had now in operation trains of this type between Kansas City and Fort Worth - Dallas, between Kansas City and Minneapolis, and, jointly with the Burlington, between Forth Worth and Houston. Rocket trains were paying for themselves and were attracting patronage. He wasn't afraid to plunge into the Colorado operation.

The Rocky Mountain Rocket was inaugurated on November 12, 1939. Before it had been in service 30 days, Farrington's vision and faith appeared fully justified.

During these developments in America's Midwest the situation in Europe became inflammable. Hitler marched into Poland and world conflict was in the making. The American economy rocked unevenly.

In Washington the Interstate Commerce Commission had before it three plans for the reorganization of the railroad. One was the Brown plan of the debtor company, another was the Rock Island, Arkansas and Louisiana bondholders' separation deal, and a third had been proposed by the protective committee for the first and refunding mortgage 4 percent and secured 4½ percent bonds.

On September 22 the examiner for the Commission submitted his report, after the long hearings on the various proposals, and recommended a plan which would cut the then existing capitalization of the debtor company from $458,000,-000 to $306,000,000. This plan would eliminate completely all equity of the stockholders.

The creditors, secured and general, filed exceptions and the corporate officers protested vigorously. Briefs were submitted and oral arguments were heard on December 7 and 8, after which the Commission took the whole subject under advisement.

Branch-line abandonment along the Rock Island progressed to the point where now since 1936 approximately 265 miles of unprofitable operations had been discontinued, with the approval of both the Commission and the Court. Farrington, shortly after coming to the railroad, had set up a committee to study the branch lines and to make reports so that proper consideration could be given to abandonment. Thus, after two and a half years, this feature of his planning for progress was making acceptable headway.

The railroad was beginning to look good. But it still had a long way to go.

4⓪ Into the black

The Japanese air squadrons came out of the morning sky on Sunday, December 7, 1941, to blast the Nation's Pacific fleet out of the water at Pearl Harbor. War had come to the United States, and overnight every resource of the country was being readied to meet the emergency.

The first line of national defense was the Nation's railroads. The Rock Island system, now showing the results of Farrington's five years of progressive improvement to roadbed and equipment, was rounding into first-class physical shape. Major line relocations between Davenport and Kansas City were on the drawing boards, and one important line change was under construction.

As of the moment, however, the main-line rail relay and the bridge rebuilding projects were beginning to pay off. A better use of the road's big engines was resulting in heavier freight trains and much swifter movement. People in railroad circles and those closely allied with transportation were beginning to say: "Watch this Rock Island. Watch this Farrington."

During 1940 industrial activity in the United States had increased with so-called defense needs. Rock Island's revenues had crossed the $80,000,000 mark and the deficit had dropped to $5,600,000. The close of 1941 saw a $16,000,000 increase in gross income to put the figure at $96,900,000—the highest in the 10 years of the road's bitter struggle for survival. The road earned its heavy interest charges and showed a black figure of $4,600,000—the first since 1930 when Brown and

Hayden had paid out $8,800,000 in dividends with only $7,700,000 earnings after fixed charges.

It was, indeed, a different Rock Island.

Its reorganization, however, was bogged down. The Interstate Commerce Commission, on October 31, 1940, had come out with a modified plan in which was prescribed a maximum capitalization of $351,180,912. This plan, too, eliminated any equity of the stockholders. Again the usual objections were filed and the Commission took them under advisement as the year closed.

Jim Gorman, as president of the debtor corporation, reviewed the proceedings in his 1940 annual report with a bitter attack on the Commission's reasoning. In defense of the debtor company's plan which had been proposed with its effective date stipulated at January 1, 1937, Gorman pointed out that, at the time, $44,000,000 in interest had been accumulated.

"The Commission's plan," Gorman wrote, "proposes an effective date of January 1, 1941, which choice of date alone adds some $53,000,000 to the amount of claims for unpaid interest which must be dealt with in the plan. The date proposed by the First and Refunding Committee was January 1, 1939, at which time the amount of unpaid interest was approximately $69,000,000."

Gorman pointed out that by the Commission's own records the actual investment in the property as of December 31, 1937, was more than $504,000,000. The present capitalization, exclusive of unpaid interest, was approximately $458,000,000.

"The Commission," Gorman said, "apparently has adopted the policy of reducing capitalization arbitrarily to accord with its own estimates of what the future earning power of the carrier will be. In the case of your company the Commission estimated a normal year's earnings in the future at $11,000,000 in spite of the fact that for 10 years prior to the early 1930's depression the average available for interest was $27,047,129. This is a disastrous policy for the roads undergoing reorganization, and involves a great danger to the securities of now solvent roads . . .

"One of the tragic features of it is that the destruction is permanent. The stockholders' equity is gone forever. It is possible that the Country some day may emerge from the fog that enshrouds it; but no amount of returning prosperity will resurrect the stockholders' investment."

Gorman pledged that the company would fight the plan before the court.

By now there was a new judge on the bench. Michael L. Igoe had succeeded Judge Wilkerson upon the latter's retirement. Perhaps Igoe would see the justice in the position of the debtor corporation.

The Commission certified to Judge Igoe, in August 1941, a modified plan with a supplemental report. The new plan upped the proposed capitalization to $386,127,410, and proposed January 1, 1942, as the effective date. Again no provision was made for the stockholders.

Igoe held hearings from October 13 to 17. The first and refunding group, the Choctaw, Oklahoma and Gulf committee and the Reconstruction Finance Corporation all voiced their support of the plan, but the preferred stock groups and others entered their objections.

Shortly after the court took the case under advisement two circuit courts of appeals upset the orders of lower courts approving the reorganization plans of the Western Pacific and the Milwaukee. In both cases the appellate courts held that the Commission had not made findings adequate to justify its orders. Applications immediately were made to the United States Supreme Court for certiorari. The Rock Island case would not be decided until the Supreme Court acted.

The Supreme Court decisions in the Western Pacific and Milwaukee proceedings were handed down on March 15, 1942. The plans as certified by the lower courts were upheld. The Commission's valuation of the companies and the capitalization as proposed got the Supreme Court's sanction. Changed circumstances brought about by wartime earnings were not sufficient, the Supreme Court held, to upset the judgment of the Commission as to proper capitalization.

It was a blow to the hopes of the Rock Island's debtor corporation.

Ten days later, on March 25, 1942, James E. Gorman died at the age of 78. High tribute was paid by his associates on the Rock Island Board to his "amazing knowledge of traffic and transportation matters." He was praised for his "patience, courtesy and kindliness." His friends in transportation, industry, and commerce, numbered literally in the thousands, mourned his passing.

Judge Igoe decided not to name a trustee to replace Gorman. Durham had now only Joe Fleming and Frank Lowden to work with under the direction of the court. Lowden was 81 years old and was failing.

With the death of Gorman, Edward N. Brown took over the post as president of the debtor corporation in addition to his duties as chairman of the board. He was determined to keep fighting to the last ditch to protect the equity of the stockholders in the Rock Island reorganization, no matter how many years it might take.

As summer approached and the war-actuated pace of commerce and industry quickened, the Rock Island appeared to be in for a good year. There was an optimistic feeling in some quarters about the reorganization, and the possibility that before the year's end the termination of the bankruptcy would be in sight.

Ned Durham didn't share this view. He knew how these things worked, and how court delays could pile month upon month and year upon year.

Durham wasn't satisfied with his progress. It wasn't easy to deal with court appointees who had not the faintest idea of what it took to make a railroad run. There had been differences of opinion with the trustees both as to expenditures and procedures. Durham was now 65. For many years he had laid plans to retire at that age. He was financially independent, and he wanted to play golf and do a little gardening and sort of let down.

He had accomplished, in his tenure of office on the Rock Island, far more than he had dreamed possible. Much of it had been done under extreme difficulties. John Farrington could carry it on.

Durham decided to take his retirement. His resignation was accepted, effective July 1, and Farrington was picked to step into the post as chief executive officer.

Farrington immediately moved Bill Hillis into the top operating spot, made a few other shifts in the official family and took over complete executive authority with much confidence but some qualms.

The monthly increases in earnings as a result of the war traffic meant to Farrington that he'd at last have cash to pursue his modernization program. He had to get the work on the southern Iowa sector under way just as soon as possible. The line between Ainsworth and Trenton, Missouri, with its grades and curves, simply had to be straightened out if the Rock Island hoped to perform at its best in the movement of the increasing war freight traffic.

True, the first segment of the four-segment line relocation program had been completed. This involved the building of 15.1 miles of new railroad between Mercer and Mill Grove, Missouri, on that section of the railroad between Allerton, Iowa, and Kansas City. Here the density of traffic was much greater than on the Chicago line east of Allerton in that the traffic from and to the Twin Cities in addition to the Chicago - Kansas City traffic used this portion of the railroad.

To complete the other three sections Farrington would need considerable money, a lot of rail, ties and ballast, and new signaling.

The deterrent factor in accomplishing what the Rock Island boss had in mind lay in Washington. As the result of the Nation's entry into war, Washington had already mushroomed into a vast bureaucracy. Under President Franklin D. Roosevelt's series of executive orders numerous agencies had been established to control the national economy, to conserve the Country's resources, to restrict and price the output and sale of consumer goods, and to designate what industries would be favored with the allocation of steel and other materials essential to the war effort.

Railroads, in 1942, failed to come under the classification of essential industries, and the procurement of rail, steel for cars and locomotives, and many other materials necessary to keep wheels turning got involved in a wide variety of Government red tape.

Farrington got a taste of what Washington was like when the railroad had to go before one branch of the War Production Board to get authorization for the continuation of its line relocation work. The Rock Island was accused by one bureaucrat of seeking to use its war profits to improve its property at the expense of the war effort.

The Office of Defense Transportation, under the direction of Commissioner Joseph B. Eastman, of the Interstate Commerce Commission, turned out a little better than most of the other agencies with which the railroads had to deal because Eastman insisted on getting, in his key jobs, top-caliber talent to deal with rail transportation problems.

For John Farrington and the Rock Island the going wasn't too rough until Frank Lowden died on March 20, 1943. The infirmities of his advanced years had caught up with the one-time governor of Illinois at his wintering place at Chandler, Arizona. During the last months of his life he had been unable to travel, and it had been necessary for the trustees' meetings to be held at Lowden's Arizona retreat.

Joe Fleming was now alone in his administration of Rock Island affairs and the Rock Island's chief executive had no trouble in getting along with this very shrewd and successful attorney at law. Over the period of time since Farrington first rolled up his sleeves in the La Salle Street Station he had inspired the complete confidence of the trustees and by now they had learned that the man they had in the driver's seat knew exactly how to drive.

Judge Mike Igoe, in the District Federal Court, announced on April 19 the appointment of Aaron Colnon, Chicago real estate operator and president of the Fort Dearborn Mortgage Company, as Rock Island trustee to succeed Lowden. It was necessary for the Interstate Commerce Commission to ratify this selection.

Pending the ratification Colnon entered the Rock Island picture on May 4 to attend the trustees' meeting and to shake hands with the chief executive officer. It was a sort of get-acquainted call. Colnon right then could take no official part in the matters under discussion.

The Commission's ratification of Colnon's appointment was made on May 20, and the court order that made the appointment final was entered five days later. Colnon began his official duties as co-trustee with Joe Fleming at the May 28 meeting of the trustees, and that date marked a new milestone in Rock Island's hectic history.

Farrington didn't realize it then, but he was about to enter upon the roughest, toughest road he would ever have to follow.

41 Big traffic—big trouble

Aaron Colnon had a dominant presence, a certain charm that he could turn on at will, a disturbing arrogance, and an unbridled determination to be the one big duck on the pond and all the other ducks had better understand it.

It didn't take him long to get his feet thoroughly planted

on the property. What he saw was enough to imbue him with a variety of grandiose ideas that, but for the dogged stubbornness of John Farrington, coupled with his waiting out the unpredictable turns of circumstances, might have gone a long way to wreck every constructive thing Farrington and Ned Durham had accomplished.

That Colnon firmly believed he stood hand in glove with Judge Igoe was demonstrated repeatedly in episode after episode. It wasn't long before Colnon made it quite plain to Trustee Joe Fleming that he, Aaron Colnon, was running the show, and that Fleming could object to Colnon's ideas until he was blue in the face but it would do Fleming no good. Igoe, Colnon implied, would approve whatever Colnon brought up in the administration of the railroad's affairs—an implication that the judge undoubtedly would have vigorously disaffirmed.

Before the end of 1943 Farrington had Colnon's measure. By that time, too, leaders of the protective committees of the various creditor groups in the reorganization proceedings had generally sized up the new trustee and privately expressed themselves as not being too happy about him. Colnon might claim to be the Federal judge's man in this picture, but Farrington had the support of the powerful creditor committees. If Colnon had any idea that he'd like to dump Farrington he was bright enough to know that the bondholders would appeal the action to the Circuit Court and Farrington would land right back in his lap.

The next best thing Colnon could do to make things uncomfortable for the railroad's chief executive officer was to resort to invective and personal abuse. Maybe Farrington would get a bellyful and quit of his own accord.

Farrington just wasn't that soft. He wasn't going to throw away seven years of unbelievable accomplishments and leave the Rock Island system to be manipulated for the personal glory, and indirectly for the private profit, of any new set of pirates. All he had to do was turn back the pages of the railroad's history to refresh his memory of what had happened as the result of previous manipulator control.

Shortly after Colnon took office, Judge Igoe entered an order approving generally the plan of reorganization which previously had been certified by the Commission. However, there were a couple of features he didn't like about it. He sent it back to the Commission with a request for certain changes —changes that were to have far-reaching repercussions. What the judge asked for was authority to approve or reject the reorganization managers who might be proposed by the various creditor groups.

E. N. Brown, representing the debtor company, promptly filed objections to the court's approval and asked the Commission for reconsideration of the stockholders who, under the plan, were completely eliminated.

The year 1943 passed into the records on a rising note of tension inside the trustees' meeting room. From the operating and earning viewpoint, John Farrington could be happy. His new and rerolled rail now extending over vast stretches of the property, his deeper and heavier ballast, his growing fleet of diesel power, his new car deliveries, all combined had enabled the system to meet the increasing demands of war traffic and troop movements.

Gross revenues set a new record for the railroad at $176,644,-685. Military travel was reflected in a $15,000,000 jump in passenger revenues over 1942's high of $24,700,000. The shortage of manpower was felt seriously in certain branches of the service and the bars of maximum age limits for hiring, that had formerly prevailed, were let down.

How Farrington's increased operating efficiencies were working out was graphically attested to by the fact that he was moving, with a total of 836 locomotives and 29,983 freight cars of all classes, 15 billion ton-miles of freight as compared with 1929's record year of 10 billion ton-miles when the road operated 1,453 locomotives and owned 43,093 freight cars of all types.

The diesel fleet had now grown to 19 of the most modern passenger locomotives and 82 switchers, and their economy of operation spurred the chief executive to planning further increases in this type of power. He planned for the day when the diesel would supplant steam entirely, but that would be long in the future.

The way was cleared for the line-shortening project between Perlee and Eldon, Iowa. Here the ground was broken for construction of 20.74 miles of new railroad that would shorten the present line by almost 4 miles, reduce the ruling grade of 1.6 percent to 0.6 percent, and eliminate 560 degrees of time-consuming, tonnage-restricting curves.

Farrington could do nothing to add to his streamlined passenger equipment which, as of the end of 1942, stood at 52 cars of various classes. The Office of Defense Transportation had cracked down on the allocation of steel for cars of this type. There was now in service in addition to the Peoria, Des Moines, Rocky Mountain, Twin Cities, and Texas Rocket runs, the Choctaw Rocket between Memphis and Amarillo, and the Zephyr Rocket between St. Louis and the Twin Cities in connection with the Burlington.

Any further extension of streamlined passenger service would have to be deferred until after the war unless the Government had a change of heart on the equipment restrictions.

There was nothing, however, to prevent the Rock Island's chief executive from turning his attention to dieselizing his principal main-line freight runs. Accordingly, he got the agreement of the trustees in May, 1944, to go to the court for an order authorizing the purchase of nine diesel freight locomotives and 10 modern 4-8-4 steam locomotives. These together with an order for 500 new steel box cars would cost $5,900,000 and would be handled with cash and equipment trust notes.

The whole program of planned progress by now had become a subject of national interest. Most interested was Henry Luce's *Fortune* magazine. The editorial board decided that in the revived Rock Island there must be one whale of a story. Accordingly, Gilbert Burck, one of Luce's top writers and editors, was assigned to cover the Rock Island property, interview Farrington, dig into the history, and see what he could make of it.

The story "Rock Island Revived" broke in the December, 1944, issue of *Fortune*, and created nothing short of a sensation among railroad analysts, investors, banking houses, industrialists, and employees.

However, the publicity didn't help Farrington in the growing rift between him and Trustee Aaron Colnon.

But Colnon by now had developed certain ideas of his own, which, if they worked, would eventually cut Farrington down to the size that Colnon thought he should be. Colnon's schemes were worked around the Commission's reorganization plan.

This plan, modified as Judge Igoe had insisted, was again certified to the court, and Igoe held the final hearings on it on June 23, 1944, after which he took it under further advisement.

The plan stipulated in its revised form that the names of the reorganization managers proposed by the various creditor groups would be subject to ratification by the court. Igoe thereby could reject any person the creditors proposed if he so desired, even though he himself could not actually name the managers.

This provision was enough for Colnon. He was determined that the names proposed would first of all be acceptable to himself—and the best way to accomplish this would be to confer with the creditor committees and "suggest" certain persons as their nominees, persons known to him as more than likely being acceptable to the judge. Colnon's reasoning was simple. If he could get the reorganization managers he personally wanted to see on the job, he could dictate procedures. This board of managers would have the say as to the selection of a board of directors. The directors would then meet and elect officers. It was no secret that Colnon wanted to be either chairman of the board, or president, and he had men picked for other jobs on the executive level. John Farrington's name was nowhere in the picture.

Colnon went so far as to approach his co-trustee, Joe Fleming, with the suggestion that Fleming could be vice-president and general counsel if he wanted to coöperate with Colnon.

Colnon spent the fall and early winter of 1944 turning his charm on the protective committee members. He later denied that he had actually put certain names before the committees as reorganization managers. But when the names came out and four of them were known close personal friends of either Colnon or the judge, the Chicago *Sun* in one of a series of articles on the Rock Island case reported that an influential member of one of the large creditor committees told the *Sun*, "the names of prospective reorganization managers actually were forced upon us in one of the most high-handed procedures in the history of railroad reorganization."

The *Sun*, further quoting an unnamed spokesman, said, "The obvious inference was that the reorganization plan would not be approved unless we agreed in advance to a hand-picked list of reorganization managers acceptable to the court, without the privilege of exercising our lawful rights to make voluntary appointments. The associations of some of the appointees for the reorganization board with Mr. Colnon or with Judge Igoe leave tell-tale tracks."

Farrington got through 1944 with new revenue and traffic records. The reborn Rock Island piled up $190,000,000 in gross, of which $131,000,000 was freight and $44,500,000 was passenger. His Perlee - Eldon line change was completed, and across the muddy Missouri, work was pushing ahead on a new bridge that, with certain minor operational changes, would give the Rock Island a completely new entrance into Kansas City and enable it to cut a full hour out of through schedules. The bridge was being built jointly by the Rock Island and the Milwaukee.

The big question that confronted Farrington now was what was going to happen to the reorganization. He was becoming more and more impatient with this long delay.

42 Widows and orphans

Judge Igoe, after almost a year during which Colnon was active in conferring with the protective committees and lining up his slate of "acceptable" reorganization managers, finally announced on May 14, 1945, his formal order of approval. It will be remembered that it was on June 23 of the previous year that he had held the last hearings.

Of course, the first thing Edward N. Brown, chairman of the debtor corporation did was file an appeal in the Circuit Court to set aside Igoe's approval of the plan. He was aided in this move by the preferred-stock committee.

There the matter stood, insofar as the reorganization was concerned, through the remainder of 1945. But on August 28, Colnon, just to show the creditors that he was on their side, and that they had nothing to fear from having gone along with him in the matter of reorganization managers, petitioned the court for authority to pay, out of treasury cash, $34,279,-750 to the bondholders. The distribution of this sum was provided for in the reorganization plan, but only at the time of consummation. What Colnon asked for, and got, was the authority to jump the gun in a grandstand play to make the distribution in advance.

The new bridge across the Missouri and 4.42 miles of new line from Birmingham across the bridge to a connection with the Kansas City Terminal Railway were completed in June. It was named after Harry S. Truman, who had succeeded the deceased F. D. R. to the Presidency of the United States. The span was constructed at a total cost of $3,500,000, of which the Rock Island shared half with the Milwaukee.

The bridge was another engineering triumph for John Farrington. It meant that no more would Rock Island's passenger trains have to be turned completely in the Kansas City terminal to get into or out of that Union Station.

Impatient with waiting until new equipment could be ordered to make up another topnotch Rocket train for through Twin Cities-Texas service, Farrington pieced together such cars as he could—some streamlined and some conventional with new dress, and inaugurated the now-famous Twin Star Rocket between Minneapolis, St. Paul, and Houston.

A new rail re-laying policy was adopted by which 131-pound rail would be put down in areas of the greatest density of traffic. With the launching of this program the use of 112-pound steel in main lines generally continued and another 229 miles of this new steel went into the 1945 re-lays.

Not to be overlooked in Farrington's progressive planning was the ever-increasing mileage of automatic block signals and centralized traffic control. At the time Farrington first came to the property, this particular improvement had been sadly neglected. There was but 191.20 miles of CTC on the railroad and the block signals covered but 1,266.48 miles. Now the block signaling system extended over 2,061 miles of main line and the highly efficient centralized traffic control was in service on both double- and single-track operations to the extent of 428.5 miles.

The chief executive, in his planning, had overlooked nothing in the way of up-to-the-minute technological advances to make this railroad second to none in its territory, and certainly on a par with any major system in the United States.

But there were many things beyond his control—things that the trustee Colnon, with the approval of the court, made the most of. Colnon was not only taking a lead in the reorganization plans—a function which as a trustee he had no business assuming—but in taking the purchase of materials and supplies out of the railroad's long-established policy of competitive bidding, and awarding juicy contracts to his personal friends.

As an example, Colnon arbitrarily took the railroad's insurance contract away from the Baltimore firm of Alexander and Alexander, which had won it on competitive bidding over a period of years, and appointed the Chicago firm of Marsh and McLennon as sole agent for the Rock Island's insurance business. Colnon acknowledged that the head of the firm was a close personal friend of his and had solicited the business shortly after Colnon was appointed a trustee. Another friend, Ivo Buddeke, according to Colnon, solicited him at the same time, but Colnon felt Buddeke's organization would be unable to handle the contract.

"As the court record shows," Colnon told the Chicago *Sun*, "I got an order from Judge Igoe appointing Marsh and Mc-Lennon sole agent for Rock Island insurance and I fixed it with them to give Buddeke part of the commissions as a personal favor to me because of my friendship with Buddeke. I don't know whether he does anything for Marsh and Mc-Lennon in connection with Rock Island insurance, but I know they give him only a small cut out of their commissions."

Colnon pooh-poohed the idea of competitive bidding insofar as insurance was concerned and called such a procedure outmoded. His procedure added about $25,000 to Rock Island's 1945 insurance costs.

This trustee's high-handed distribution of patronage extended into several important railway-supply fields and Colnon crassly demanded to know why he should not favor his friends wherever he could. He insisted that he favored no one unless the price of the commodity in question was right.

All through the transportation industry, as Rock Island reached new earning heights at the close of 1945, the dissension inside the trustee situation on the Rock Island was a subject of much discussion. Trustee Joe Fleming stood by Farrington, and Colnon sneered at them both. The question was, how long can John Farrington run his railroad and still take that abuse?

Rock Island's $192,000,000 gross for 1945, a new high, reflected a $3,500,000 increase in freight revenue.

Victory over Germany, and then VJ Day's wild climax saw the end of the shooting war, and almost at once passenger revenues suffered from the sharp cutback in military movements.

Now, as 1946 dawned, Farrington should be able to turn his attention to the property, determine what effects the bang and rattle, and the wear and tear, occasioned by the extraordinary demands, war traffic had made on road and equipment. He was thinking of postwar progress. He was tense and on edge over the delays to the property's reorganization.

Then, as if he didn't have troubles enough, something grim and ominous was taking shape in Washington that, if successful, might keep this railroad and other bankrupt properties in the hands of the courts forever.

It had started in a previous session of Congress when a charming and lovable old ex-judge, Sam Hobbs, who for years had represented the Fourth Congressional District of Alabama, and who on more than one occasion had shown himself to be friendly to the railroads, began to worry audibly about widows and orphans. Somebody implanted in Sam's mind the idea that stocks in bankrupt railroads were held mainly by forlorn and bereaved old ladies, or parentless children, whose very bread and butter and book learning depended solely upon the dividends paid.

Sam tried to save these unfortunate people from a sad fate by drawing up a bill that would change the application of the bankruptcy laws insofar as railroads were concerned. Sam's bill, while not very strong or clear in itself, was a sort of trial balloon. If enough legislators started to worry about the widows and orphans something really concrete might be done with legislation that would take these bankrupt railroads out of Section 77's provisions.

The concrete was poured by Burton K. Wheeler, then Democratic senior senator from the great and good state of Montana. Wheeler late in 1945 dumped a bill into the hopper designated as S.1253. The purpose of the legislation was to nullify pending plans of reorganization of bankrupt railroads, as developed by the Commission, return these properties to the stockholders, put the functions of management back in the hands of the debtor corporations, and allow the stockholders under court supervision to work out their own reorganization with the various creditor groups.

War earnings on most railroads now in the hands of the Federal courts, Wheeler reasoned, had proved sufficient to give the stock issues, declared without equity by the Commission, full reinstatement.

Wheeler, chairman in the 79th Congress of the Senate Interstate Commerce Committee, scheduled hearings on the bill in the spring of 1946. The hue and cry went around Capitol Hill that everything must be done for the widows and orphans.

During the hearings it developed that the main widow and orphan in the picture were Robert R. Young and his Alleghany Corporation. Young, who in 1932 had outsmarted the Morgan banking firm and the Guaranty Trust Company, of New York, to gain control of Alleghany, had gathered in with the other cats and dogs in the package the majority of the Missouri Pacific's common stock. Since Young had picked up Alleghany with an investment of only slightly more than $3,500,000 it was pretty certain that the apportionment of this outlay to Missouri Pacific common represented no more than a few cents a share.

Young appeared personally to testify and so did Alleghany's general counsel. Witnesses were gathered up from all over the country, most of them pleading for widows and orphans who didn't exist.

Senator Clyde Reed, Republican of Kansas, was the ranking minority member of the Senate Interstate Commerce Committee and sat in on most of the hearings. He wasn't too much in favor of S.1253 because it would upset the reorganization of the Denver and Rio Grande which, at that time, seemed to be about ready to come out of the wringer. Senator Ed C.

Johnson, of Colorado, an astute Democrat, held the same views.

Wheeler saw that unless he made a deal with Reed and Johnson to get an amendment into the bill that would eliminate the Denver and Rio Grande, these two gentlemen would make a lot of trouble on the Senate floor.

Attorneys representing a wide variety of railroad creditors appeared against the measure.

While the hearings progressed in Washington, the United States Circuit Court of Appeals in Chicago, on May 23, 1946, affirmed Judge Igoe's approval of the Commission's reorganization plan. Immediately the debtor corporation applied to the Supreme Court for a writ of certorari. This was promptly denied.

During the period in which the plan was before the Appellate Court, a ballot was taken among all classes of Rock Island creditors. When the results were tabulated it was shown that all groups, with the exception of the holders of the convertibles and the Hot Springs and Western (subsidiary) bonds, were in favor of the confirmation of the plan.

Igoe held hearings to determine whether the plan should be allowed to go through, despite the two groups that opposed it, and counsel for the debtor made a strong plea against confirmation.

Before Igoe rendered a decision, the Senate, on June 15, 1946, passed on a voice vote the Wheeler Bill. Ed Johnson got the Denver and Rio Grande exempted from its provisions and the bill promptly went to the House.

Less than two weeks later—on June 28—while the Wheeler Bill and the House version of this legislation awaited the House action, Igoe did a turn-about-face and signed the order proposed by the debtor corporation denying confirmation of the reorganization plan. He referred it back to the Interstate Commerce Commission for reconsideration in the light of recent earnings.

The Commission told the various Rock Island groups that

they would have until September 14 to file new plans, and hearings would start on September 24.

The senior bondholders went once more to the Court of Appeals to have Igoe's most recent ruling set aside, and the plan ordered confirmed.

The House, in Washington, passed a conference compromise of the Wheeler Bill in July and it went to the President for signature. The legislation came in the last minute rush to close up the 79th Congress so that its members could get back to the bushes for campaigning.

When President Truman got around to consideration of Burt Wheeler's railroad reorganization bill, early in August, 1946, John Snyder, his Secretary of the Treasury, advised him against signing on the grounds that the impact of such a law on railroad credit would be extremely serious. The Interstate Commerce Commission also advised in favor of a veto.

But the death knell was sounded by Representative Francis Walter, Democrat of Pennsylvania, who had been bitterly opposed to such legislation. Walter called the President by telephone, called the bill scandalous, and purportedly told Truman that if it were made into law by his signature it might very well cause an investigation of Democratic congressmen—and the party, at this time, with a new congress to be elected in the fall, certainly couldn't stand another national scandal.

Truman vetoed the bill. The President said he wasn't opposed to the basic principle of the legislation but, in its present form, he didn't like the "limitations and discriminations" it contained. He made it clear that he did not necessarily favor any of the reorganization plans of the various bankrupt railroads as projected by the Commission. He told the bill's proponents that he hoped they would work out a better bill in the next session.

With Igoe's action in returning the proposed plan for the Rock Island to the Commission, and in view of further possible legislative action, the creditor groups who had gone along with the trustee Colnon on his proposed board of reorganization managers now revoked the nominations. If and when this plan might finall/ get confirmation the board of managers would certainly be a quite different group—a group of the creditors' own choosing.

Colnon, meanwhile, became more and more interested in the future of legislative activity. He apparently figured that Young's Alleghany Corporation would be a good ally in the event a bill similar to Burt Wheeler's work of art could be drawn—one that would have Truman's sanction. Colnon would move heaven and earth to keep a spot for himself in the Rock Island's future affairs where he could hold a whip hand. He considered the Commission's plan, formerly approved by Igoe and then returned to the Commission, completely dead despite the fact that the Court of Appeals had made no ruling on the judge's refusal to confirm the plan.

Thus, while a decision was pending in the Circuit Court, Colnon filed with Judge Igoe, on September 30, 1946, a plan of his own. Under his proposal he would retire divisional mortgages by using cash in the treasury to buy in the St. Paul and Kansas City Short Line bonds at $635 per $1,000 bond; the Rock Island, Arkansas and Louisiana bonds at $740; Burlington, Cedar Rapids and Northern at $580; and Choctaw at full $1,000 value. His way of dividing up $32,000,000 of treasury cash for these issues meant that he would offer for them from $220 to $335 per $1,000 bond more than they were selling for in the market, which apparently made some sort of sense to Colnon although it made no sense to anybody else.

Colnon said he was offering his plan "as an aid to the Interstate Commerce Commission in formulating whatever new plan" it might have in mind.

When Colnon went before the Court on November 1 to argue for his proposal he found Attorneys Wilkie Bushby and Edward Bourne, of New York, representing the principal creditor groups, all lined up to fight him.

Others in the argument were the preferred stockholders

and the debtor corporation. They each had their plans which they pleaded should be given further consideration.

Bushby and Bourne argued that Igoe had no authority to consider Colnon's plan or any other proposals. They stood on the ground that Igoe's order of June 28 returning the once-approved plan to the Commission had been appealed to the Circuit Court and that until such appeal should be decided nothing in the way of a new plan had any right to be considered.

Colnon denied that his proposal actually was a new reorganization plan, insisting it was merely a set of suggestions to guide the Commission. He wanted authority from Igoe to submit his proposal to the creditors for a vote. He charged that the groups represented by Bushby and Bourne had one interest only, and that was getting control of the railroad for the big insurance companies and savings banks. He accused the creditors of bad faith.

Bourne unloaded on Colnon with the statement that insofar as the general mortgage bondholders had any power to designate reorganization managers "the only objective is to have a management that will preserve and command respect.

"If Colnon thinks we are concerned over his control over the Rock Island, he is entirely right!"

Robert Purcell, chief counsel for Robert Young's widow and orphan, the Alleghany Corporation, sided in with Colnon and his ideas. As Judge Igoe announced he would take the plans under advisement, Colnon was certain that he, with Alleghany support, was firmly and unassailably entrenched in a big-league operation.

Meanwhile what was happening to the Rock Island railroad? By the middle of 1946 the postwar recession was being acutely felt. Freight revenues were dropping off steadily and passenger receipts were declining sharply. Those things were to be expected.

With Government restrictions lifted, Farrington bought 10 more of the big 5100-series freight locomotives of the 4-8-4 class. He bought 7 more diesel passenger engines and 4 additional diesel freight haulers. He added 24 lightweight sleeping cars to his streamlined equipment and 500 additional all-steel box cars to his freight-car ownership.

The diesel fleet had now grown to 137 locomotives, of which 16 were in freight service, 26 in passenger service, and 95 in switching work.

In the big Iowa line relocation program, the year 1945 had seen completed the 21-mile segment between a point east of Paris westward to Centerville. This shortened the main line by 3.93 miles and reduced the grade from 1 percent to 0.50 percent. This was followed immediately in 1946 by work on the next segment east from Paris to Floris with a grade reduction from 1.40 percent to 0.50 percent. Curves of 1,204 degrees were cut out and the line shortened 1.37 miles. Construction got under way on the final section in the program between Brighton and Ainsworth.

With Farrington there was no letup to the progressive improvements. He knew that this 1946 postwar slump would not last long. Industry was busy re-tooling to supply the needs of the consumers of the nation who so long had had to defer such things as new cars, refrigerators, radios, home appliances, and other items of both necessity and luxury. Once the peacetime economy got adjusted, Farrington was sure, the Rock Island, along with its neighbors, would have plenty of business. He wanted his entire railroad in top physical condition to meet the flow of traffic.

Before the end of 1946 his modern coach shop and yard at 47th Street, Chicago, were completed, and the research laboratory nearby was getting its finishing touches. This latter facility was being equipped with the last word in all sorts of testing machines that would tell an accurate story on the many varieties of materials and devices that went into modern railroad construction and maintenance.

Freight business dropped 13 percent and passenger business was off 30 percent as compared with 1945. The drop in gross from $192,000,000 to $159,900,000 didn't bother John Farrington too much.

What did bother him was this business of facing another year of uncertainties insofar as the reorganization was concerned. He was increasingly discouraged over the court delays and certainly he was taking more than seemed possible in the nature of personal abuse from the trustee Colnon.

43 Solid track at last

January, 1947, ushered in for the Rock Island a year of crises.

The new 80th Congress met and organized with Republican majorities in both houses. How would this overturn in political control affect the railroads still in the bankruptcy courts? Subsequent to the veto of the Wheeler Bill, the Frisco and the Seaboard had gotten out of the hands of the courts through final consummation of their respective reorganizations.

Of the major properties left there were the Rock Island, the New Haven, and the Missouri Pacific. The Denver and Rio Grande was on the verge of getting out. Would proponents of legislation similar to the Wheeler Bill consider the game had stakes high enough to fight on?

The answer came quickly. Robert R. Young and Orphan Alleghany pulled the strings. Alleghany now had a sizeable amount of Rock Island bonds and how much of the old common stock nobody knew. It was rumored that Young had picked up a lot of it, and that it was being held in blocks by brokers. You couldn't pin it down. The rumors said he'd bought the stock for as little as 25 cents a share.

The decisive defeat of Burt Wheeler in the Montana elections where the voters replaced him in the Senate with Zales Ecton, Republican, brought no solace to the opponents of reorganization legislation. Wheeler promptly moved into Washington, opened a law firm with his son, Eddie, and took over representation of the Robert R. Young interests.

Chauncey Reed, Republican representative from West Chicago, Illinois, who had steered the compromise version of the Wheeler Bill through the House in the closing days of the 79th Congress, began drafting a new piece of legislation that was to become known as the Reed Bill. Over on the Senate side he had solidly lined up with him Clyde Reed, of Kansas; Tobey, of New Hampshire; Tom Stewart, Democrat of Tennessee; and four other members of that party on the powerful Senate Interstate and Foreign Commerce Committee. Wallace White, of Maine, was the chairman, and noncommittal.

Reed, of Illinois, high ranking on the House Judiciary Committee which, in 1947, would launch the bill, conferred with the White House. He was determined that before he put the bill in the hopper he would be sure of President Truman's support. Backstage, Burt Wheeler was wielding a mighty hand.

Farrington, in Chicago, had little hope but that there would ensue more court delays in the Rock Island case, since the trustee Colnon already was laying plans to go to Washington, if he got a chance, and there to testify in favor of whatever legislation Chauncey Reed would concoct.

The tension mounted. Here was a case where the chief executive officer of the Rock Island, determined to save his railroad physically and financially, was in sharp opposition to a trustee who had pitched his lot with groups of speculators in a drive to control the property. And speculators, they were. In early 1947 less than 10 percent of the old stock of the Rock Island was held by the original owners. It had sold in lots of thousands for as little as a dime a share, according to experts in the field. Whatever widows and orphans there might have been, they long ago had parted with their holdings.

In Chicago, on January 30, 1947, the Circuit Court of Appeals held hearings on the plea of the senior creditors in the Rock Island case to overturn Judge Igoe's refusal to confirm the Commission plan. The Circuit Court also heard arguments on appeals from the Igoe order permitting the trustee Colnon to submit his own proposals to the security holders for a vote.

Alleghany's counsel asked permission to intervene as a friend of the court in support of Igoe's refusal to confirm. Again Edward Bourne and Wilkie Bushby appeared for the senior creditors and pleaded that the Colnon plan violated the Bankruptcy Act. Sherman Minton, one of the three judges hearing the arguments, commented that the Rock Island, along with other lines, all were once over-capitalized and "full of water."

"Now," said Minton, "when we want to take a little of the water out, the fellows who own the water want to pump it back in."

The result of the Circuit Court's deliberations came on February 21. Igoe was ordered to confirm immediately the plan that he had returned to the Commission, and to vacate his order approving Aaron Colnon's recapitalization plan.

Once again the hopes of John Farrington and others in the Rock Island official family were raised somewhat, although Farrington was conscious of the many things impending that could bring about further delay.

Judge Igoe took his time about complying with the Circuit Court's order to confirm "forthwith."

The creditor groups went about the business of naming a new slate of reorganization managers and taking all the steps they could toward getting the Rock Island launched under a new corporate structure.

However, it wasn't until May 6, 1947, that the lawyers in the case appeared in Igoe's court with motions to confirm the plan and to appoint the reorganization managers. The new slate was made up of Edward E. Brown, chairman of the board of Chicago's First National Bank; Mark A. Brown, then vice-president of the Harris Trust and Savings Bank, Chicago; James Norris, of Norris Grain Company; and Roy C. Ingersoll, then president of Ingersoll Steel and Disc Company. The fifth man was to be named by the court. Norris later withdrew his name, and Charles D. Wiman, president of Deere and Co., at Moline, Illinois, took his place.

Igoe blasted the New York attorneys for the creditors for coming into Chicago and taking up his time without due prior notice. He heard the junior creditors and stockholders plead for delay until a writ of certiorari could be applied for in the Supreme Court. He then continued until May 13 arguments on the reorganization.

Meanwhile, Chauncey Reed, in the House in Washington, brought in his reorganization bill, designated as HR 3237 but later reintroduced as HR 3980. He immediately announced that hearings before the House Judiciary Committee would begin on May 12, and thereby caught the railroad interests opposed to the legislation something more than flatfooted.

Reed contended that the committee should be guided by the voluminous amount of testimony taken the previous year on the Wheeler Bill, and gave every indication that he intended to move fast with his measure. He admitted that he expected considerable opposition and was prepared to meet it.

What Representative Reed hadn't figured on was the terrific opposition leadership that was to come from Senator Albert Hawkes, of New Jersey, from Representative Francis A. Walter, Pennsylvania, a member of Reed's committee, and from Representative Ross Rizley, Oklahoma, on the House Rules Committee.

As the hearings proceeded, the opposition took definite form. This was intensified by the series of events that built up in Judge Igoe's court and through the trustee Colnon's activities. Congressman Walter kept a sharp eye on the Rock Island reorganization proceedings.

The flame in Congress grew high on May 22 when Judge Igoe tossed new fuel onto the glowing embers. On that day the lawyers for the creditors appeared in the Chicago District Court to hear the judge announce that he was confirming the Rock Island plan, but—it would be strictly on his terms. He was taking unto himself the right to appoint three of the five reorganization managers. He told the lawyers that the creditors would have until May 27 to withdraw the names of their nominees, and he would hold the next hearing on May 28. Igoe came out with a nine-page opinion attached to his six-page confirmation order.

The fight started. Ed Bourne, of New York, blew the lid off with the accusation that Igoe "is directly interested in controlling the reorganization."

"What you have said is untrue," Igoe stormed back from the bench. He then held Bourne in contempt and taxed him with a hundred-dollar fine. Arguments were held up while Bourne took up a collection in the courtroom from his friends. Then he continued with his statements.

Igoe, in handing down his opinion said the reorganization managers would stand in a fiduciary relationship to all parties and should therefore "be free from any special allegiance to any single class or group of creditors."

He blasted Harry Haggerty, vice-president of the Metropolitan Life Insurance Company, as the man behind the appointments of the reorganization managers who had been proposed by the creditors, and declared that the present nominees would be serving special interests rather than the bondholder committees and the public.

It was then that Bourne brought out the allegation that the trustee Colnon had only recently been in New York soliciting a number of brokerage firms to join in the formation of a new bondholders' protective committee.

Senator Hawkes followed the story. He passed it on to others. Francis Walter, in the House, discussed it with his associates. Whispers that a full-dress Congressional investigation of Judge Igoe's court and his method of handling bankruptcy cases was contemplated were beginning to be heard.

While the House Judiciary Committee continued to hear witnesses on the Reed Bill, the attorneys for the Rock Island creditors stopped Igoe from appointing three reorganization managers of his own choice. On May 27 Bourne and his colleagues appeared before the Circuit Court of Appeals and asked for a writ of mandamus, ordering full approval of the plan without Igoe's qualifications.

Igoe was ordered by Judge Otto Kerner to appear before the Circuit Court on the following day to show cause why the writ should not be granted.

Meanwhile, in Washington, another fire in the Rock Island case had broken out with the appearance of the trustee Colnon before the House Judiciary Committee in support of the Reed Bill. After more than two hours of testimony, Congressman Albert Reeves, of Missouri, expressed himself as being entirely amazed that this trustee could have taken upon himself this task without Judge Igoe's knowledge and consent.

Reeves and others summed up Colnon's presentation of the Rock Island story as "confused" and ostensibly filled with "half truths or complete misstatements of the facts." Colnon used the personal pronoun "I" as if no one else on the Rock Island had any say in the management of the property, or had ever had any part in the financial and operational activities of the road. The general opinion among Chauncey Reed's supporters was that Colnon's appearance contributed nothing to aid the legislation, but a great deal to harm it.

The hearings moved over to the Senate, and while they gathered momentum there, Judge Evan A. Evans, of the Circuit Court of Appeals, had before him a petition from the Rock Island bondholders asking him to remove Igoe from the Rock Island case. Igoe, at the same time, asked the Executive Committee of the Senior Judges of the District Court to take him off the proceedings, which, after a brief discussion, the committee refused to do.

On June 5, in Washington, Haggerty, of Metropolitan, and Lawyer Bourne were two chief witnesses against the Reed Bill before Senator Reed and his Senate Interstate and Foreign Commerce Committee. Haggerty spared no language in his charge before the group that Igoe and Colnon sought to control the Rock Island on its emergence from trusteeship, and alleged that Igoe, by setting himself up to appoint the majority of the reorganization managers could, through Colnon, dictate the selection of a board of directors and the officers who would be elected to manage the property.

Nor did Haggerty spare Colnon for his testimony before the House Committee in support of this legislation. He seriously questioned the propriety of a man appointed by the court to conserve the estate, playing footsie with supporters of this legislation.

"In fact," Haggerty told the committee, "Igoe and Colnon are urging legislation to defeat a plan which Judge Igoe had approved and later refused to confirm until ordered to do so by the Appeals Court."

Haggerty excoriated Robert R. Young and the Alleghany Corporation for their part in the affair.

"I am sick and tired," Haggerty said, "of reading and listening to rabble-rousing attacks, particularly by Robert Young and his associates. We do not need Robert Young or any other self-appointed guardian to take care of the interests of our policy-holders."

Edward Bourne told the committee that "during more than 25 years of practice I have never known such important proceedings in any court in which there was such complete disregard of the law as there was in connection with the initiation of Mr. Colnon's plan and its approval by Judge Igoe."

He charged that Alleghany's principal interest in Missouri Pacific, Central of Georgia, and Rock Island reorganization plans "is to increase the power of Alleghany Corporation as a holding company, and of those who dominate it."

In an attack on Burton K. Wheeler, the defeated Montana senator, Bourne pointed to Alleghany's employment of Wheeler's son in 1946 to plug for the Wheeler Bill at the time the ex-senator was working to get the legislation passed.

The Circuit Court of Appeals in Chicago issued its writ of mandamus in June, directing that Igoe confirm the Rock Island plan as originally certified by the Commission. This meant that Igoe now could no longer delay, nor could he have his say in appointing the majority of the reorganization managers.

As to the appeal before Judge Evans in the Circuit Court to remove Igoe from the case, Evans refused. He said he did not agree that Igoe had arbitrarily delayed the completion of the case, but, about the trustee Aaron Colnon, Judge Evans said he "was not so sure."

"Trustee Colnon," Judge Evans said, "has said and done things which would justify a conclusion that he has been bent upon delaying the execution of the plan and changing it to the interests of the junior creditors. Statements of Colnon which appear in the record . . . indicate he has misconceived his duties and entertained magnified ideas about the part he is to play in this reorganization."

Judge Evans criticized certain creditor groups in which he included Alleghany Corporation, and the stockholders, when he said, "I received the impression that (they) are not seeking to carry out the plan of reorganization, but that they applaud Trustee Colnon because he is blocking it and doing all he can to prevent its execution. I do not respect their action or their motive." He asked the bondholders again to urge Judge Igoe to ratify their appointment of four of the five reorganization managers.

Igoe confirmed the plan in accordance with the mandamus on June 26, 1947. Immediately thereafter the reorganization managers took over their duties and it looked as if, at long last, the Rock Island was on its way out of its tangle.

There was still the threat of the Reed Bill, but most of its questionable import was removed when, on July 15, the House Judiciary Committee voted 12 to 11 to report the bill out favorably.

Led by Representative Walter, the minority report was written all through the hours of a hot sticky night. It was delivered by Walter to the printer the following morning and became part of the whole committee report in the nick of time.

The members of the committee who had so doggedly fought approval of the bill tried to assure their railroad friends that with such a big minority signing the report there was little chance, if any, that the bill would ever get to the floor of the House.

The Senate approval came on July 3, and eight days later Senator Hawkes turned in the Senate Committee's minority report. Hawkes had 6 of the 13 members, so again the minority was strong against bringing the bill up for Senate consideration.

Would it get to the floor of either house? The first session of the 80th Congress was droning to a close in that July of 1947, and each day was a day of suspense. Finally with but a few days to go before the set day for adjournment, Chauncey Reed, of Illinois, went before the House Rules Committee to clear the way for his bill to get to the floor. Walter, of Pennsylvania, led the opposition.

No vote was ever announced. One member said that the Rules Committee decided to defer the granting of a rule. What did that mean? It was the kiss of death to Chauncey Reed's HR 3980. Almost at the same time the Senate policy group decided that the companion legislation in the Senate would not be brought to the floor.

The legislation was properly buried on the early evening of July 27 when the first session of the 80th Congress passed into history.

Chauncey Reed took the defeat with a grin. But not Senator Clyde Reed, of Kansas. He later issued a blast against the Interstate Commerce Commission and threatened a full-dress investigation of that body.

Meanwhile the application of the debtor corporation and the junior creditors to the Supreme Court for a writ of certiorari was on the docket. Again the anxiety began to mount. By this time not only the Rock Island officers were praying to get this business over with, but the employees were beginning to wonder. They had read enough and heard enough about the court delays and the congressional maneuvers to become greatly concerned.

Then, on October 14, a strange thing happened. With the petition for certiorari before the Supreme Court under active consideration, the Interstate Commerce Commission wrote a letter to Supreme Court Justice Vinson in which it said, in effect, that if it were the Court's pleasure to overrule the Court of Appeals and reopen the Rock Island case the Commission would immediately set it down for hearings.

It was, in the opinion of congressmen, lawyers, and railroad leaders, the most amazing switch in the history of the Interstate Commerce Commission. It was unprecedented. The idea that a Government agency should write such a letter to the Nation's highest court at such a time was regarded as a backhanded attempt to influence a judicial decision. The Commission was criticized by editorials in many large dailies as having gotten scared by the threat of Senator Reed to investigate it.

The Supreme Court, on October 20, denied the petition for a writ, and that was the end of it insofar as the old debtor corporation was concerned.

John Farrington, guiding the destinies of the Rock Island from his Chicago office, could now breathe a little easier. With the reorganization managers at work, all the legal technicalities should be completed before the end of November so that, by December 1, the new corporation could take over the property.

Things appeared to be going more or less on schedule, when, on October 29, the reorganization managers presented to Judge Igoe their request for the order that would grant authority to file with the Commission their application for approval of the new charter, the mortgages, and all other things within the structure of the plan. They also asked the Court's approval of the charter and by-laws of the new corporation.

The managers had filed with the judge, five days before, copies of all these documents, so they expected that immediate issuance of the proper orders would be but a mere formality.

The judge dropped a large bucket of cold water on the whole proceedings by announcing that he had before him a telegram from the Attorney General of Texas, asking to be heard for the purpose of intervening against the plan's consummation.

Instead of complying with the petition of the managers, Judge Igoe announced that he would continue the case two weeks to give the Texas Attorney General a chance to be heard.

Counsel for the managers exploded. The thing was impossible. They argued that the Texas Attorney General had no standing in the plan to be heard on any question. The judge wasn't moved. He set November 12 for the new hearing.

The Assistant Attorney General for the Lone Star State showed up in court on the appointed date and the matter of intervention was argued lustily by both sides. The lawyers for the reorganization managers made a strong case that the Texas objections had to do with matters that already were in the plan and that any recognition of the Texas contentions would have the effect of altering the plan. Under the law, the court had no power to make such alteration.

Despite the facts in law, Judge Igoe gave the Texas attorney 10 days in which to file a brief, and the managers 5 days in which to answer. The delay made tempers short. The whole thing seemed incredibly preposterous.

When, eventually, on December 30, Judge Igoe ruled out the position of the representative of the Texas Attorney General, and signed the order consummating the Rock Island plan, that gentleman promptly petitioned the Circuit Court of Appeals for an order to stay the signing over of the Rock Island property to the new corporation until such time as he could argue the merits of his position.

The machinery had been set up to convey the property on January 1, 1948, and this latest move looked like another monkey wrench that without the least doubt might have serious effects.

The suspense was again at fever pitch on December 31, 1947, when the Circuit Court, with three judges sitting, heard the arguments on the Texas position.

Finally, at 3 o'clock on that dreary afternoon, the final break came. The circuit judges denied the Texas request for a stay. The last legal obstacle had been removed.

The embattled Rock Island, after 15 years, 6 months and 23 days in the hands of the Federal court and under the trying reorganization proceedings, was at last on sound financial ground—was at last free to take its place as a solvent, highly progressive railroad system under as strong a management as any railroad could ever know.

The blasting of whistles and the ringing of bells that New Year's Eve marked the close of one of the darkest and the opening of one of the brightest periods in the system's 95 years of life.

44 Bright dawn—bright hope

The Rock Island was in all respects a vastly different railroad on New Year's morning, 1948, compared with the property that sought the protection of the bankruptcy court in that long-ago June of 1933.

John Farrington took over as president, a fitting reward indeed for the long and sometimes seemingly futile battle he had fought. Making up his board of directors was a powerful group of business leaders, *not* representative of Eastern banking interests as Judge Igoe had predicted they would be. With the exception of one, all had business interests in cities located on the Rock Island system.

Farrington, as the new president, also was chairman of the board. The reorganization managers—Edward E. Brown, chairman of the First National Bank, Chicago; Roy Ingersoll, president of Ingersoll Steel Disc Division of Borg-Warner, Chicago; Charles D. Wiman, president of Deere and Co., Moline; Mark Brown, executive vice-president of Harris Trust and Savings Bank, Chicago; and William E. Fay, president of the Champion Machinery Company, Joliet—took their places as directors. The remainder of the board was made up of Henry Crown, chairman of Material Service Corporation, Chicago; Harry Darby, chairman of the board, the Darby Corporation, Kansas City, Kansas; Herbert L. Horton, board chairman of the Iowa - Des Moines National Bank and Trust Company, Des Moines; Frederick M. Mayer, president, Continental Supply Company, Dallas; Robert McKinney, then a rancher and investor of Tucumcari, New Mexico; Louis B. Neumiller, president, Caterpillar Tractor Company, Peoria; James Norris, president of Norris Grain Company, Chicago; William F. Peter, vice-president and general counsel of the Rock Island; Dudley Swim, of Pebble Beach, California.

Fay had been the appointee of the court as a reorganization manager, and McKinney and Swim represented the holdings of the Robert R. Young interests.

Farrington, with the full confidence of his board, could look over the new Rock Island with justifiable pride. In its last year in trusteeship it had continued its progress. The final segment of the big Iowa line change had been completed so that now he could point to a total of 120 miles of line relocations at various points on the system that had eliminated 3,800 degrees of curvature and 1,200 feet of rise and fall. He had abandoned 650 miles of unprofitable branch lines since he had taken over in 1936.

The rail relay now added up to a total of 3,951 miles of which 2,401 miles was in new steel and the remainder rerolled rail. The 1,463 miles of automatic block signals in operation in 1936 had grown to 3,261 miles, of which 592 miles was centralized traffic control.

Through the modern reclamation plant and general scrap dock at Silvis the sales of scrap now stood at $12,900,000.

During these 12 years Farrington had added 6,285 modern freight cars of all classes to Rock Island ownership, and with the continued increase in the use of diesel power the number of locomotives in service had decreased from 1,160 in 1936, to 632. With this power the road in 1947 had handled 73.58 percent more gross ton-miles of freight and 148.92 percent more passengers one mile than had been handled in 1936.

Industrial development had brought to the system during the past 12 years 2,084 new industries producing an estimated $22,800,000 annually in freight revenues. At Dallas, on Rock Island tracks, the Alford refrigerator warehouse, largest in the world, was opened for business.

Altogether the Rock Island had spent $130,800,000 in this gigantic rehabilitation program, of which $69,800,000 had gone into the road, and $61,000,000 into the modernization, building, and purchase of equipment.

The reorganization had pared down annual fixed charges for interest on the funded debt from $13,000,000 to $1,700,-000. The new capitalization stood at $324,667,932 as compared with the old company's $431,575,282. The new preferred stock issue was $70,538,193, and the common was $140,934,649 of no par value, but stated at $100 per share.

Under the reorganization plan the subsidiaries had been consolidated into the corporate structure of the new Chicago, Rock Island and Pacific Rail*road* Company.

The gross earnings of 1947 totaling $178,000,000 had shown a comfortable increase over the $159,900,000 of the previous year. With the hope that these revenues would continue to improve with the upward trend in the general economy, Farrington and the Rock Island could now face the future with a renewed faith in the ever-growing importance of the system to the territory it served, to its patrons, and to its neighbors on the farms and in the cities and towns along its bustling right-of-way.

Great though its gains had been during these past 12 years, there would be no halt to the railroad's progressive expansion. As a prelude of what was to come, the Rock Island's big name train—the Golden State—modernized and diesel-powered, was set up on a 45-hour schedule between Chicago and Los Angeles and took its place among the nation's extra-fare luxury runs. Delivery of the last of 57 lightweight streamlined chair and sleeping cars, on order since 1945, would enable the road to improve its entire Rocket fleet with the finest in comfort, color, and design.

While further grade-reduction programs continued, along with the renewing and rebuilding of bridges, ground was broken at Armourdale Yard, Kansas City, Kansas for the installation of the railroad's first hump-retarder facility. The plan called for 40 classification tracks on which could be expedited the handling of 4,000 freight cars daily. The yard would be equipped with radio communication between office and engines and talk-back stations at strategic points. The railroad had been among the first to experiment with radio and electronics, and this modern technological development was meeting with success.

Farrington had notified the stockholders in the new company that only after a complete study by the directors would a decision be made on what the dividend policy of the company should be.

The first announcement came at the June meeting of the board at which was declared a mid-year dividend of $2.50 per share on the preferred. This was followed in July by a dividend of 75 cents a share on the common stock. It was the intention to place the common on an annual $3.00 basis together with the $5.00 yearly dividend on the preferred. Reduction of debt in the hands of the public received serious attention.

The first year out of the trusteeship saw Farrington's fleet of diesels increased to a total of 163 locomotives. His program looking toward complete dieselization was rapidly stepped up.

A new departure in acquainting the public with the railroad, its equipment, and its vast progress was brought about through Rock Island's participation in the Chicago Railroad Fair, the first of its kind in history. Among the 40 major railroads participating, Rock Island's Rocket Village, in the middle of the 35-acre area, featured a variety of entertainment, including dining on the colorful Fiesta car from the Golden State, and a preview of the last word in observation-lounge cars.

That first year out of trusteeship set a record for gross revenues. The year ended with earnings of $197,404,990. Only the heavy tax bill kept the net railway operating income of $21,800,000 from reaching a record peak. The dividend policy was firmly established.

Rock Island was roaring its way to new achievements with a wide-open throttle and the signal lights all green.

45 Test and triumph

John Farrington, in his second year as Rock Island's president, was a good deal like a general in the field, in the manner in which he planned the future of his railroad. With the experiences of the past still fresh in his mind—the policies and circumstances that led to the 1933 debacle—Farrington was determined to use a strategy that would guarantee against anything like that in the future, no matter what the general economy might have to stagger through.

Never again would the Rock Island railroad be called a "granger" line, dependent for more than half its income from agriculture and thereby subject to wide fluctuations in earnings, depending on crop conditions. And never again would there be a mounting debt in the hands of the public with ever-increasing interest charges.

The continued placing of more and more industries along the rails was one strengthening phase that was forging ahead in an aggressive manner. The other was the debt-reduction program.

This project gained momentum from its inception in 1948. As 1949 neared its close the $100,853,150 in first mortgage and general mortgage bonds in the hands of the public January 1, 1948, had been reduced to $59,404,500. The board of directors was convinced that this would be an opportune time to issue new first-mortgage bonds in the amount of $55,000,000. With the money derived from the sales of these securities, plus some additional cash from the treasury, what remained of the old issues could be completely wiped out. The stockholders approved, and by January 1, 1950, the buying in of the first-mortgage and general-mortgage issues was well under way. Halsey, Stuart & Co., Inc., was awarded the bid on the new issue, and the interest rate of 2⅞ percent was highly favorable. The former first-mortgage bonds carried interest at 4 percent, and the general-mortgage bonds earned 4½ percent.

The road in 1949 put under construction its second great hump-retarder yard at Silvis, near East Moline, Illinois. This 50-track facility would be larger than the 40-track layout at Kansas City, Kansas, and it would handle the reclassification of freight cars for the North, West, and Southwest.

Here again the installation of radio communications was technological development at its best. And while the communications forces were at work on this, the Rock Island launched the first microwave experiment ever to be conducted on any railroad. The engineers picked the high, open plains country of northwest Kansas to erect their towers and reflectors and their concrete relay housing on the 100-mile section of the Colorado main line between Norton and Goodland. This was an area where the sweeping storms of snow, ice, and high winds too frequently disrupted wire communications. If the microwave could be made to work, its use stood an excellent chance of opening up a whole new era of railroad dispatching and message transmission.

The Rock Island scored another first with the receipt from the builders of new lightweight streamlined suburban cars. There were 20 of these, 8 of them air-conditioned for the longer express runs. They were especially designed with coil-spring trucks and shock-absorbing devices for smooth riding and operation. Their double doors, pneumatically controlled, were in the sides instead of the ends of the cars. Roller bearings, high-speed electric brakes, and tight-lock couplers combined to make these 100-passenger-capacity cars something no Chicago suburbanite had ever seen before. Even in this branch of service, a prodigious money-loser at best, Farrington took the view that everything possible should be done to modernize it, to provide comfort, convenience, and economical transportation for the suburban patrons.

The Rock Island closed another successful 100 days of participation in the second year of the Chicago Railroad Fair, and while more hundreds of thousands of visitors were seeing railroad history at first hand along Chicago's lake front, Republic Pictures, down in Oklahoma, was making a de luxe color feature on the early days of the railroad's building. This would be something for millions of people to see in theaters all over the land.

During the eventful year of 1949 the acquisition of 46 new diesels brought the road's ownership of this type of power to 209 locomotives. Forty-five of these were now in passenger service, 44 hauling main-line Rocket freights and 120 assigned to the switching chores. Retirement of 67 more steam locomotives left in service 502 of this fading fleet.

The 1949 earnings dipped 6.5 percent from 1948's high of

$197,400,000 to $184,656,845—not too serious in view of the national average of the Class I carriers which experienced an 11.3 percent drop. The inauguration of the 40-hour week for the vast majority of the company's employees and the wage increases for both operating and nonoperating people had their impact to hold down the year's net to $19,800,000.

Purchase of the Pullman Railroad, an important switching line on Chicago's south side, along with 364 acres of land for industrial development, marked further progress in this particular field. Over in Denver the industrial department acquired 355 acres for new development, and at Colorado Springs 70 acres was bought and made ready for the installation of new factories. The Denver program was part of the new line-building project that would be called the Denver Cutoff and would take Rock Island freight trains from a junction east of the city directly to new North Yard which was used jointly with the Denver and Rio Grande.

Planned progress, to John Farrington, was real and vital— not just a play on words in the company's advertising campaign. Everywhere you looked over the 8,000-mile system you saw the evidence. You saw the men in a hurry to complete first one project, then another. You saw the spirit of progress in the morale; the spark of new pride, the glow of accomplishment.

As the road drove through the first half of 1950 it seemed as if nothing could stop this great momentum of improvement and growth.

However, the system's switchmen stopped it, head on. At 6 o'clock in the morning, on June 25, the Rock Island for the first time in its 98 years of historic struggle completely ceased all operations.

The switchmen's organization had been negotiating for a 40-hour week and certain wage increases on a number of railroads where its membership had the bargaining rights. The dispute finally went to the Presidential Fact-Finding Board, provided under the Railway Labor Act. This board granted the 40-hour week and an 18-cent increase. This finding was accepted by the Rock Island and all the other railroads. The union refused to entertain the decision and called the strike.

Attempts at negotiation and settlement were continued, but for two weeks not a wheel turned. President Truman pleaded with the union leadership and insisted the men return to work. He called the strike wholly unjustified. His pleas were ignored.

Finally, on Saturday, July 8, Truman ordered the U.S. Army to take over, and the Attorney General went into the United States District Court to obtain a restraining order against the Switchmens Union of North America.

The following day the Rock Island resumed operations. A settlement eventually was accepted by the union that gave its members the 40-hour week, an increase of 18 cents an hour as recommended by the fact-finding board, plus an additional 5 cents suggested by the Government. The new contract provided a cost-of-living formula for certain subsequent increases in return for a three-year moratorium on changes in rules and rates of pay.

The ill-advised 14-day strike was a costly one. It took months to recover the road's full volume of business. Otherwise, from the viewpoint of earnings, it undoubtedly would have been a very good year. The gross was $179,652,325, a decrease of 2.7 percent. The cut in operating expenses from 1949's $135,300,-000 to $130,700,000 marked an outstanding achievement despite the cost of the strike and the fact that 1950 was the first full year in which the road could feel the full effects of the 40-hour week and the previously awarded wage grants.

The vast progress the Rock Island had made under John Farrington's planning to get away from too much dependence on agriculture as the main source of its revenue met its full test in the middle of 1951.

The crop failure in the Southwest in 1950 had its impact, but that wasn't too serious compared to the labor troubles and the wage increases. The spring of 1951, however, gave cause for great concern. The rains in Kansas and Oklahoma came early. Vast sections were affected by rising waters. Here and there a bridge would wash out. Quick repairs followed at first one point and then another.

In the light of events that were to follow, Farrington's new operating vice-president was in for a grand-scale baptism. His name was Downing B. Jenks. He had come from the post of operating vice-president on the Chicago and Eastern Illinois, in the previous December, as assistant operating chief of the Rock Island under Bill Hillis. On July 1, the elevation of Hillis to the newly created office of senior vice-president was announced, and Jenks succeeded to the top operating spot.

Jenks, a native of Portland, Oregon, had seen plenty of service on various divisions of the Great Northern, where he, in a manner of speaking, had cut his teeth on an air-hose gasket. After graduating from Yale's Engineering School he had worked his way through the jobs of trainmaster and division superintendent from Minnesota to Washington before being called to the Army. He had battled sleet and mud and snow. But all this water—he hadn't seen so much since he'd crossed the Atlantic aboard a troopship.

He walked into the flood problems with a lot of determination to keep the railroad open. If he found something that puzzled him he had Hillis to call on for counsel.

The weeks of rain finally culminated in the great flood of the Kansas River. The crisis set in at Kansas City, Kansas, on the early morning of July 12. The Rock Island's bridge at Topeka, after day and night battling to save it, had gone under the swirling waters as they rose on their eastward course.

The Government engineers at the junction of the Kansas and Missouri Rivers had said there would be no danger to the Rock Island's still-new facilities at Armourdale Yard in Kansas City, Kansas.

But a yard clerk, on his way to work over the viaduct at the east end of Armourdale, looked back over his shoulder as the water began to flow in. He hurried to reach the yard office and spread the warning.

However, time was too short. The yard men got the diesel engines to high ground. But in the path of the flood stood hundreds of loaded freight cars and other hundreds of empties. They couldn't be saved.

By the night of July 12 the Armourdale Yard was completely submerged. The water washed over the tops of the heavily loaded cars that held on the tracks. Other cars were toppled over and floated off their trucks. By noon of July 13 it was a scene of vast devastation.

It took several days for the water to recede, and John Farrington, together with Jenks and his operating officers, was on the ground to witness the worst physical disaster in the Rock Island's 99 years. Not only did the road face the loss to its facilities, but hundreds of its workmen who lived nearby had been made homeless.

Through superhuman efforts the work of rehabilitation was begun. Switchmen, firemen, clerks, and mechanics joined shoulder to shoulder with maintenance men to swing shovels and dig through the muck. Heroic were their efforts, and the railroad's directors voted a resolution expressing their appreciation of the fine demonstration of loyalty.

Operations through the stricken area were resumed in record time. The cost in physical damage neared the $5,500,000 mark and was charged out currently to operating expenses. Farrington estimated that the loss in traffic that had to be diverted to other roads aggregated more than $9,000,000.

Piled on to the flood losses was another crop failure in the Texas and Oklahoma Panhandle and in southwest Kansas.

Still, Farrington could pridefully point out in his annual report, commenting on flood losses and crop failures:

"This unprecedented situation, together with the impact of the inflationary spiral of wages, materials, and supplies, resulted in increasing our operating expenses from $130,700,000 in 1950 to $150,900,000 in 1951, an increase of 15.5 percent. Included therein is an increase in wages alone of $8,749,000. Our net income for the year totaled $15,419,099, a decrease of 13.8 percent—a disappointing figure and yet one which compares favorably with the majority of Western railroads which were unaffected by the great flood. The fact that your railroad, in the face of these major economic disturbances, was able to absorb currently the costs involved and still make a creditable showing in earnings, is strongly indicative of its vitality and the soundness of its financial position."

Yes, with 1951's gross reaching a new high of $198,500,000, this showing could not have been made were it not for the vast diversification in traffic that had been brought about through increased industrial development over the years, the stepped-up operating efficiencies that had been achieved through the enormous sums spent in additions and betterments, and the wise reduction in funded debt.

The crises faced in 1951 proved, beyond all doubt, that Farrington had built a railroad that could withstand virtually anything short of complete demolition. He felt now that he could face the system's centennial year, 1952, with optimism.

46 End of a century and of an era

The Rock Island, with John Farrington's hard hand at the controls, rocketed into its hundredth year with the high iron singing under the spinning brightness of its rolling wheels.

Up and down the railroad civic leaders in cities and towns and villages worked with Rock Island men from the right-of-way and from cabs and cabooses, from offices, yards and shops, to devise ways and means of paying fitting tribute to the iron road that had been their friend and neighbor. It would be a birthday party that would draw them all closer together, that would give them a deeper insight into the railroad, past and present, and it would give the railroad an opportunity to tell its friends and patrons the depth of its appreciation for the contributions of industry, agriculture, and commerce to its own success.

The wheels of progress rolled on. At Council Bluffs the new East Yard was completed. East of that point work was progressing on the last big line change in Farrington's plans —the Atlantic Cutoff. This involved the building of nearly 35 miles of new railroad between Atlantic, Iowa, and the Missouri River. It was designed to shorten the old line by some 10 miles and give new competitive strength to the Chicago-Colorado main line through the elimination of 1,629 degrees of curvature and the abandonment of a very poor and broken grade line. It, of course, would not be completed until perhaps the late summer of 1953, so there would be nothing to focus upon there in the nature of a centennial celebration.

The program of dieselization was the thing that occupied Farrington as the year advanced. The orders had all been placed for the units that would bring about the completion of his diesel planning.

At Silvis the new diesel shop was completed, a conversion of the big locomotive facility that was built originally to service the steam power.

All through the spring and summer the centennial fever increased. It spread to 117 towns and cities where civic clubs, fraternal organizations, chambers of commerce, and mayors and city councils perfected their plans.

The celebrations—whether they were simply a Rotary or Kiwanis or Lions Club observing Rock Island Day with an appropriate speaker to tell the Rock Island Centennial story, or whether they centered around an all-day outing with parades, picnics, and other festivities—were scheduled to take place for the most part in the week between October 5 and 12.

The focal point of all the observances was at Rock Island, Illinois, with Davenport, Moline, and East Moline joining in. It was at Rock Island that the idea of this railroad was conceived, and it was at Rock Island where the plans for its first charter were drawn.

Chicago's South Side suburban area staged the first big celebration. It came on September 9 when the publisher of the *Southtown Economist* staged a party attended by more than 600 men and women, leaders in the area's civic and business life. The railroad provided an eight-car suburban train on which the party traveled over suburban and industrial sections of the railroad. Many were in the costumes of a hundred years ago, and school bands along the way serenaded the special.

On October 9, the eve of the system's birthday, a marker was unveiled on the courthouse lawn at Joliet to commemorate the anniversary and to honor Joliet pioneer Nelson D. Elwood, one of the founding fathers of the road. The championship Joliet high school band furnished the music, and immediately afterward the combined civic clubs tendered a luncheon to the Rock Island president and his official staff.

The climax came on the following day when Farrington and the company's officers and directors arrived at Rock Island aboard a special train, accompanied by many of Chicago's foremost businessmen. For months the plans had been in the making and now the day was here.

The weather was made to order—clear October sky, deep blue, and bright sunshine. Huge crowds met the special and the visitors were escorted by an old-time German band to the Masonic Temple. There 600 of the leading service club members from the Quad Cities paid tribute to the railroad and its past with a luncheon.

Farrington told the audience briefly of the railroad's long struggle and of its modern achievements. Other speakers gave some of the historical background.

The high schools of Davenport, Rock Island, Moline, and East Moline assembled their bands, and banks and industries joined with Rock Island employees to provide floats for a two-hour long parade on the theme of a Century of Service. Old-timers said it was the city's biggest turnout.

The ceremonies were finished off with the dedication of a

monument at the newly modernized Rock Island passenger
station. Over the loudspeakers, and over a radio hookup,
Farrington paid tribute to the countless employees and officers
of the railroad, past and present, for their contribution to its
progress and success. He received as a gift in memory of the
occasion, a gavel made from the wood of the first bridge to
span the Mississippi.

Outside observers, familiar with the vast extent of the sys-
tem-wide ceremonies, expressed themselves as somewhat
amazed that in the majority of instances the citizens of the
communities gave the party to the railroad instead of it being
the other way round.

The trade magazines, *Railway Age* and *Modern Railroads*,
devoted, in October, full issues to the many facets of the Rock
Island's march of progress. It was in all respects a centennial
birthday that would be long remembered.

But more to make its mark in history was the railroad's full
performance as its hundredth year drew to a close.

If Farrington had hoped that this 1952 would be a very
good year, he saw that hope realized as the curtain came down
on December 31. He saw a new all-time record set for gross
income—$213,938,266. With no untoward operating emer-
gencies such as had stricken his railroad in 1950 and 1951,
he saw his net income top $22,600,000 for earnings of $32.43
per share on the preferred and $13.57 on the common.

He could write in his annual report that his diesel program now was finished with the delivery through November
and December of the last of 88 additional locomotives. When
the figures were all added, he had a total of 413 diesels in
service. Seventy-seven were assigned to the Rockets and other
passenger runs, 168 were hauling all the freight trains on the
system proper, and 168 were doing the yard work. Only 119
steam locomotives remained, and these were being kept in
shape for stand-by service. With the passing of a century, it
was to the Rock Island also the passing of the great iron horse.
Soon now the kids at the Main Street crossing or down in the
corner of the pasture fence could no longer stand in awe at the

swirling blur of the main rods flashing in the prairie sun, nor watch the trailing smoke plume drift across the fields. It was the end of an era.

John Farrington could look back over sixteen and a half bright and bitter years—the hardest and most rewarding of his life—and feel the inner glow that comes with the realization of a job well done. He could do that, but he wouldn't. There would never be a time when he could shake off the feeling that, in one way or another, he might have done it better.

But the record stands for itself—the record of the hustling, bustling and sometimes discouraging years in which this beaten and dying giant of a railroad was brought back completely to a new and highly useful and eminently successful life.

From the first scrap drive through the rust and the weeds in 1936 to the unveiling of the Centennial Monument at Rock Island, the story of the revival, the recovery and the rebuilding of this 8,000-mile railway system was deeply etched in the records—the story of the vision, the courage and the drive of John Dow Farrington.

When, before the arrival of Ned Durham and Farrington on the scene, Engineer Moulton reported to the bondholders that it would take $30,000,000 to put this railroad in shape to hold up its head competitively, outsiders thought the estimate too high.

Now, at the close of the sixteen-and-a-half-year chapter of Farrington's progress, the cost was all down on paper. From the day the first cash had been realized from scrap sales to the end of 1952, the railroad had paid out for roadway and structures, and for new and rebuilt equipment, $236,221,740. This huge expenditure was accomplished at the same time the funded debt was being reduced to where it now stood at less than $51,000,000.

Farrington had to show for it a thoroughly modern railroad that ranked second to none among the leaders of the Nation. In addition to his dieselization, his succession of line relocations and line shortening, and his more than 5,000 miles of rail relays, he had built or bought through those years 16,400 new freight cars of all classes—more than half his ownership. His automatic block signals and centralized traffic control now served 3,615 track miles. Besides his testing laboratory, his hump-retarder yards, modern mechanized freight houses, icing docks and numerous other facilities all designed to speed traffic and result in higher operating efficiencies, he had seen the growth of industry on the system's lines achieve a remarkable expansion.

From January 1, 1937, to the close of 1952, more than 3,300 plants of various types had located along the Rock Island. This represented the investment of private capital reaching $732,500,000. Freight revenue derived from tonnage into and out of these plants was estimated at more than $70,000,000 annually.

Little wonder that the experts and the analysts in commerce and finance, in their evaluation of Farrington's progressive planning and achievements, have called the Rock Island's accomplishments nothing short of miraculous. And the record, according to these observers, will long stand as a historic monument not only to the man who was responsible, but to the American system of free enterprise.

The first hundred years are the hardest!

The firm mouth set above Farrington's big stubborn chin twists into a crooked smile when he thinks of this homely adage and wonders if it hadn't long ago originated with some cracker-barrel philosopher who knew the Rock Island well.

Bibliography

BOOKS:

Burrows, J. M. D., *Fifty Years in Iowa*. Davenport, Glass & Co., 1888.

Crosby, George H., *Corporate History of the Rock Island*. Chicago, privately printed, 1902.

Farnum, Henry, *Henry Farnum*. New Haven, privately printed, 1889.

Foreman, Grant, *A History of Oklahoma*. Norman, Okla., University of Oklahoma Press, 1942.

Gue, Benjamin F., *History of Iowa from the Earliest Times to the Beginning of the 20th Century*. New York, Century History Co., 1903.

James, Marquis, *Cherokee Strip*. New York, Viking Press, 1945.

Leonard, Levi O. and Johnson, Jack T., *A Railroad to the Sea*. Iowa City, Midland House, 1939.

May, Earl Chapin, *Principio to Wheeling*. New York, Harper & Bros., 1945.

Meyer, Balthasar Henry, *History of Transportation in the United States before 1860*. Washington, Carnegie Institution of Washington, 1948. Reprinted by permission of Peter Smith.

Riegel, Robert Edgar, Ph.D., *The Story of the Western Railroads*. New York, The Macmillan Co., 1926.

Spencer, J. W., *Reminiscences of Pioneer Life in the Mississippi Valley*. Davenport, Griggs, Watson & Day, 1872.

Starr, John W., Jr., *Lincoln and the Railroads*. New York, Dodd, Mead & Co., 1927.

Chicago, Rock Island and Pacific Railway System and Representative Employees, Chicago, Biographical Publishing Co., 1900.

297

By the '89ers, *Oklahoma, The Beautiful Land.* Oklahoma City, Times-Journal Publishing Co., 1943.

Official state histories of each of the fourteen states served by the Rock Island Lines and also of Arizona, California and Utah, have been consulted.

PERIODICALS:

Chicago Tribune
Chicago Sun
Chicago Journal of Commerce
Wall Street Journal, New York
Fortune Magazine
Congressional Record
The Railway Gazette
    (Predecessor of the *Railway Age*)
The Railway Age
Modern Railroads
The Commercial and Financial Chronicle, New York

OTHER DATA:

Interstate Commerce Commission transcripts of various hearings
Transcripts of Senate and House Committee hearings
Annual reports of the Rock Island Railroad (complete)
Official records of the Rock Island Railroad
The Rock Island Employees' Magazine
The Rock Island Lines News-Digest

Index

299